German
Phrasebook &
Culture Guide

1st Edition

WILEY

Wiley Publishing, Inc.

Published by:

Wiley Publishing, Inc.

111 River St.
Hoboken, NJ 07030-5774

ISBN-13: 978-0-470-22859-3

Editor: Jennifer Polland
Japanese Editor: Jim Cohen
Series Editor: Maureen Clarke
Travel Tips & Culture Guide: Jane Yager
Illustrations by Maciek Albrecht
Photo Editor: Richard H. Fox

Translation, Copyediting, Proofreading, Production, and Layout by:
Lingo Systems, 15115 SW Sequoia Pkwy, Ste 200, Portland, OR 97224

For information on our other products and services or to obtain technical support,
please contact our Customer Care Department within the U.S. at 800/762-2974,
outside the U.S. at 317/572-3993 or fax 317/572-4002.
Wiley also publishes its books in a variety of electronic formats. Some content that
appears in print may not be available in electronic formats.

Manufactured in the United States of America

5   4   3   2   1

Contents

An Invitation to the Reader

In researching this book, we discovered many wonderful sayings and terms useful to travelers in German-speaking countries. We're sure you'll find others. Please tell us about them so we can share them with your fellow travelers in upcoming editions. If you were disappointed about any aspect of this book, we'd like to know that, too. Please write to:

Frommer's German Phrasebook & Culture Guide, 1st Edition
Wiley Publishing, Inc.
111 River St. • Hoboken, NJ 07030-5774

An Additional Note

The packager, editors and publisher cannot be held responsible for the experience of readers while traveling. Your safety is important to us, however, so we encourage you to stay alert and aware of your surroundings. Keep a close eye on cameras, purses, and wallets, all favorite targets of thieves and pickpockets.

Frommers.com

Now that you have the language for a great trip, visit our website at **www.frommers.com** for travel information on more than 3,600 destinations. With features updated regularly, we give you instant access to the most current trip-planning information available. At Frommers.com you'll also find the best prices on airfares, accommodations, and car rentals—and you can even book travel online through our travel booking partners. Frommers.com also features:

- Online updates to our most popular guidebooks
- Vacation sweepstakes and contest giveaways
- Newsletter highlighting the hottest travel trends
- Online travel message boards with featured travel discussions

INTRODUCTION: HOW TO USE THIS BOOK

More than 80 million people in Germany, Switzerland, Austria, and Luxembourg are native speakers of German. Tens of millions more speak it as a second language. German is the language of music, art, philosophy, science, and literature. Like English, German is a Germanic language, and they share many cognates, or words that look alike with similar meanings.

Our intention is not to teach you German; a class or audio program is better for that. Our aim is to provide a portable travel tool that's easy to use. The problem with most phrasebooks is that you practically have to memorize the contents before you know where to look for the term you need on the spot. This phrasebook is designed for fingertip referencing, so you can whip it out and find the words you need fast.

Part of this book organizes terms by chapters, like the sections in a Frommer's guide—getting a room, getting a good meal, etc. Within those divisions, we tried to organize phrases intuitively, according to how frequently most readers would be likely to use them. The most unique feature, however, is the two-way PhraseFinder dictionary in the back, which lists words as well as phrases organized by key word. Say a taxi driver hands you €5 instead of €10. Look up "change" in the dictionary and discover how to say: "Sorry, but this isn't the correct change."

To make best use of the content, we recommend that you spend some time flipping through it before you depart for your trip. Familiarize yourself with the order of the chapters. Read through the pronunciations section in chapter one and practice pronouncing random phrases throughout the book. Try looking up a few phrases in the phrasebook section as well as in the dictionary. This way, you'll be able to locate phrases faster and speak them more clearly when you need them.

What will make this book most practical? What will make it easiest to use? These are the questions we asked ourselves repeatedly as we assembled these travel terms. Our immediate goal was to create a phrasebook as indispensable as your passport. Our far-ranging goal, of course, is to enrich your experience of travel. And with that, we wish you *Viel Spass!* (Have a great trip!)

CHAPTER ONE

SURVIVAL GERMAN

If you tire of toting around this phrasebook, tear out this chapter.
You should be able to navigate your destination with only the
terms found in the next 29 pages.

BASIC GREETINGS

For a full list of greetings, see p115.

Hello.	**Hallo.**
	Hah-LOH.
How are you?	**Wie geht es Ihnen?**
	Vee GHEHHT as eehnen?
I'm fine, thanks.	**Mir geht es gut, danke.**
	Mere ghehht as GOOT, dunk-eh.
And you?	**Und Ihnen?**
	Oonnd EEHNEN?
My name is ____.	**Ich heiße ____.**
	Ee[ch] HYE-sseh ____.
And yours?	**Wie heißen Sie?**
	Vee hye-ssenn ZEE?
It's a pleasure to meet you.	**Freut mich, Sie kennen zu lernen.**
	Froyd mi[ch], zee CANON tsoo lehr-nen.
Please.	**Bitte.**
	BIT-eh.
Thank you.	**Danke.**
	DUNK-eh.
Yes.	**Ja.**
	Yahh.
No.	**Nein.**
	Nine.
Okay.	**OK.**
	Okay.

No problem.	**Kein Problem.**
	Kyne proh-BLEHM.
I'm sorry, I don't understand.	**Entschuldigung, ich verstehe Sie nicht.**
	Ennt-SHOOLL-dee-ghoong, ee[ch] fair-SHTEH-heh zee ni[ch]t.
Would you speak slower please?	**Könnten Sie bitte etwas langsamer sprechen?**
	K[oe]nn-ten zee bit-eh at-vahs LUNG-sah-mehr shpre-[ch]en?
Would you speak louder please?	**Könnten Sie bitte etwas lauter sprechen?**
	K[oe]nn-ten zee bit-eh at-vahs LOU-tehr shpre-[ch]en?
Do you speak English?	**Sprechen Sie Englisch?**
	Shpre-[ch]en zee ENG-lish?
Do you speak any other languages?	**Sprechen Sie irgendeine andere Sprache?**
	Shpre-[ch]en zee irr-ghend eye-ne UN-deh-reh shpra-[ch]eh?
I speak ____ better than German.	**Ich spreche besser ____ als Deutsch.**
	Ee[ch] shpre-[ch]eh bess-er ____ ahlls doytsh.
Would you spell that?	**Könnten Sie das bitte buchstabieren?**
	K[oe]nn-ten zee dahs bit-eh bu[ch]-shtah-BEE-ren?
Would you please repeat that?	**Könnten Sie das bitte wiederholen?**
	K[oe]nn-ten zee dahs bit-eh veeder-HOH-len?
Would you point that out in this dictionary?	**Könnten Sie mir das bitte in diesem Wörterbuch zeigen?**
	K[oe]nn-ten zee mere dahs bit-eh in dee-sem V[OE]R-tehr-boo[ch] tsai-ghen?

THE KEY QUESTIONS

With the right hand gestures, you can get a lot of mileage from the following list of single-word questions and answers.

Who?	**Wer?**
	Vehr?
What?	**Was?**
	Vahs?
When?	**Wann?**
	Vahnn?
Where?	**Wo?**
	Voh?
To where?	**Wohin?**
	Voh-HINN?
Why?	**Warum?**
	Vah-ROOM?
How?	**Wie?**
	Vee?
Which?	**Welcher (m) / Welche (f) / Welches (n)?**
	VELL-[ch]err / VELL-[ch]eh / VELL-[ch]ess?
How many? / How much?	**Wie viele?**
	Vee FEE-leh?

THE ANSWERS: WHO

For full coverage of pronouns, see p20.

I	**Ich**
	Ee[ch]
you	**Sie (formal, sing. + pl.) / du (informal, sing.) / ihr (informal, pl.)**
	zee / doo / eehr
him	**er**
	air
her	**sie**
	zee
us	**wir**
	veer
them	**sie (pl.)**
	zee

THE ANSWERS: WHEN
For full coverage of time, see p11.

now	**jetzt**
	yetst
later	**später**
	SHP[AE]-tehr
in a minute	**gleich**
	glye[ch]
today	**heute**
	HOY-teh
tomorrow	**morgen**
	MORR-ghenn
yesterday	**gestern**
	GHESS-tehrn
in a week	**in einer Woche**
	in eye-nehr VOH-[ch]eh
next week	**nächste Woche**
	n[ae][ch]s-teh VOH-[ch]eh
last week	**letzte Woche**
	lets-teh VOH-[ch]eh
next month	**nächsten Monat**
	n[ae][ch]s-ten MOH-naht
At ____	**Um ____**
	Oomm ____
ten o'clock this morning.	**zehn Uhr heute Morgen.**
	TSEHN oohr hoy-teh MORR-ghenn.
two o'clock this afternoon.	**zwei Uhr heute Nachmittag.**
	TSVAIH oohr hoy-teh NAH[CH]-mitt-tahhg.
seven o'clock this evening.	**sieben Uhr heute Abend.**
	ZEE-ben oohr hoy-teh AHH-bend.

For full coverage of numbers, see p7.

THE ANSWERS: WHERE

here	**hier**	
	hear	
there	**dort**	
	dohrrt	
near	**in der Nähe von**	
	in dehr N[AE]H-heh fonn	
closer	**näher**	
	N[AE]H-herr	
closest	**am nächsten**	
	umm N[AE][CH]s-ten	
far	**weit weg**	
	VYTE vegg	
farther	**weiter weg**	
	VYE-tehr vegg	
farthest	**am weitesten weg**	
	umm VYE-tess-ten vegg	
across from	**gegenüber von**	
	ghe-ghenn-[UE]H-behr fonn	
next to	**neben**	
	NEH-ben	
behind	**hinter**	
	HINN-tehr	
straight ahead	**geradeaus**	
	ghe-rah-deh-OUS	
left	**links**	
	links	
right	**rechts**	
	re[ch]ts	
up	**aufwärts**	
	OUF-v[ae]rts	
down	**abwärts**	
	UPP-v[ae]rts	
lower	**niedriger (height) / geringer (price)**	
	NEE-drigger / ghe-RING-er	

higher	**höher**
	H[OE]-hehr
forward	**vorwärts**
	FOHR-v[ae]rts
back	**zurück**
	tsoo-R[UE]KK
around	**herum**
	heh-ROOMM
across the street	**auf der anderen Straßenseite**
	ouf dehr UN-deh-renn SHTRAH-ssen-sye-teh
down the street	**am Ende der Straße**
	umm enn-deh dehr SHTRAH-sseh
on the corner	**an der Ecke**
	unn dehr EKKEH
kitty-corner	**schräg gegenüber**
	shr[ae]gg gheh-ghenn-[UE]H-behr
____ blocks from here	____ **Straßen von hier**
	SHTRAH-ssen fonn hear

For a full list of numbers, see the next page.

THE ANSWERS: WHICH

this one	**dieser (m) / diese (f) / dieses (n)**
	DEE-sehr / DEE-seh / DEE-sess
that (that one, close by)	**dieser (m) / diese (f) / dieses (n)**
	DEE-sehr / DEE-seh / DEE-sess
(that one, in the distance)	**jener (m) / jene (f) / jenes (n)**
	YEH-nehr / YEH-neh / YEH-ness
these	**diese**
	DEE-seh
those (those there, close by)	**diese (pl.)**
	DEE-seh

NUMBERS & COUNTING

one	**Eins** *Aihnts*	seventeen	**Siebzehn** *ZEEB-tsehn*
two	**Zwei** *Tsvaih*	eighteen	**Achtzehn** *A[CH]-tsehn*
three	**Drei** *Drrye*	nineteen	**Neunzehn** *NOYN-tsehn*
four	**Vier** *Feer*	twenty	**Zwanzig** *TSVANN-tsigg*
five	**Fünf** *F[ue]nff*	twenty-one	**Einundzwanzig** *AIHNN-oonnd-tsvann-tsigg*
six	**Sechs** *Zeks*	thirty	**Dreißig** *DRRYE-sigg*
seven	**Sieben** *ZEE-ben*	forty	**Vierzig** *FEER-tsigg*
eight	**Acht** *A[ch]t*	fifty	**Fünfzig** *F[UE]NFF-tsigg*
nine	**Neun** *Noyn*	sixty	**Sechzig** *ZE[CH]-tsigg*
ten	**Zehn** *Tsehn*	seventy	**Siebzig** *ZEEB-tsigg*
eleven	**Elf** *Ellf*	eighty	**Achtzig** *A[CH]-tsigg*
twelve	**Zwölf** *Tsv[oe]llf*	ninety	**Neunzig** *NOYN-tsigg*
thirteen	**Dreizehn** *DRRYE-tshen*	one hundred	**Einhundert** *AIHN-hoonn-dehrt*
fourteen	**Vierzehn** *FEER-tsehn*	two hundred	**Zweihundert** *TSVAIH-hoonn-dehrt*
fifteen	**Fünfzehn** *F[UE]NFF-tsehn*	one thousand	**Eintausend** *aihn-TOWSEND*
sixteen	**Sechzehn** *ZE[CH]-tsehn*		

FRACTIONS & DECIMALS

one eighth	**ein Achtel**
	aihn A[CH]-tell
one quarter	**ein Viertel**
	aihn FEER-tell
one third	**ein Drittel**
	aihn DRITT-tell
one half	**die Hälfte**
	dee H[AE]LLF-teh
two thirds	**zwei Drittel**
	tsvaih DRITT-tell
three quarters	**drei Viertel**
	drrye FEER-tell
double	**doppelt**
	DOP-pellt
triple	**dreifach**
	DRRYE-fah[ch]
one tenth	**ein Zehntel**
	aihn TSEHN-tell
one hundredth	**ein Hundertstel**
	aihn HOON-derts-tell
one thousandth	**ein Tausendstel**
	aihn TOW-sends-tell

MATH

addition	**Addition**
	AH-dee-tsee-ohn
2 + 1	**zwei plus eins**
	tsvaih plooss aihnts
subtraction	**Subtraktion**
	ZOOBB-trahkk-tsee-ohn
2 - 1	**zwei minus eins**
	tsvaih mee-nooss aihnts
multiplication	**Multiplikation**
	MUHLL-tee-plee-kah-tsee-ohn

2 x 3	**zwei mal drei**
	tsvaih mahl drye
division	**Division**
	DEE-vee-see-ohn
6 ÷ 3	**sechs geteilt durch drei**
	zekks gheh-TYLET doorr[ch] drye

ORDINAL NUMBERS

first	**erster (m) / erste (f) / erstes (n)**
	AIHRS-tehr / AIHRS-teh / AIHRS-tess
second	**zweiter (m) / zweite (f) / zweites (n)**
	TSVAIH-tehr / TSVAIH-teh / TSVAIH-tess
third	**dritter (m) / dritte (f) / drittes (n)**
	DRITT-ehr / DRITT-eh / DRITT-tess
fourth	**vierter (m) / vierte (f) / viertes (n)**
	FEER-tehr / FEER-teh / FEER-tess
fifth	**fünfter (m) / fünfte (f) / fünftes (n)**
	F[UE]NFF-tehr / F[UE]NFF-teh / F[UE]NFF-tess
sixth	**sechster (m) / sechste (f) / sechstes (n)**
	ZEKS-tehr / ZEKS-teh / ZEKS-tess
seventh	**siebter (m) / siebte (f) / siebtes (n)**
	ZEEB-tehr / ZEEB-teh / ZEEB-tess
eighth	**achter (m) / achte (f) / achtes (n)**
	A[CH]-tehr / A[CH]-teh / A[CH]-tess
ninth	**neunter (m) / neunte (f) / neuntes (n)**
	NOYN-tehr / NOYN-teh / NOYN-tess
tenth	**zehnter (m) / zehnte (f) / zehntes (n)**
	TSEHN-tehr / TSEHN-teh / TSEHN-tess
last	**letzter (m) / letzte (f) / letztes (n)**
	LETS-tehr / LETS-teh / LETS-tess

MEASUREMENTS

millimeter	**Millimeter**	*MIL-lee-meh-tehr*
centimeter	**Zentimeter**	*TSENN-tee-meh-tehr*
meter	**Meter**	*MEH-tehr*
kilometer	**Kilometer**	*KEE-loh-meh-tehr*
squared	**quadriert**	*kvah-DREEHRT*
short	**kurz**	*koorrts*
long	**lang**	*lahng*

VOLUME

milliliters	**Milliliter**	*MIL-lee-lee-tehr*
liter	**Liter**	*LEE-tehr*
kilo	**Kilo**	*KEE-loh*
cup	**Tasse**	*TAHSS-eh*

QUANTITY

some	**etwas**	*AT-vahs*
none	**nichts**	*ni[ch]ts*
all	**alles**	*AHLL-ehs*
many / much	**viele / viel**	*FEEL-eh / feel*

a little bit (can be used for quantity or for time)	**etwas** *AT-vahs*
dozen	**Dutzend** *DUTT-send*

SIZE

small	**klein** *klyne*
the smallest	**der / die / das Kleinste** *dehr / dee / dahs KLYNES-teh*
medium	**mittel** *MITT-ell*
big	**groß** *grohs*
fat	**dick** *dick*
wide	**breit** *brryte*
narrow	**schmal** *shmahl*

TIME

Time in German is referred to, literally, by the clock. "What time is it?" translates literally as "How much clock is it?"
For full coverage of number terms, see p7.

HOURS OF THE DAY

What time is it?	**Wie spät ist es?** *Vee SHP[AE]HT isst as?*
At what time?	**Um wie viel Uhr?** *Oomm VEE-feel oohr?*
For how long?	**Wie lange?** *Vee LUNG-eh?*
It's one o'clock.	**Es ist ein Uhr.** *As isst AIHN oohr.*

It's two o'clock.	**Es ist zwei Uhr.**
	As isst TSVAIH oohr.
It's two thirty.	**Es ist halb drei.**
	As isst hahllb DRRYE.
It's two fifteen.	**Es ist Viertel nach zwei.**
	As isst feer-tell nah[ch] TSVAIH.
It's a quarter to three.	**Es ist Viertel vor drei.**
	As isst feer-tell fohr DRRYE.
It's noon.	**Es ist Mittag.**
	As isst MITT-tahgg.
It's midnight.	**Es ist Mitternacht.**
	As isst MITT-ehr-na[ch]t.
It's early.	**Es ist früh.**
	As isst FR[UE]HH.
It's late.	**Es ist spät.**
	As isst SHP[AE]HT.
in the morning	**morgens**
	MORR-ghenns
in the afternoon	**nachmittags**
	NA[CH]-mitt-tahggs
at night	**nachts**
	na[ch]ts
dawn	**Morgendämmerung**
	MORR-ghenn-d[ae]mm-eh-roong

DAYS OF THE WEEK

Sunday	**Sonntag**
	ZONN-tahgg
Monday	**Montag**
	MOHN-tahgg
Tuesday	**Dienstag**
	DEENS-tahgg
Wednesday	**Mittwoch**
	MITT-voh[ch]
Thursday	**Donnerstag**
	DONN-airs-tahgg

Friday	**Freitag**
	FRYE-tahgg
Saturday	**Samstag**
	ZAMMS-tahgg
today	**heute**
	HOY-teh
tomorrow	**morgen**
	MORR-ghenn
yesterday	**gestern**
	GHESS-tehrn
the day before yesterday	**vorgestern**
	FOHR-ghess-tehrn
one week	**eine Woche**
	eye-neh VOH-[ch]eh
next week	**nächste Woche**
	n[ae][ch]s-teh VOH-[ch]eh
last week	**letzte Woche**
	lets-teh VOH-[ch]eh

MONTHS OF THE YEAR

January	**Januar**
	YAHNN-oo-ahr
February	**Februar**
	FEHH-broo-ahr
March	**März**
	M[ae]rts
April	**April**
	ah-PRILL
May	**Mai**
	Maih
June	**Juni**
	YOU-nee
July	**Juli**
	YOU-lee
August	**August**
	ou-GHOOSST

September	**September**
	zepp-TEMM-behr
October	**Oktober**
	okk-TOH-behr
November	**November**
	no-FEMM-behr
December	**Dezember**
	deh-TSEMM-behr
next month	**nächsten Monat**
	n[ae][ch]s-ten MOH-naht
last month	**letzten Monat**
	lets-ten MOH-naht

SEASONS OF THE YEAR

spring	**Frühling**
	FR[UE]H-linng
summer	**Sommer**
	ZOMM-ehr
autumn	**Herbst**
	Herrbst
winter	**Winter**
	VINN-tehr

Falsche Freunde

If you try winging it with Denglish, beware of false cognates, known as "*falsche Freunde*" (false friends)—German words that sound like English ones, but with different meanings. Here are some examples of false cognates.

bald	soon
kahl	bald
Menü	today's special
Speisekarte	menu
Gift	poison
Geschenk	gift
Billion	trillion
Milliarde	billion
Puff	bordello
Hauch / Zug	puff
konsequent	consistent(ly)
folglich	consequently
Dom	cathedral
Kuppel	dome
aktuell	current
eigentlich, wirklich	actual
also	thus, therefore
auch	also
Art	kind, type
Kunst	art
Bad	bath, spa
schlecht	bad
blenden	dazzle, blind
mischen	blend
brav	well behaved
tapfer	brave

GERMAN GRAMMAR BASICS

Like English, German is a Germanic language. Both languages have the same basic alphabet of 26 letters. German has three additional letters with the addition of the umlaut (the two dots over the a, o and u). German is a very phonetic language, meaning words are generally (though not always) pronounced the way they look.

THE ALPHABET

German is a straightforward language with a simple alphabet. It has 29 letters: all of the same letters found in the English alphabet, plus three additional vowels formed by adding an umlaut (two dots) over a, o and u. The umlaut changes the pronunciation of these vowels in a small but important way.

Letter	Name	Pronunciation
a	a	*ah (as in "fAther")*
ä	aeh	*aeh (as in "hEAven")*
b	beh	*b (as in "brave")*
c	tseh	*k (as in "caviar");*
("ch" at beginning of word: hard "k" sound (as in "character"), "ch" in the middle or at the end of a word: softer sound (as in Scottish pronunciation of "Loch"))		
d	deh	*d (as in "day")*
e	ehh	*eh (as in "help")*
f	eff	*f (as in "friend")*
g	gheh	*gh (as in "ghost")*
h	hah	*h (as in "hand")*
stresses all vowels; for combinations with "c" see letter "c"		
i	eeh	*ee (as in "bee")*
j	yott	*y (as in "yellow")*
k	kah	*c (as in "can")*
l	ell	*l (as in "lake")*
m	emm	*m (as in "mother")*

Letter	Name	Pronunciation
n	enn	n (as in "name")
o	ohh	o (as in "often")
ö	oeh	u (as in "burger")
p	peh	p (as in "page");

the combination "ph" is pronounced as "f" (as in "philosophy")

q	coo	q (as in "quest")
r	err	r (as in "ERRor";

however, the German "r" has to be spoken as a rolling "r"

s	ess	s (as in "stay");

the combination "st" at the beginning of a word is pronounced as "sh" (as in "shuttle"), while in the middle or at the end of a word it is pronounced as "st" (as in "stick"); the combination "sch" is pronounced as "sh" (as in "shelf")

t	teh	t (as in "tea");

the combination "tio" is pronounced as "tsee-yoh" (as in the German word "Aktion" - akk-tsee-YOHN)

u	ooh	ooh
ü	ueh	ueh (a slight variant of the "ooh" sound)
v	fauh	f (as in "front")
w	vehh	v (as in "value")
x	ikks	x (as in "extra")
y	YP-see-lohn	ueh (see letter "ü")
z	tsett	ts (as in "iTS")

PRONUNCIATION GUIDE

Vowels

a	ah as the a in father:	Vater (FAH-tehr)
ä	eh like the ea in heaven:	hätte (hat-teh)
au	ow as in cow:	Haus (hows)
ai	aye as in "All in favor, say aye":	Mai (my)
e	long as the a in tame:	zehn (tsayn)
eu	oy as in toy:	euch (oy[ch])

i	ee as in feed
o	oh as in boat
ö	ew as in blue
u	oo as in coo
ü	like the oo in cool

Consonants

b	as in bean: Boot *(boht)*
ch	like the "ch" in loch (as in Loch Ness)
d	as the d in day
f	as in fox: Feuer *(FOY-er)*
g	as in guy: Geist *(guyst)*
h	as in hay: hallo *(HALL-oh)*
j	pronounced like the "y" as in yes: Ja *(yahh)*
k	as in English: Kilometer *(KEE-lo-may-ter)*
l	as in English: links
m	as in English: Mai *(my)*
n	as in English: nein *(nine)*
p	as in English: Pass *(pahs)*
q	qu is pronounced as kv: Quittung *(KVih-toong)*
r	as in English but more rolled: rot *(rote)*
s	at the beginning of words (followed by a vowel) pronounced as z; in the middle and at or near the end of words as in English: selbst *(ZELpst)*
st, sch	like the "sh" in shoe: Stein *(shtine)*; Schule *(SHOO-la)*
ß	like English "s": Straße *(SHTRAH-sseh)*
t	as in English: Tee *(tay)*
v	like the "f" in fox, but more explosive: verwirrt *(fehr-VIRRT)*
w	like the "v" in vase: weiss *(vice)*
x	like English x: extra *(EX-tra)*
z	like "ts" or the "zz" in pizza: Zoo *(tsoh)*

WORD PRONUNCIATION

Syllables in words are also accented in a standard pattern. Generally, in words with two syllables the first syllable is stressed. For longer words, an accent mark is shown to indicate the stress.

Ending in -ieren

studieren   *shtoo-DEE-ren*

Loan word

Computer   *com-PEW-ter*

Compound adjective with hin, her, da or wo

damit   *da-MIT*

GENDER, ADJECTIVES, MODIFIERS

Each noun takes a masculine, feminine or neutral gender and is most often accompanied by a masculine, feminine or neutral definite article, like the English "the" (*der, die* or *das*), or by an indefinite article, like the English "a" or "an" (*ein* or *eine*). Definite articles ("the"), indefinite articles ("a," "an"), and related adjectives change their endings depending on whether they are the subject, direct or indirect object, or possessive. For example, "*Ich bin ein Mann*" (I am a man) becomes "*Ich sehe einen Mann*" (I see a man) because "Mann" is the subject of the first sentence and the direct object of the second. (What is being seen? The man.)

The Definite Article ("the")

	Masculine	Feminine	Neutral
Singular	*der* Hund (the dog)	*die* Katze (the cat)	*das* Tier (the animal)
Plural	*die* Hunde (the dogs)	*die* Katzen (the cats)	*die* Tiere (the animals)

The Indefinite Article ("a" or "an")

	Masculine	Feminine	Neutral
Singular	*ein* Hund (a dog)	*eine* Katze (a cat)	*ein* Tier (an animal)

PERSONAL PRONOUNS

	LIEBEN: "to love"	
I love.	*Ich* liebe.	LEE-beh
You (singular familiar) love.	*Du* liebst.	leebst
He / She / It loves. You (singular formal) love.	*Er / Sie / Es* liebt. Sie lieben.	leebt / LEE-ben
We love.	*Wir* lieben.	LEE-ben
You (plural familiar) love.	*Ihr* liebt.	leebt
They / You (plural formal) love.	*Sie / Sie* lieben.	LEE-ben

Hey, you!

German has two words for "you"— *du*, spoken among friends and familiars, and *Sie*, used among strangers or as a sign of respect toward authority figures. When speaking with a stranger, expect to use *Sie*, unless you are invited to do otherwise. The second-person familiar plural form (*ihr*) is used among friends and family. The second-person formal plural is the same as the second-person formal singular: *Sie*. Both the singular and plural forms of the second-person formal are always written with an upper-case S: "*Sie*."

REGULAR VERB CONJUGATIONS

Most German verbs end in "-en" (*lieben, geben, kommen,* etc.). To conjugate the present tense of regular verbs, drop the -en and add the following endings:

Present Tense

Regular verbs	GEHEN "to go"	
I go.	Ich gehe.	GHEH-heh
You (singular familiar) **go.**	Du geh*st*.	ghehst
He / She / It goes.	Er / Sie (singular feminine) / Es geh*t*.	gheht
You (singular formal) **go.**	Sie (singular formal) geh*en*.	GHEH-hen
We go.	Wir geh*en*.	GHEH-hen
You (plural familiar) **go.**	Sie geh*en*.	GHEH-hen
They / You (plural formal) **go.**	Sie / Sie geh*en*.	GHEH-hen

Simple Past Tense

These are the simple past tense conjugations for regular verbs.

Regular verbs	LIEBEN "To Live"	
I lived.	Ich lebte.	LEHB-te
You (singular familiar) **lived.**	Du lebte*st*.	LAYb-test
He / She / It lived.	Er / Sie / Es lebte.	LAYb-tah
You lived. (singular formal)	Sie lebte*n*.	LAYb-tahn
We lived.	Wir lebte*n*.	LAYb-ten
You (plural familiar) **lived.**	Ihr lebte*t*.	LAYb-tet
They / You (plural formal) **lived.**	Sie / Sie lebte*n*.	LAYb-ten

The Future

For novice German speakers, the easiest way to express the future is to conjugate the verb WERDEN (to go) + any infinitive ("I am going to speak", "you are going to speak", etc.).

I am going to speak.	Ich *werde* reden.	VER-de
You (singular familiar) are going to speak.	Du *wirst* reden.	Virrst
He / She / It is going to speak.	Er / Sie / Es *wird* reden.	Virrd
You (singular formal) are going to speak.	Sie *werden* reden.	Verr-den
We are going to speak.	Wir *werden* reden.	Verr-den
You (plural familiar) are going to speak.	Ihr *werdet* reden.	Verr-det
They / You (plural formal) are going to speak.	Sie / Sie *werden* reden.	Vehrr-den

TO BE OR NOT TO BE (SEIN)

The German verb for "to be," SEIN, is irregular. It is conjugated as follows:

Present Tense

SEIN "To Be"		
I am.	Ich *bin.*	bin
You (singular, familiar) **are.**	Du *bist.*	bist
He / She / It is.	Er / Sie / Es *ist.*	ist
You (singular formal) **are.**	Sie sind.	zint
We are.	Wir *sind.*	zint
You (plural familiar) **are.**	Ihr *seid.*	zeit
They / You (plural formal) **are.**	Sie *sind.*	zint

Simple Past Tense

SEIN "To Be"		
I was.	Ich *war.*	vahr
You were.	Du *warst.*	vahrst
He / She / It was.	Er / Sie / Es *war*	vahr
You (formal) were.	Sie *waren.*	VAHR-en
We were.	Wir *waren.*	VAHR-en
You were.	Ihr *wart.*	vahrt
They / You (plural formal) **were.**	Sie *waren.*	VAHR-en

IRREGULAR VERBS

German has numerous irregular verbs that stray from the standard -EN conjugations. Rather than bog you down with too much grammar, we're providing the present tense conjugations for the most commonly used irregular verbs.

HABEN "To Have"

I have.	Ich *habe*.	HAH-beh
You (singular familiar) **have.**	Du *hast*.	hahsst
He / She / It has.	Er / Sie / Es *hat*.	haht
You (singular formal) **have.**	Sie *haben*.	HAH-ben
We have.	Wir *haben*.	HAH-ben
You (plural familiar) **have.**	Ihr *habt*.	hahbt
They / You (plural formal) **have.**	Sie / Sie *haben*.	HAH-ben

Haben

Haben means "to have," but it's also used to describe conditions such as hunger and thirst. For example:
Ich habe Hunger. I'm hungry.
(Literally: I have hunger.)
Ich habe Durst. I'm thirsty.
(Literally: I have thirst.)

SPRECHEN "To Speak, To Talk"

I speak.	Ich spreche.	SHPRE[CH]-eh
You (singular familiar) **speak.**	Du sprichst.	shpri[ch]st
He / She / It speaks.	Er / Sie / Es spricht.	shpri[ch]t
You (singular formal) **speak.**	Sie sprechen.	SHPRE[CH]-en
We speak.	Wir sprechen.	SHPRE[CH]-en
You (plural familiar) **speak.**	Ihr sprecht.	shpre[ch]t
They / You (plural formal) **speak.**	Sie / Sie sprechen.	SHPRE[CH]-en

WOLLEN "To Want"

I want.	Ich will.	vill
You (singular familiar) **want.**	Du willst.	villsst
He / She / It wants.	Er / Sie / Es will.	vill
You (singular formal) **want.**	Sie wollen.	VOHLL-en
We want.	Wir wollen.	VOHLL-en
You (plural familiar) **want.**	Ihr wollt.	vohllt
They / You plural formal) **want.**	Sie / Sie wollen.	VOHLL-en

KOENNEN "To Be Able"

I can.	Ich kann.	KHANN
You (singular familiar) can.	Du kannst.	khannst
He / She / It can.	Er / Sie / Es kann.	khann
You (singular formal) can.	Sie können.	KH[OE]NN-en
We can.	Wir können.	KH[OE]NN-en
You (plural familiar) can.	Ihr könnt.	kh[oe]nnt
They / You (plural formal) can.	Sie / Sie können.	KH[OE]NN-en

KENNEN vs. WISSEN: There are two ways to say "To Know" in German: *kennen* and *wissen*. *Kennen* is to know someone or something, while *wissen* is to know a fact. For example, "*Ich kenne Peter.*" (I know Peter.) BUT "*Ich weiß, wo das Restaurant ist.*" (I know where the restaurant is.)

KENNEN "To Know" (someone)

I know.	Ich kenne.	KHENN-eh
You (singular familiar) know.	Du kennst.	khennst
He / She / It knows.	Er / Sie / Es kennt.	khennt
You (singular formal) know.	Sie kennen.	KHENN-en
We know.	Wir kennen.	KHENN-en
You (plural familiar) know.	Ihr kennt.	khennt
They / You (plural formal) know.	Sie / Sie kennen.	KHENN-en

WISSEN "To Know" (something)		
I know.	**Ich weiß.**	vice
You (singular familiar) **know.**	**Du weißt.**	vyesst
He / She / It knows.	**Er / Sie / Es weiß.**	vice
You (singular formal) **know.**	**Sie wissen.**	VISS-en
We know.	**Wir wissen.**	VISS-en
You (plural familiar) **know.**	**Ihr wisst.**	visst
They / You (plural formal) **know.**	**Sie / Sie wissen.**	VISS-en

Stem-changing Verbs

Some irregular verbs change their stem in addition to their ending. For example:

ESSEN (To Eat)
Ich esse (I eat)
Du isst (You eat)
Er / Sie / Es isst (He / She / It eats)
Wir essen (We eat)
Ihr esst (You eat) (informal)
Sie / Sie essen (You eat / They eat) (formal / pl.)

Notice that the stem only changes in the first three conjugations (I, you, and he/she/it). All of the plural forms are conjugated like regular verbs by adding the correct ending to the stem.

Gefallen

To say you like something, use the verb *gefallen*. *Gefallen* is different from other verbs because the person doing the liking is the subject of the sentence, not the object. For example, to say you like music, you would say:

Mir gefällt Musik. I like music.
(Literally: Music is pleasing to me.)

When what is liked is plural, the verb is plural:

Mir gefallen die Blumen. I like the flowers.
(Literally: The flowers are pleasing to me.)

The person doing the liking is represented by an indirect object pronoun placed in front of the verb, as illustrated below. Remember, gefallen can only be conjugated in two ways: *gefällt* (for singular things that are liked) and *gefallen* (for plural things that are liked). The pronoun changes to reflect who is doing the liking.

GEFALLEN "To Like"

I like Germany.	*Mir* gefällt Deutschland.	geh-FELT
You (informal singular) **like Germany.**	*Dir* gefällt Deutschland.	geh-FELT
He / She/ It likes Germany.	*Ihm / Ihr / Ihm* gefällt Deutschland.	geh-FELT
You (formal singular) **like Germany.**	*Ihnen* gefällt Deutschland.	geh-FELT
We like Germany.	*Uns* gefällt Deutschland.	geh-FELT
You (informal plural) **like Germany.**	*Euch* gefällt Deutschland.	geh-FELT
They / You (formal plural) **like Germany.**	*Ihnen* gefällt Deutschland.	geh-FELT

REFLEXIVE VERBS

German has many reflexive verbs (when the subject and object both refer to the same person or thing). The following common verbs are used reflexively: *sich anziehen* (to get dressed, literally to dress oneself), *sich rasieren* (to shave, literally to shave oneself), *sich duschen* (to shower, literally to shower oneself), and *sich treffen* (to meet, literally to meet one another).

SICH ANZIEHEN "To Dress"

I get dressed.	Ich ziehe mich an.	tsee-he mee[ch]UN
You (singular familiar) get dressed.	Du ziehst dich an.	tseeh-st di[ch] UN
He / She / It gets dressed.	Er / Sie / Es zieht sich an.	tseet si[ch] UN
You (singular formal) get dressed.	Sie ziehen sich an.	tsee-hen si[ch] UN
We get dressed.	Wir ziehen -uns an.	tsee-hen oonns UN
You (plural familiar) get dressed.	Ihr zieht euch an.	tseet oy[ch] UN
They / You (plural formal) get dressed.	Sie / Sie ziehen sich an.	tsee-hen si[ch] UN

ESSENTIALS CHECKLIST

Do you have:

- A current **passport**? Leave a copy of the identification page with someone at home, or bring a copy with you and store it separately from your passport.
- The address and phone number of your country's **embassy or consulate**?
- A copy of your **itinerary**, with contact numbers, with someone at home?
- A current **ATM card**? Is your PIN four-digits? Most European ATMs only accept cards with four-digit numeric PINs. Ask your bank for one.
- Your **e-ticket** documentation (a printout of the reservation confirmation and your itinerary)?
- Documentation for **traveler's checks**, stored separately from the checks?
- An extra pair of **glasses and/or contact lenses** and enough **prescription medications** to last the trip?
- Do you have your **credit card** PINs? Is there a daily withdrawal limit on credit card advances? Did you notify your credit card companies that you are traveling abroad?
- An **adapter and/or transformer** for electrical appliances?
- Your health **insurance card**?
- Your **camera** and an extra set of camera batteries?
- Any **ID cards** that could entitle you to discounts, such as AAA, AARP or ISIC student IDs?

FUN FACTS

- At 137,821 sq. miles (357,000 sq. km), Germany is **about the size of Montana**.
- Germany is home to **more cell phones than people**: a population of 82 million owns 83.9 million mobile phones.

- Nine countries **border Germany**: Poland, the Czech Republic, Austria, Switzerland, France, Luxembourg, Belgium, the Netherlands, and Denmark.
- Germany has the world's **third-largest economy**, behind the U.S. and Japan.
- Berlin, Germany's **capital and largest city**, has a population of 3.4 million—and a municipal debt of €60 billion.
- Linguists can't agree on the **longest German** word, but one top candidate is 63-letter **Rindfleischetikettierungsüberwachungsaufgabenübertragungsgesetz**, which won a 1999 award for German Word of the Year and translates to "beef labeling regulation and delegation of supervision law."
- The **unemployment rate** is 9.8% nationwide, 15.7% in the former East Germany, and 16.7% in Berlin.
- About two-thirds of German autobahns have **no speed limit**.
- In 2007, Germans surpassed the British as the **fattest people in Europe**: 75.4% of men and 58.9% of women are overweight.
- The average German consumes **117.8 liters of beer and 8.3kg (18.5lb) of chocolate** annually.
- In spring 2007, Knut the **celebrity polar bear cub** brought over one million visitors—and a $3.3 million increase in revenue—to the Berlin zoo.
- The **last wild bear** in Germany was killed in 1835.
- The *Stasi*, the **notorious East German secret police**, once held files on over six million people and employed an estimated one in every fifty East Germans as unofficial informants.
- The world has **German inventors** to thank for aspirin, the printing press, and the gummy bear.
- Germany is today home to the **fastest-growing Jewish community** in Europe—thanks largely to immigration from the former Soviet Union.

- **Turks**, the largest ethnic minority in Germany, make up about 3% of the population.
- Immigrants from Germany brought the traditions of the **Christmas tree, the Easter Bunny, and the kindergarten** to America.

GREAT MOMENTS

Surveying the new Berlin from the dome of the Reichstag Norman Foster's glittering glass dome atop the rebuilt Reichstag offers a sweeping vista of the reborn Berlin, a city that has transformed itself at breakneck pace since German reunification. Berlin hasn't forgotten its dark history, but with a construction crane or a newly restored building at every turn, the German capital is surging ahead as one of Europe's most dynamic cities.

Whiling away a midsummer evening in a Munich beer garden The unpretentious cheer of a *Biergarten* offers the perfect complement to a mug of German beer and a hearty platter of sausages. These family-friendly watering holes, decked with trellises, climbing vines, and Chinese lanterns, offer low-cost fun on summer nights. Standout beer gardens include the Augustinerkeller and the Hirschgarten.

Taking the waters at one of Germany's fabled spas Each spa resort has its own virtues, specialties, and historical associations. Whether you choose the luxury of storied Baden-Baden, the open-air thermal pools of Wiesbaden, or the saline waters of alpine Bad Reichenhall, you'll emerge from your treatment with a relaxed attitude and a sensory appreciation of German efficiency.

Nibbling your way through the Christmas market in Nürnberg There's no better way to warm up on a cold December day than with a glass of *Glühwein* (mulled wine) and a stroll under the red-and-white striped canvas roofs of the stalls at the Nürnberg Christmas market. Along with locally made crafts and wooden ornaments, the market is famous for its *Lebkuchen* (gingerbread cakes), homemade cheeses, and little Nürnberger sausages.

Lounging in a wicker beach basket on the island of Sylt With its white sand beaches, miles of hiking trails, and shifting dunes, windswept Sylt attracts celebrities and ordinary vacationing families alike. This island near the Danish border has a distinctly northern feel, and wicker baskets shelter beachgoers from bracing North Sea breezes.

Sampling wines in the lush Mosel Valley The banks of the meandering Mosel River are dotted with castles, fortresses, and vineyards. Visit between late August and mid-October, when the riverbanks light up in shades of gold and red, and workers gather buckets of grapes to press into the region's distinctive full-bodied wines.

Hiking through the Black Forest The forest that inspired the Brothers Grimm owes its name to the darkness that prevails under its thick canopy. Parts of the forest are now overrun with kiosks selling cuckoo clocks and *Lederhosen* to tourists; the best place to get an unspoiled taste of the forest and its hamlets is in the Upper Black Forest.

Glimpsing the frenzied visions of "Mad" King Ludwig at Castle Neuschwanstein Ludwig II of Bavaria devoted much of his time to building fantastical castles inspired by the operas of his beloved Wagner. The most spectacular castle built by the "Fairy-Tale King," Neuschwanstein Castle perches on an alpine crag over a gorge of the River Pöllat. With its courtyards, towers, and soaring turrets, Neuschwanstein is an orgy of opulence that nearly bankrupted the Bavarian treasury between 1868 and 1892.

CHAPTER TWO

GETTING THERE & GETTING AROUND

This section deals with every form of transportation. Whether you've just reached your destination by plane or you're renting a car to tour the countryside, you'll find the phrases you need in the next 30 pages.

AT THE AIRPORT

I am looking for ____	**Ich suche ____** *Ee[ch] su[ch]e ____*
a porter.	**einen Träger für mein Gepäck.** *eye-nen tr[ae]ger f[ue]r mine ghe-P[AE]CK.*
the check-in counter.	**den Abfertigungsschalter.** *dehn AB-fertigungs-shahlter.*
the ticket counter.	**den Kartenschalter.** *dehn KAHRR-ten-shahlter.*
arrivals.	**den Ankunftsbereich.** *dehn AN-kunfts-beh-rei[ch].*
departures.	**den Abreisebereich.** *dehn AB-rise-eh-beh-rei[ch].*
gate number ____.	**Gate ____.** *Gate ____.*

For full coverage of numbers, see p7.

the waiting area.	**den Wartebereich.** *dehn WARTEH-beh-rei[ch].*
the men's restroom.	**die Herrentoilette.** *dee hair-renn-toi-LET-teh.*
the women's restroom.	**die Damentoilette.** *dee dah-menn-toi-LET-teh.*
the police station.	**die Polizeidienststelle.** *dee poli-TSAI-deenst-shtelle.*
a security guard.	**einen Sicherheitsbeamten.** *eye-nen SI[CH]ER-heights-beh-ahmten.*

the smoking area.	**den Raucherbereich.**
	dehn RAU[CH]-er-beh-rei[ch].
the information booth.	**den Informationsstand.**
	dehn informahtsihons-stahnd.
a public telephone.	**ein öffentliches Telefon.**
	aihn [oe]ffentli[ch]es tehleh-PHON.
an ATM.	**einen Geldautomaten.**
	eye-nen GELD-auto-MAH-ten.
baggage claim.	**die Gepäckausgabe.**
	dee ghe-P[AE]CK-ousgah-beh.
a luggage cart.	**einen Gepäckwagen.**
	eye-nen ghe-P[AE]CK-wah-ghen.
a currency exchange.	**eine Geldwechselstube.**
	eye-neh GELD-whecksel-shtoobeh.
a café.	**ein Café.**
	aihn kaff-EHH.
a restaurant.	**ein Restaurant.**
	aihn restau-RONG.
a bar.	**eine Bar.**
	eye-neh bar.
a bookstore or newsstand.	**eine Buchhandlung oder einen Zeitungsstand.**
	eye-neh BOO[CH]-hahnd-lung ohdehr eye-nen TSITE-oongs-shtahnd.
a duty-free shop.	**einen Duty-Free-Shop.**
	eye-nen duty-FREE shop.
Is there Internet access here?	**Gibt es hier einen Internetzugang?**
	Gheebt as heer eye-nen INTERNET-tsoo-gahng?
I'd like to page someone.	**Ich möchte jemanden ausrufen lassen.**
	Ee[ch] m[oe][ch]teh yeh-mahn-denn OUS-roofen lahssen.
Do you accept credit cards?	**Akzeptieren Sie Kreditkarten?**
	Acktsep-TEEREN zee cre-DEET-kahrr-ten?

CHECKING IN

I would like a one-way ticket to ____.	**Ich hätte gern ein einfaches Ticket nach ____.** *Ee[ch] HAT-teh ghern aihn AIHN-fa[ch]es ticket nah[ch] ____.*
I would like a round trip ticket to ____.	**Ich hätte gern ein Ticket nach ____ inklusive Rückreise.** *Ee[ch] HAT-te ghern aihn AIHN-fa[ch]-as ticket nah[ch] ____ inclu-ZEE-veh R[UE]CK-rise-eh.*
How much are the tickets?	**Wie viel kosten die Tickets?** *Vee-feel costen dee tickets?*
Do you have anything less expensive?	**Haben Sie auch etwas Günstigeres im Angebot?** *Ha-ben zee au[ch] at-WAHS G[UE]NS-tee-gheh-res im ahn-ghe-BOHT?*
How long is the flight?	**Wie lange dauert der Flug?** *Vee lahng-eh dauert dehr floog?*
What time does flight ____ leave?	**Welche Abflugzeit hat Flug Nummer ____?** *VELL-[ch]eh UP-floog-tsite hut floog noommer ____?*
What time does flight ____ arrive?	**Welche Ankunftszeit hat Flug Nummer ____?** *VELL-[ch]eh UN-koonfts-tsite hut floog noommer ____?*
Do I have a connecting flight?	**Gibt es einen Anschlussflug?** *Gheebt as eye-nen AN-shluss-floog?*
Do I need to change planes?	**Muss ich umsteigen?** *Muhss ee[ch] UM-shteye-ghenn?*
My flight leaves at __:__.	**Mein Flug geht um __:__ Uhr.** *Mine floog gheht oomm __:__ oor.*

For full coverage of numbers, see p7.
For full coverage of time, see p11.

Common Airport Signs

Ankunft	Arrivals
Abreise	Departures
Terminal	Terminal
Gate	Gate
Tickets	Ticketing
Zoll	Customs
Gepäckausgabe	Baggage Claim
Drücken	Push
Ziehen	Pull
Rauchen verboten	No Smoking
Eingang	Entrance
Ausgang	Exit
Herren	Men's
Damen	Women's
Pendelbusse	Shuttle Buses
Taxis	Taxis

What time will the flight arrive?

Welche Ankunftszeit hat der Flug?
VELL-[ch]eh UN-koonfts-tsite hut dehr floog?

Is the flight on time?

Ist der Flug pünktlich?
Ist dehr floog P[UE]NKT-li[ch]?

Is the flight delayed?

Hat der Flug Verspätung?
Hut dehr floog fair-SP[AE]-toong?

From which terminal is flight _____ leaving?

Welches Abflugterminal hat Flug _____?
VELL-[ch]ess UP-floog-terminal hut floog _____?

From which gate is flight _____ leaving?

Welches Abfluggate hat Flug _____?
VELL-[ch]ess UP-floog-gate hut floog _____?

How much time do I need for check-in?

Wie lange dauert das Einchecken?
Vee lahng-eh douert dahs EYN-checken?

Is there an express check-in line?	**Gibt es einen schnelleren Check-In?** *Gheebt as eye-nen SHNELL-eren check-in?*
Is there electronic check-in?	**Gibt es einen elektronischen Check-In?** *Gheebt as eye-nen ehlec-TROH-nishen check-in?*

Seat Preferences

I would like ____ ticket(s) in ____	**Ich hätte gern ____ Ticket(s) in ____** *Ee[ch] HUT-te ghern ____ Ticket(s) in ____*
first class.	**der ersten Klasse.** *dehr AIR-sten klasseh.*
business class.	**Business-Klasse.** *business klasseh.*
economy class.	**Economy-Klasse.** *economy klasseh.*
I would like ____	**Geben Sie mir bitte einen ____** *Ghehben zee mere bit-eh eye-nen*
Please don't give me ____	**Geben Sie mir bitte keinen ____** *Ghehben zee mere bit-eh k-eye-nen ____*
a window seat.	**Fensterplatz.** *FAN-stir-plahts.*
an aisle seat.	**Gangplatz.** *GAHNG-plahts.*
an emergency exit row seat.	**Platz an einem Notausgang.** *plahts un eye-nem NOHT-ous-gahng.*
a bulkhead seat.	**Fensterplatz.** *FAN-stir-plahts.*
a seat by the restroom.	**Platz in der Nähe der Toiletten.** *plahts in dehr N[AE]-he dehr toi-LET-ten.*
a seat near the front.	**Platz im vorderen Teil.** *plahts im FOR-deren tile.*

a seat near the middle.	**Platz im mittleren Teil.**
	plahts im MITT-leren tile.
a seat near the back.	**Platz im hinteren Teil.**
	plahts im HIN-teren tile.
Is there a meal on the flight?	**Gibt es Verpflegung während des Flugs?**
	Gheebt as fair-PFLEH-goong v[ae]h-rend des floogs?
I'd like to order ____	**Ich hätte gern ____**
	Ee[ch] hut-te ghern ____
a vegetarian meal.	**ein vegetarisches Essen.**
	aihn veh-gheh-TA-rishes essen.
a kosher meal.	**ein koscheres Essen.**
	aihn KO-sheres essen.
a diabetic meal.	**ein Essen für Diabetiker.**
	aihn essen f[ue]r dee-ah-BEH-ticker.
I am traveling to ____.	**Ich bin auf dem Weg nach ____.**
	Ee[ch] bin ouf dehm vehg na[ch] ____.
I am coming from ____.	**Ich komme gerade aus ____.**
	Ee[ch] com-me ghe-RA-de ous ____.
I arrived from ____.	**Ich bin aus ____ angekommen.**
	Ee[ch] bin ous ____ UN-gheh-com-menn.

For full coverage of country terms, see English / German dictionary.

I'd like to change / cancel / confirm my reservation.	**Ich möchte meine Reservierung ändern / stornieren / bestätigen.**
	Ee[ch] m[oe][ch]te mine-eh rehsehr-VEE-rung [ae]n-dern / shtor-NEE-ren / beh-ST[AE]H-ti-ghen.
I have ____ bags to check.	**Ich habe ____ Taschen aufzugeben.**
	Ee[ch] hah-beh ____ tashen OUF-tsoo-GEH-ben.

For full coverage of numbers, see p7.

Passengers with Special Needs

Is that wheelchair accessible?	**Ist dieser Rollstuhl frei?** *Isst DEE-sehr ROLL-shtool frei?*
May I have a wheelchair / walker please?	**Könnte ich bitte einen Rollstuhl / eine Gehhilfe bekommen?** *K[oe]nnte ee[ch] bit-eh eye-nen ROLL-shtool / eye-neh GHEH-hilfeh beh-COM-men?*
I need some assistance boarding.	**Ich benötige Hilfe beim Einsteigen.** *Ee[ch] beh-N[OE]-tiggeh HILL-feh buym AIHN-shty-ghen.*
I need to bring my service dog.	**Ich bin auf die Begleitung meines Blindenhundes angewiesen.** *Ee[ch] bin ouf dee beh-GLEYE-toong minus BLIN-den-hoon-des un-gheh-VEE-sen.*
Do you have services for the hearing impaired?	**Haben Sie Angebote für Hörgeschädigte?** *Hah-ben zee un-gheh-BOH-teh f[ue]r H[OE]R-gheh-SH[AE]H-digg-teh?*
Do you have services for the visually impaired?	**Haben Sie Angebote für Sehbehinderte?** *Hah-ben zee un-gheh-BOH-teh f[ue]r SEH-behhinderteh?*

Trouble at Check-In

How long is the delay?	**Wie viel beträgt die Verspätung?** *Vee feel beh-TR[AE]GT dee fair-SHP[AE]H-tung?*
My flight was late.	**Mein Flug hatte Verspätung.** *Mine floog hut-eh fair-SHP[AE]H-tung.*
I missed my flight.	**Ich habe meinen Flug verpasst.** *Ee[ch] hah-beh my-nen floog fair-PASSED.*
When is the next flight?	**Wann geht der nächste Flug?** *Vann gheht dehr n[ae][ch]s-teh floog?*

May I have a meal voucher?	**Bekomme ich einen Essensgutschein?** *Beh-COM-meh ee[ch] eye-nen ESSENCE-goot-shine?*
May I have a room voucher?	**Bekomme ich einen Zimmergutschein?** *Beh-COM-meh ee[ch] eye-nen TSIMMER-goot-shine?*

AT CUSTOMS / SECURITY CHECKPOINTS

I'm traveling with a group.	**Ich bin Mitglied einer Reisegruppe.** *Ee[ch] bin mit-GLEED eye-ner RISE-EH-gruppeh.*
I'm on my own.	**Ich reise allein.** *Ee[ch] rise-eh ah-LINE.*
I'm traveling on business.	**Ich befinde mich auf Geschäftsreise.** *Ee[ch] beh-FINN-deh mi[ch] ouf gheh-SHAFTS-rise-eh.*
I'm on vacation.	**Ich mache Urlaub.** *Ee[ch] ma[ch]eh OOR-laub.*
I have nothing to declare.	**Ich habe nichts zu verzollen.** *Ee[ch] hah-beh ni[ch]ts tsoo fair-TSOLLEN.*
I would like to declare ___.	**Ich habe ___ zu verzollen.** *Ee[ch] hah-beh ___ tsoo fair-TSOLLEN.*
I have some liquor.	**Ich habe etwas Alkohol dabei.** *Ee[ch] hah-beh AT-vahs alkohol dah-BY.*
I have some cigars.	**Ich habe ein paar Zigarren dabei.** *Ee[ch] hah-beh aihn pahr tsi-GARREN dah-BY.*
They are gifts.	**Das sind Geschenke.** *Dahs sind gheh-SHENK-eh.*
They are for personal use.	**Sie sind für den Privatgebrauch.** *Zee sind f[ue]r dehn pree-VAAT-gheh-brau[ch].*

GETTING THERE

That is my medicine.
Das ist meine Medizin.
Dahs isst my-neh mehdi-TSIHN.

I have my prescription.
Ich habe ein Rezept.
Ee[ch] hah-beh aihn reh-TSEPT.

My children are traveling on the same passport.
Meine Kinder reisen mit demselben Ausweis.
My-neh KIN-der rise-en mit dehm selben OUS-vise.

I'd like a male / female officer to conduct the search.
Ich hätte gern, dass die Durchsuchung von einem Mann / einer Frau durchgeführt wird.
Ee[ch] hat-teh ghern, dahss dee dur[ch]-SUH-[ch]ung fonn eye-nem mahnn / eye-ner frau dur[ch]-gheh-F[UE]HRT wird.

Trouble at Security

Help me. I've lost ____
Könnten Sie mir bitte helfen? Ich habe ____
K[oe]nnten zee mere bit-eh HELL-fen? Ee[ch] hah-beh ____

my passport.
meinen Ausweis verloren.
my-nen OUS-vise fer-LOH-ren.

my boarding pass.
meine Bordkarte verloren.
my-ne BORT-kahrr-teh fer-LOH-ren.

my identification.
meine Papiere verloren.
my-ne pa-PEE-reh fer-LOH-ren.

my wallet.
meine Geldbörse verloren.
my-ne GELD-b[oe]rseh fer-LOH-ren.

my purse.
meine Handtasche verloren.
my-ne HAHND-tasheh fer-LOH-ren.

Someone stole my purse / wallet!
Jemand hat meine Handtasche / meine Geldbörse gestohlen!
YEH-mahnd hut my-ne HANHD-tasheh / my-ne GELD-b[oe]rseh gheh-SHTOH-len!

Listen Up: Security Lingo

Bitte ziehen Sie Ihre Schuhe aus.	Please remove your shoes.
Ziehen Sie Ihre Jacke aus.	Remove your jacket / sweater.
Legen Sie Ihren Schmuck ab.	Remove your jewelry.
Legen Sie Ihre Taschen auf das Band.	Place your bags on the conveyor belt.
Treten Sie zur Seite.	Step to the side.
Wir müssen Sie abtasten.	We have to do a hand search.

IN-FLIGHT

It's unlikely you'll need much German on the plane, but these phrases will help if a bilingual flight attendant is unavailable or if you need to talk to a German-speaking neighbor.

I think that's my seat.	**Ich glaube, das ist mein Platz.** *Ee[ch] GLAU-beh, das isst MINE plahts.*
May I have _____	**Ich hätte gern _____** *Ee[ch] hat-eh ghern _____*
water?	**ein stilles Wasser.** *aihn shtilles vahsser.*
sparkling water?	**ein Wasser mit Kohlensäure.** *aihn vahsser mit COHLEN-soi-reh.*
orange juice?	**einen Orangensaft.** *eye-nen oh-RUNSHEHN-saft.*
soda?	**eine Limonade.** *eye-ne limo-NAH-deh.*
diet soda?	**eine Diätlimonade.** *eye-ne dee-ATE-limo-NAH-deh.*
a beer?	**ein Bier.** *aihn beer.*
wine?	**ein Glas Wein.** *aihn glahs vine.*

For a complete list of drinks, see p92.

a pillow?	**ein Kissen.**
	aihn KISS-en.
a blanket?	**eine Decke.**
	eye-ne DECK-eh.
a hand wipe?	**ein Tuch für die Hände.**
	aihn tuh[ch] f[ue]r dee H[AE]N-deh.
headphones?	**Kopfhörer.**
	KOPF-h[oe]rer.
a magazine or	**eine Zeitschrift oder eine Zeitung.**
newspaper?	*eye-ne TSAIT-shrift ohdehr*
	eye-ne TSAI-toong.
When will the meal be	**Wann wird das Essen serviert?**
served?	*Vann vird dahs ESSEN sehr-VEERT?*
How long until we land?	**Wie lange noch bis zur Landung?**
	Vee lahng-he no[ch] bis tsoor
	LANN-doong?
May I move to another seat?	**Dürfte ich mich bitte woanders**
	hinsetzen?
	D[ue]rfte ee[ch] mi[ch] bit-eh wo-
	AHNN-ders HIN-settsen?
How do I turn the light	**Wie kann ich das Licht einschalten**
on / off?	**/ ausschalten?**
	Vee kann ee[ch] dahs li[ch]t AIHN-
	shahllten / OUS-shahllten?

Trouble In-Flight

These headphones are	**Dieser Kopfhörer funktioniert**
broken.	**nicht.**
	DEE-sehr KOPF-h[oe]rer funktsio-
	NEERT ni[ch]t.
I spilled.	**Ich habe etwas verschüttet.**
	Ee[ch] hah-beh AT-vas fair-
	SH[UE]T-tet.
My child spilled.	**Mein Kind hat etwas verschüttet.**
	Mine kinnd hut AT-vahs fair-
	SH[UE]T-tet.

My child is sick.	**Meinem Kind ist schlecht.**
	Mine-m kinnd isst shle[ch]t.
I need an airsickness bag.	**Ich brauche eine Spucktüte.**
	Ee[ch] BRAU-[ch]eh eye-ne
	SHPUCK-t[ue]teh.
I smell something strange.	**Hier riecht etwas seltsam.**
	Hear REE[CH]T at-vahs SELLT-sahm.
That passenger is	**Dieser Passagier verhält sich**
behaving suspiciously.	**verdächtig.**
	Dee-sehr passa-SHEER fair-H[AE]LT
	si[ch] fair-D[AE][CH]-tig.

BAGGAGE CLAIM

Where is baggage claim	**Wo finde ich die Gepäckausgabe**
for flight ____?	**für Flug ____?**
	Voh fin-de ee[ch] dee ghe-P[AE]CK-
	ousgahbeh f[ue]r floog ____?
Would you please help	**Könnten Sie mir bitte mit meinem**
with my bags?	**Gepäck behilflich sein?**
	K[oe]nn-ten zee mere bit-eh mit
	mine-em ghe-P[AE]CK beh-HILLF-
	li[ch] sine?
I am missing ____ bags.	**Mir fehlen ____ Taschen.**
	Mere FEH-lenn ____ tashen.

For full coverage of numbers, see p7.

My bag is ____	**Meine Tasche ____**
	My-neh tasheh ____
lost.	**ist verschwunden.**
	isst fair-SHWOON-den.
damaged.	**wurde beschädigt.**
	voor-deh beh-SH[AE]H-
	diggt.
stolen.	**wurde gestohlen.**
	voor-deh gheh-SHTOH-len.
a suitcase.	**ist ein Koffer.**
	isst aihn COUGH-er.
a briefcase.	**ist ein Aktenkoffer.**
	isst aihn ACKTEN-cough-er.

a carry-on.	**ist eine Tragetasche.**
	isst eye-ne TRAH-gheh-tasheh.
a suit bag.	**ist ein Kleidersack.**
	isst aihn kl-EYE-dehr-sahck.
a trunk.	**ist ein Schrankkoffer.**
	isst aihn SHRANK-cough-er.
golf clubs.	**sind Golfschläger.**
	sinnd GOLF-shl[ae]h-gher.

For full coverage of color terms, see English / German Dictionary.

hard.	**ist hart.**
	isst harrt.
made out of ____	**ist aus ____**
	isst ous ____
canvas.	**Stoff.**
	shtoff.
vinyl.	**Vinyl.**
	vee-N[UE]HL.
leather.	**Leder.**
	LEH-der.
hard plastic.	**Hartplastik.**
	HARRT-plahstick.
aluminum.	**Aluminium.**
	ahlu-MIH-nium.

RENTING A VEHICLE

Is there a car rental agency in the airport?	**Gibt es am Flughafen eine Autovermietung?**
	Gheebt as ahm FLOOG-hahfen eye-ne OUTOH-fair-meetung?
I have a reservation.	**Ich habe eine Reservierung.**
	Ee[ch] hah-beh eye-ne reh-sehr-VEE-rung.

Vehicle Preferences

I would like to rent ____	**Ich möchte gern ____ mieten.**
	Ee[ch] m[oe][ch]-te ghern ____ meeten.

an economy car.	**ein sparsames Auto** *aihn SHPAHR-summes outoh*
a midsize car.	**einen Mittelklassewagen** *eye-nen MITTEL-clahsseh-wahghen*
a sedan.	**eine Limousine** *eye-ne limo-SEENEH*
a convertible.	**ein Cabrio** *aihn CAAH-bree-oh*
a van.	**einen Van** *eye-nen van*
a sports car.	**einen Sportwagen** *eye-nen SHPORT-wahghen*
a 4-wheel-drive vehicle.	**ein Auto mit Vierradantrieb** *aihn outoh mit FEAR-rahd-antreeb*
a motorcycle.	**ein Motorrad** *aihn moh-TO-rahd*
a scooter.	**einen Roller** *eye-nen roller*
Do you have one with ____	**Ist ein Fahrzeug mit ____ verfügbar?** *Isst aihn FAAR-tsoig mit ____ fair-F[UE]G-bahr?*
air conditioning?	**Klimaanlage** *CLEE-mah-un-lahgheh*
a sunroof?	**Sonnendach** *SONNEN-da[ch]*
a CD player?	**CD-Player** *TSEH-DEH player*
satellite radio?	**Satellitenradio** *sattel-ITTEN-rah-dee-oh*
satellite tracking?	**Navigationssystem** *nah-vee-ghah-TSEEONS-sys-tehm*
an onboard map?	**Straßenatlas** *SHTRAHSSEN-aht-lahss*

a DVD player?	**DVD-Player**
	DHE-FOUH-DEH player
child seats?	**Kindersitzen**
	KIN-dehr-sitsen
Do you have a ___	**Haben Sie ein ___**
	Hah-ben zee aihn ___
smaller car?	**kleineres Auto?**
	CLYE-neres outoh?
bigger car?	**größeres Auto?**
	gr[oe]ceres outoh?
cheaper car?	**günstigeres Auto?**
	GH[UE]N-stee-gheres outoh?
Do you have a non-smoking car?	**Haben Sie ein Nichtraucherauto?**
	Hah-ben zee aihn NI[CH]T-rau-[ch]er-outoh?
I need an automatic transmission.	**Ich hätte gern ein Automatikgetriebe.**
	Ee[ch] hut-teh ghern aihn outoh-MAH-tik-ghe-treebeh.
A standard transmission is okay.	**Schaltgetriebe ist in Ordnung.**
	Shallt-ghe-treebeh isst in ORD-noong.
May I have an upgrade?	**Könnte ich bitte eine höhere Kategorie bekommen?**
	K[oe]nn-te ee[ch] bit-eh eye-ne h[oe]her-eh kahte-gho-REE beh-COM-men?

Money Matters

What's the daily / weekly / monthly rate?	**Wie hoch sind die Kosten pro Tag / Woche / Monat?**
	Vee hoh[ch] sind dee COS-ten proh tahg / wo[ch]eh / MOH-naht?
What is the mileage rate?	**Wie hoch sind die Kosten pro Kilometer?**
	Vee hoh[ch] sind dee COS-ten proh KILO-mehter?

How much is insurance?	**Wie viel kostet die Versicherung?**
	Vee feel costet dee fair-SI[CH]E-roong?
Are there other fees?	**Fallen weitere Kosten an?**
	Fahllen VYE-tereh COS-ten un?
Is there a weekend rate?	**Gibt es einen Wochenendtarif?**
	Gheebt as eye-nen WO-[ch]en-end-ta-REEF?

Technical Questions

What kind of fuel does it take?	**Welche Kraftstoffart muss ich verwenden?**
	Vell-[ch]E KRAFFT-shtoff-art muss ee[ch] fair-VENN-denn?
Do you have the manual in English?	**Haben Sie ein englisches Handbuch?**
	Hah-ben zee aihn ENG-lishes hahnd-boo[ch]?
Do you have a booklet in English with the local traffic laws?	**Haben Sie eine englische Broschüre mit den örtlichen Verkehrsregeln?**
	Hah-ben zee eye-ne ENG-lisheh bro-SH[UE]-reh mit dehn [oe]rt-li-[ch]en fair-CARES-reh-gheln?

Technical Issues

Fill it up, please.	**Volltanken, bitte.**
	FOLL-tunken, bit-eh.
It is already dented.	**Das Fahrzeug ist bereits beschädigt.**
	Dahs FAAR-tsoig isst beh-raits beh-SH[AE]H-diggt.
It is scratched.	**Das Fahrzeug hat einen Kratzer.**
	Dahs FAHR-tsoig hut eye-nen KRATT-ser.

| The _____ doesn't work. | **Der / Die / Das _____ funktioniert nicht.** |
| | *Dehr / Dee / Dahs _____ funk-tsio-NEERT ni[ch]t.* |

See diagram on p51 for car parts.

The tires look low.	**Die Reifen scheinen wenig Druck zu haben.**
	Dee RYE-fan shy-nen wehnig droock tsoo hah-ben.
It has a flat tire.	**Das Fahrzeug hat einen Platten.**
	Dahs FAAR-tsoig hut eye-nen plahtten.
Whom do I call for service?	**Wo kann ich anrufen, wenn ich Hilfe benötige?**
	Voh kann ee[ch] UN-roofen, venn ee[ch] HILL-fe beh-N[OE]-tiggeh?
It won't start.	**Der Motor springt nicht an.**
	Dehr MO-tor shpringt ni[ch]t un.
It's out of gas.	**Der Tank ist leer.**
	Dehr tahnk isst lehr.
The Check Engine light is on.	**Das Lämpchen für ein Problem mit dem Motor leuchtet.**
	Dahs L[AE]MP-[ch]en f[ue]r aihn proh-BLEHM mit dehm MO-tor loy[ch]ted.
The oil light is on.	**Das Öllämpchen leuchtet.**
	Dahs [OE]HL-l[ae]mp-[ch]en loy[ch]ted.
The brake light is on.	**Die Bremsleuchte leuchtet.**
	Dee BREMS-loy[ch]teh loy[ch]ted.
It runs rough.	**Das Fahrzeug läuft unruhig.**
	Dahs FAAR-tsoig loyft OON-ruhig.
The car is over-heating.	**Das Fahrzeug überhitzt.**
	Dahs FAAR-tsoig [ue]ber-HITST.

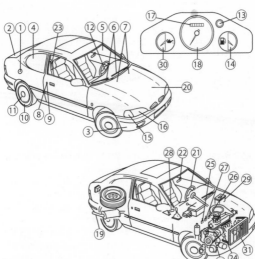

1. Tank
2. Kofferraum
3. Stoßstange
4. Fenster
5. Windschutzscheibe
6. Scheibenwischer
7. Scheibenwaschanlage
8. Tür
9. Schloss
10. Reifen
11. Radkappe
12. Lenkrad
13. Warnleuchte
14. Tankanzeige
15. Blinker
16. Scheinwerfer
17. Kilometerzähler

18. Tacho
19. Auspuff
20. Motorhaube
21. Lenkrad
22. Rückspiegel
23. Sicherheitsgurt
24. Motor
25. Gaspedal
26. Kupplung
27. Bremse
28. Handbremse
29. Batterie
30. Ölstandsanzeige
31. Kühler
32. Keilriemen

Asking for Directions

Excuse me, please.	**Verzeihung bitte.**
	Fair-TSYE-hoong bit-eh.
How do I get to ____?	**Wie komme ich zum ____?**
	Vee COMM-eh ee[ch] tsoomm ____?
Go straight.	**Gehen Sie geradeaus.**
	Ghe-hen zee ghe-RA-deh ous.
Turn left.	**Gehen Sie nach links.**
	Ghe-hen zee na[ch] links.
Continue right.	**Gehen Sie nach rechts.**
	Ghe-hen zee na[ch] re[ch]ts.
It's on the right.	**Das Ziel befindet sich auf der rechten Seite.**
	Dahs tseel beh-FIN-det si[ch] ouf dehr RE[CH]-ten SYE-teh.
Can you show me on the map?	**Könnten Sie mir das bitte auf der Karte zeigen?**
	K[oe]nn-ten zee mere dahs bit-eh ouf dehr KAHRR-teh tsye-ghen?
How far is it from here?	**Wie weit ist das von hier entfernt?**
	Vee vye-t isst dahs fonn heer ent-FAIRNT?
Is this the right road for ____?	**Ist das die Straße nach ____?**
	Isst dahs dee shtrahseh na[ch] ____?
I've lost my way.	**Ich habe mich verirrt.**
	Ee[ch] hah-beh mi[ch] fair-IRRT.
Would you repeat that?	**Könnten Sie das bitte wiederholen?**
	K[oe]nn-ten zee dahs bit-eh veeder-HOH-len?
Thanks for your help.	**Vielen Dank für Ihre Hilfe.**
	FEEL-en dunk f[ue]r ee-reh HILL-feh.

For full coverage of direction-related terms, see p5.

Road Signs

Geschwindigkeitsbegrenzung	Speed Limit
Stopp	Stop
Vorfahrt gewähren	Yield
Gefahr	Danger
Sackgasse	No Exit
Einbahnstraße	One Way
Einfahrt verboten	Do Not Enter
Straße gesperrt	Road Closed
Maut	Toll
Nur Bargeld	Cash Only
Parken verboten	No Parking
Parkgebühr	Parking Fee
Parkhaus	Parking Garage

Sorry, Officer

What is the speed limit?	**Welche Geschwindigkeitsbegrenzung gilt hier?** *Vell-[ch]eh ghe-SHWINN-digg-keits-beh-gren-tsoong guilt heer?*
I wasn't going that fast.	**So schnell bin ich nicht gefahren.** *Soh shnell bin i[ch] ni[ch]t ghe-FAH-renn.*
How much is the fine?	**Wie hoch ist die Strafe?** *Vee hoh[ch] isst dee SHTRA-fe?*
Where do I pay the fine?	**Wo muss ich die Strafe bezahlen?** *Voh muhss i[ch] dee shtra-fe beh-ZAH-len?*
Do I have to go to court?	**Komme ich vor Gericht?** *Com-me ee[ch] fohr ghe-RI[CH]T?*
I had an accident.	**Ich hatte einen Unfall.** *Ee[ch] hut-eh eye-nen OON-fahll.*
The other driver hit me.	**Der andere Fahrer hat den Unfall verursacht.** *Dehr un-dehreh FAH-rer hut dehn OON-fahll fair-OOR-sa[ch]t.*

I'm at fault.	**Es war mein Fehler.** *Ess vahr MINE fehler.*

BY TAXI

Where is the taxi stand?	**Wo ist der Taxistand?** *Voh isst dehr TAHXEE-stahnd?*
Is there a limo / bus / van for my hotel?	**Fährt eine Limousine / ein Bus / ein Van zu meinem Hotel?** *F[ae]hrt eye-ne limo-SEENHE / aihn booss / aihn van tsoo my-nem ho-TELL?*
I need to get to ____.	**Bringen Sie mich bitte zum ____.** *Bring-hen zee mi[ch] bit-eh tsoom ____.*
How much will that cost?	**Wie viel wird das kosten?** *Vee feel vird dahs costen?*
How long will it take?	**Wie lange dauert die Fahrt?** *Vee lahng-eh douert dee fahrt?*
Can you take me / us to the train / bus station?	**Können Sie mich / uns bitte zum Bahnhof / Busbahnhof bringen?** *K[oe]n-nen zee mi[ch] / oons bit-eh tsoom BAHN-hohf / BOOSS-bahn-hohf bring-hen?*
I am in a hurry.	**Ich bin in Eile.** *Ee[ch] bin in AY-leh.*

Listen Up: Taxi Lingo

Steigen Sie ein!	Get in!
Lassen Sie Ihr Gepäck stehen. Ich kümmere mich darum.	Leave your luggage. I got it.
Das kostet sieben Euro pro Tasche.	It's seven Euros for each bag.
Wie viele Fahrgäste?	How many passengers?
Sind Sie in Eile?	Are you in a hurry?

Slow down.	**Fahren Sie bitte langsamer.**
	Fah-ren zee bit-eh LAHNG-summer.
Am I close enough to walk?	**Kann ich von hier aus zu Fuß gehen?**
	Cahnn ee[ch] fonn heer ous tsoo FOOS ghe-hen?
Let me out here.	**Lassen Sie mich hier bitte aussteigen.**
	Lahssen zee mi[ch] heer bit-eh OUS-shtye-ghen.
That's not the correct change.	**Das Wechselgeld stimmt leider nicht.**
	Dahs VECK-sell-geld shtimmt lye-der ni[ch]t.

BY TRAIN

How do I get to the train station?	**Wie komme ich zum Bahnhof?**
	Vee COM-meh ee[ch] tsoom BAHN-hohf?
Would you take me to the train station?	**Könnten Sie mich bitte zum Bahnhof bringen?**
	K[oe]nn-ten zee mi[ch] bit-eh tsoom BAHN-hohf bring-hen?
How long is the trip to ____?	**Wie lange dauert die Fahrt nach ____?**
	Vee lahng-eh douert dee fahrt na[ch] ____?
When is the next train?	**Wann geht der nächste Zug?**
	Vahnn gheht dehr n[ae][ch]s-teh tsoog?
Do you have a schedule / timetable?	**Haben Sie einen Fahrplan?**
	Hah-ben zee eye-nen FAAR-plahn?
Do I have to change trains?	**Muss ich umsteigen?**
	Muhss ee[ch] OOMM-shtye-ghen?
a one-way ticket	**ein einfaches Ticket**
	aihn AIHN-fa-[ch]es ticket

| a round-trip ticket | **ein Hin- und Rückreiseticket** |
| | *aihn hin oonnd R[UE]CK-rise-eh-ticket* |

| Which platform does it leave from? | **Von welchem Gleis fährt der Zug ab?** |
| | *Fonn vell-[ch]emm glise f[ae]hrt dehr tsoog ab?* |

| Is there a bar car? | **Gibt es einen Barwagen?** |
| | *Gheebt as eye-nen BAR-vah-ghen?* |

| Is there a dining car? | **Gibt es einen Speisewagen?** |
| | *Gheebt as eye-nen SHPY-seh-vah-ghen?* |

| Which car is my seat in? | **In welchem Wagen befindet sich mein Platz?** |
| | *In VELL-[ch]em VAH-ghen beh-FIN-det si[ch] mine PLAHTS?* |

| Is this seat taken? | **Ist dieser Platz besetzt?** |
| | *Isst DEE-sehr plahts beh-SETST?* |

| Where is the next stop? | **Wo ist der nächste Halt?** |
| | *Voh isst dehr n[ae][ch]s-teh HALLT?* |

| How many stops to ____? | **Wie viele Haltestellen noch bis ____?** |
| | *Vee fee-leh HALLT-teh-shtell-en noh[ch] biss ____?* |

| What's the train number and destination? | **Welche Zugnummer und welchen Zielort hat dieser Zug?** |
| | *Vell-[ch]eh TSOOG-noommer oonnd vell-[ch]enn TSEEL-ort hut deeser tsoog?* |

BY BUS

| How do I get to the bus station? | **Wie komme ich zum Busbahnhof?** |
| | *Vee COM-meh ee[ch] tsoom BOOSS-bahn-hohf?* |

Would you take me to the bus station?	**Könnten Sie mich bitte zum Busbahnhof bringen?**
	K[oe]nn-ten zee mi[ch] bit-eh tsoom BOOSS-bahn-hohf bring-hen?
May I have a bus schedule?	**Könnte ich bitte einen Busfahrplan bekommen?**
	K[oe]nn-teh ee[ch] bit-eh eye-nen BOOSS-faar-plahn beh-COM-men?
Which bus goes to ____?	**Welcher Bus fährt nach ____?**
	Vell-[ch]er booss f[ae]hrt na[ch] ____?
Where does it leave from?	**Von wo fährt er ab?**
	Fonn VOH f[ae]hrt ehr ab?
How long does the bus take?	**Wie lange dauert die Fahrt?**
	Vee LAHNG-eh douert dee fahrt?
How much is it?	**Wie viel kostet das?**
	Vee feel COSS-tet dahs?
Is there an express bus?	**Gibt es einen Expressbus?**
	Gheebt as eye-nen ex-PRESS-booss?
Does it make local stops?	**Hält der Bus unterwegs?**
	H[ae]llt dehr booss oonter-VEHGS?
Does it run at night?	**Fährt der Bus nachts?**
	F[ae]hrt dehr booss NA[CH]TS?
When does the next bus leave?	**Wann geht der nächste Bus?**
	Vann gheht dehr n[ae][ch]s-teh BOOSS?
a one-way ticket	**ein einfaches Ticket**
	aihn AIHN-fa-[ch]es ticket
a round-trip ticket	**ein Hin- und Rückreiseticket**
	aihn hin oonnd R[UE]CK-rise-eh-ticket
How long will the bus be stopped?	**Wie lange steht der Bus?**
	Vee lahng-eh SHTEHT dehr booss?
Is there an air conditioned bus?	**Gibt es einen klimatisierten Bus?**
	Gheebt as eye-nen kleema-tee-SEER-ten booss?

Is this seat taken?	**Ist dieser Platz besetzt?**
	Isst DEE-sehr plahts beh-SETST?
Where is the next stop?	**Wo ist der nächste Halt?**
	Voh isst dehr n[ae][ch]s-teh HALLT?
Please tell me when we reach ____.	**Könnten Sie mir bitte sagen, wann wir ____ erreichen?**
	K[oe]nn-ten zee mere bit-eh SAH-ghen, vann veer ____ err-RYE-[ch]en?
Let me off here.	**Lassen Sie mich hier bitte aussteigen.**
	Lahssen zee mi[ch] heer bit-eh OUS-shtye-ghen.

BY BOAT OR SHIP

Would you take me to the port?	**Könnten Sie mich bitte zum Hafen bringen?**
	K[oe]nn-ten zee mi[ch] bit-eh tsoom HAH-fenn bring-hen?
When does the ship sail?	**Wann legt das Schiff ab?**
	Vann lehgt dahs shiff ab?
How long is the trip?	**Wie lange dauert die Reise?**
	Vee lahng-eh douert dee rise-eh?
Where are the life preservers?	**Wo befinden sich die Schwimmwesten?**
	Voh beh-fin-den si[ch] dee SHVIMM-vess-ten?
I would like a private cabin.	**Ich hätte gern eine Einzelkabine.**
	Ee[ch] h[ae]tteh ghern eye-ne AIHN-tsell-kah-beeneh.
Is the trip rough?	**Ist mit hohem Seegang zu rechnen?**
	Isst mit HOH-hemm SEH-gahng tsoo re[ch]nen?
I feel seasick.	**Ich bin seekrank.**
	Ee[ch] bin SEH-krahnk.

I need some seasick pills.	**Ich benötige Tabletten gegen Seekrankheit.** *Ee[ch] beh-N[OE]-tiggeh tah-BLETT-en ghe-ghen SEH-krahnk-height.*
Where is the bathroom?	**Wo finde ich die Toiletten?** *Voh fin-deh ee[ch] dee toi-LET-ten?*
Does the ship have a casino?	**Gibt es auf dem Schiff ein Casino?** *Gheebt as ouf dehm shiff aihn kah-ZEE-noh?*
Will the ship stop at ports along the way?	**Legt das Schiff unterwegs an?** *Lehggt dahs shiff oonter-vehggs AN?*

BY SUBWAY

Where's the subway station?	**Wo finde ich die U-Bahn-Haltestelle?** *Voh fin-deh ee[ch] dee OOH-bahn-hallt-eh-shtell-eh?*
Where can I buy a ticket?	**Wo kann ich ein Ticket kaufen?** *Voh cann ee[ch] aihn ticket COW-fehn?*
Could I have a map of the subway?	**Könnte ich bitte einen Plan des U-Bahn-Netzes bekommen?** *K[oe]nn-teh ee[ch] bit-eh eye-nen plahn dess OOH-bahn-netsess beh-COM-men?*
Which line should I take for ____?	**Welche Linie fährt nach ____?** *Vell-[ch]eh LEE-nee-eh f[ae]hrt nah[ch] ____?*
Is this the right line for ____?	**Ist das die Linie nach ____?** *Isst dahs dee LEE-nee-eh na[ch] ____?*
Which stop is it for ____?	**An welcher Haltestelle muss ich für ____ aussteigen?** *Un vell-[ch]er HALL-teh-shtell-eh muhss ee[ch] f[ue]r ____ OUS-shtye-ghen?*

SUBWAY TICKETS

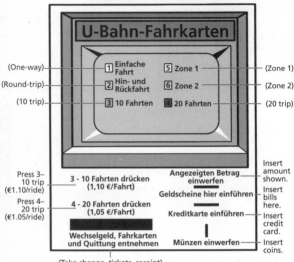

U-Bahn-Fahrkarten

(One-way) — 1 Einfache Fahrt
(Round-trip) — 2 Hin- und Rückfahrt
(10 trip) — 3 10 Fahrten

5 Zone 1 — (Zone 1)
6 Zone 2 — (Zone 2)
4 20 Fahrten — (20 trip)

Press 3–
10 trip
(€1.10/ride) — 3 - 10 Fahrten drücken (1,10 €/Fahrt)

Press 4–
20 trip
(€1.05/ride) — 4 - 20 Fahrten drücken (1,05 €/Fahrt)

Wechselgeld, Fahrkarten und Quittung entnehmen
(Take change, tickets, receipt)

Angezeigten Betrag einwerfen — Insert amount shown.
Geldscheine hier einführen — Insert bills here.
Kreditkarte einführen — Insert credit card.
Münzen einwerfen — Insert coins.

How many stops is it to ____?	**Wie viele Haltestellen noch bis ____?** *Vee feeleh HALL-teh-shtell-en noh[ch] biss ____?*
Is the next stop ____?	**Ist ____ die nächste Haltestelle?** *Isst ____ dee n[ae][ch]s-teh HALL-teh-shtell-eh?*
Where are we?	**Wo befinden wir uns gerade?** *Voh beh-FIN-denn veer oons ghe-RAH-deh?*
Where do I change to ____?	**Wo muss ich nach ____ umsteigen?** *Voh muhss ee[ch] nah[ch] ____ OOMM-shtye-ghen?*

What time is the last train to ___?	**Wann geht der letzte Zug nach ___?** *Vann gheht dehr LETS-teh tsoog nah[ch] ___?*

CONSIDERATIONS FOR TRAVELERS WITH SPECIAL NEEDS

Do you have wheelchair access?	**Ist der Zugang behindertengerecht?** *Isst dehr TSOO-gahng beh-HIN-dehr-ten-gheh-re[ch]t?*
Do you have elevators? Where?	**Gibt es Aufzüge? Wo?** *Gheebt as OUF-ts[ue]-gheh? Voh?*
Do you have ramps? Where?	**Haben Sie Rampen? Wo?** *Hah-ben zee RAHM-penn? Voh?*
Are the restrooms wheelchair accessible?	**Sind die Toiletten behindertengerecht?** *Sinnt dee toi-LET-ten beh-HIN-dehr-ten-gheh-re[ch]t?*
Do you have audio assistance for the hearing impaired?	**Haben Sie Audioinformationen für Hörgeschädigte?** *Hah-ben zee OU-dee-oh-informahtsiho-nen f[ue]r H[OE]R-gheh-sh[ae]-digg-teh?*
I am deaf.	**Ich bin taub.** *Ee[ch] bin TAUP.*
May I bring my service dog?	**Kann ich meinen Blindenhund mitnehmen?** *Kann ee[ch] my-nen BLIN-den-hoonnd mit-nehmen?*
I am blind.	**Ich bin blind.** *Ee[ch] bin BLINND.*
I need to charge my power chair.	**Ich muss meinen elektrisch betriebenen Rollstuhl aufladen.** *Ee[ch] muhss my-nen eh-LECK-trish beh-TREE-bennen ROLL-shtool ouf-lah-denn.*

TRAVEL TIPS

Flying Times
To Berlin
...From New York, Newark, and Boston, 8½ hours
...From Chicago, 10½ hours
...From Los Angeles, 13½ hours
To Munich
...From New York and Newark, 8¼ hours
...From Chicago, 8¾ hours
...From Los Angeles, 13¼ hours (with one stopover)
To Frankfurt
...From New York and Newark, 8 hours
...From Boston, 7 hours
...From Chicago, 8½ hours
...From San Francisco, 11 hours

Travel Times Between Major Cities

City	Distance	Flying Time	Train Time	Driving Time
Berlin to Dresden	193km/120 miles	no flights	3 hr	2 hr
Berlin to Munich	585km/364 miles	1 hr, 10 min	6 hr	5½ hr
Berlin to Hamburg	288km/179 miles	no flights	2 hr	3 hr
Berlin to Frankfurt	454km/339 miles	1 hr, 10 min	4½ hr	5 hr
Berlin to Köln	575km/357miles	1 hr, 5 min	4½ hr	5¼ hr
Frankfurt to Hamburg	495km/308 miles	1 hr	3¾ hr	4½ hr
Frankfurt to Köln	194km/121 miles	no flights	1½ hr	2 hr
Frankfurt to Munich	392km/244 miles	1 hr 10 min	3½ hr	3½ hr
Hamburg to Köln	427km/265 miles	55 min	4 hr	4 hr
Köln to Munich	577km/358 miles	1 hr 10 min	4¾ hr	5¼ hr

HOW TO FIND THE BEST AIRFARE

- Plan ahead and be flexible with your travel dates. Passengers who book their tickets long in advance, who can stay over Saturday night, or who fly midweek or during less-trafficked hours get the best fares. Leaving or returning a day or two earlier or later may save you hundreds of dollars.

- Rather than flying directly to Germany from North America, many travelers find it cheaper to fly into London, then continue from there on a low-cost European airline such as EasyJet or RyanAir. Be aware, however, that you may need to take an hour-plus bus journey from Heathrow Airport, where transatlantic flights arrive and depart, to a smaller outlying airport.

- Flexibility with your flight destination can also save you money: it may be significantly cheaper to fly into Berlin rather than Hamburg, or into Frankfurt rather than Munich.

- Avoid the busiest holiday periods. Christmas and Easter are especially expensive times to travel to Germany, but remember that prices also rise during holidays that may be less known to the international traveler, such as Pentecost (late May or early June) and the Day of German Unity (Oct. 3).

- Be a low-season traveler. You'll spend less to get to Germany, and have fewer crowds to cope with, if you visit October through November or January through May.

- Check out travel websites. You don't necessarily have to book online, but these sites provide a handy way to do comparison shopping. Type in various dates and various departure and arrival cities and see what you come up with. An advantage of booking on an airline's website is that you often get extra frequent flier miles for doing so. Some sites to check: www.frommers.com; www.travelocity. com; www.lastminute.com; www.expedia.com; www. cheaptickets.com; www.smarterliving.com.

GETTING AROUND

By Plane   From Frankfurt, most **Lufthansa** (www.lufthansa.com) destinations in Germany can be reached in an average of 50 minutes, with at least four flights daily. Less expensive carriers such as **Air Berlin** (www.airberlin.com) and **German Wings** (www.germanwings.com) also offer an extensive network of internal flights within Germany.

By Train   The trains of German Rail deserve their reputation for comfort, cleanliness, and punctuality. All are modern and fast, although not necessarily cheaper than flying. InterCity (IC) and InterCity Express (ICE) trains serve major cities, with the latter reaching speeds of 186mph. Comfortable night trains fan out from Berlin and connect major German cities to each other as well as to Paris, Copenhagen, Prague, and Venice. Slower regional trains serve small towns in Germany. For information about schedules and rail passes, check out the excellent website of **German Rail** (www.bahn.de/p/view/international/englisch/international_guests.shtml).

By Bus   An excellent, efficient bus network reaches the few parts of Germany that are inaccessible by train. The most popular bus rides are along the Romantic Road, along the Castle Road, and in the Black Forest. For more information, contact a travel agent or **Deutsche Touring GmbH** (www.deutsche-touring.com).

By Car   A rental car offers the easiest way to explore the German countryside, and is indispensable if you plan to tour the Fairy-Tale Road. In general:

- **Rental car rates** are fairly steep, but stiff competition between rental companies means that comparison shopping can save you money. Major rental companies are **Avis** (© 800/331-1212; www.avis.com), **Budget** (© 800/472-3325; www.budget.com), **Hertz** (© 800/654-3131; www.hertz.com), and **Auto Europe** (© 888/223-5555; www.autoeurope.com).

- **Gasoline** (known as **benzin**) prices are much higher than in the U.S., typically around €1.30 per liter (about €5.20 per gallon). Service stations are plentiful along autobahns, and the cheapest gas is at stations marked SB-TANKEN (self-service).
- Roads are very well marked and well maintained. The speed limit is 50kmph (about 30mph) in congested areas and 100 kmph (about 60mph) on all other roads except autobahns. In theory, most autobahns have no speed limit in the left (fast) lane, but the government recommends a limit of 130kmph (81mph).
- Use of **seat belts** is compulsory, and children are not allowed to ride in the front seat.
- U.S. and Canadian drivers need only a valid domestic **driver's license** to drive a rental car in Germany, but require an **international insurance certificate**, known as a green card (*Grüne Karte*). Any car rental agency will automatically provide one of these as a standard part of the rental contract.
- The major automobile club in Germany is the **AvD** (Automobilclub von Deutschland; ☎ **800/990-9909**; www. avd.de). If you have a **breakdown** on the autobahn, you can call them from one of many emergency phones, spaced about a mile apart. If you don't belong to an auto club, call ☎ **0180/222-2222** for road service assistance. Emergency service is free, but you pay for parts and materials.

CHAPTER THREE

LODGING

This chapter will help you find the right accommodations, at the right price, and the amenities you might need during your stay.

ROOM PREFERENCES

Please recommend ____	**Bitte empfehlen Sie mir ____** *Bit-eh em-PFEHH-len zee meer ____*
a clean hostel.	**eine saubere Jugendherberge.** *eye-ne SOU-beh-reh YOU-ghend-hair-bair-gheh.*
a moderately priced hotel.	**ein Hotel der mittleren Preiskategorie.** *aihn ho-TELL dehr MITT-leh-ren PRYES-kah-teh-gho-ree.*
a moderately priced B&B.	**eine Pension der mittleren Preiskategorie.** *eye-ne pen-SION dehr MITT-leh-ren PRYES-kah-teh-gho-ree.*
a good hotel / motel.	**ein gutes Hotel / Motel.** *aihn GOO-tess ho-TELL / mo-TELL.*
Does the hotel have ____	**Verfügt das Hotel über ____** *fair-F[UE]GHT dahs ho-TELL [ue]-behr ____*
a pool?	**einen Pool?** *eye-nen pool?*
a casino?	**ein Kasino?** *aihn kah-ZEE-noh?*
suites?	**Suiten?** *SWEE-ten?*

66

a balcony?	**einen Balkon?**
	eye-nen bahll-COHN?
a fitness center?	**ein Fitness-Center?**
	aihn FIT-ness-center?
a spa?	**ein Heilbad?**
	aihn HYLE-bahd?
a private beach?	**einen Privatstrand?**
	eye-nen pree-VAHT-shtrahnd?
a tennis court?	**einen Tennisplatz?**
	eye-nen TENN-is-plahts?
I would like a room for ____.	**Ich hätte gern ein Zimmer für ____.**
	Ee[ch] hat-teh ghern aihn TSIM-mer f[ue]r ____.

For full coverage of number terms, see p7.

I would like ____	**Ich hätte gern ____**
	Ee[ch] hat-teh ghern ____
a king-sized bed.	**ein breites Doppelbett.**
	aihn brye-tess DOPPEL-bet.
a double bed.	**ein Doppelbett.**
	aihn DOPPEL-bet.

LODGING

Listen Up: Reservations Lingo

Wir haben nichts mehr frei. *Veer ha-ben ni[ch]ts mehr fraih.*	We have no vacancies.
Wie lange möchten Sie bleiben? *Vee lahng-he m[oe][ch]-ten zee BYLE-ben?*	How long will you be staying?
Raucher oder Nichtraucher? *RAU-[ch]er oh-dehr NI[CH]T-rau-[ch]er?*	Smoking or nonsmoking?

twin beds.	**zwei Betten.**
	tswaih bet-ten.
adjoining rooms.	**angrenzende Zimmer.**
	AHN-grenn-tsenn-deh tsimmer.
a smoking room.	**ein Raucherzimmer.**
	aihn RAU-[ch]er-tsimmer.
a non-smoking room.	**ein Nichtraucherzimmer.**
	aihn NI[CH]T rau-[ch]er-tsimmer.
a private bathroom.	**ein eigenes Bad.**
	aihn EYE-ghenn-es bahd.
a shower.	**eine Dusche.**
	eye-ne DOO-sheh.
a bathtub.	**eine Badewanne.**
	eye-ne BAH-deh-vann-eh.
air conditioning.	**eine Klimaanlage.**
	eye-ne CLEE-mah-un-lahgheh.
television.	**einen Fernseher.**
	eye-nen FEHRN-sehh-her.
cable.	**Kabelfernsehen.**
	KAH-bell-fehrn-sehhn.
satellite TV.	**Satellitenfernsehen.**
	sattel-IT-ten-fehrn-sehhn.
a telephone.	**ein Telefon.**
	aihn tehleh-PHON.
Internet access.	**einen Internetzugang.**
	eye-nen IN-ternet-tsoo-gahng.
high-speed Internet access.	**einen schnellen Internetzugang.**
	eye-nen SHNELL-en IN-ternet-tsoo-gahng.
a refrigerator.	**einen Kühlschrank.**
	eye-nen K[UE]HL-shrahnnk.
a beach view.	**Blick auf den Strand.**
	blick ouf dehn SHTRAHND.

a city view.	**Blick auf die Stadt.**
	blick ouf dee SHTAHTT.
a kitchenette.	**eine Kochnische.**
	eye-ne KO[CH]-nee-sheh.
a balcony.	**einen Balkon.**
	eye-nen bahll-COHN.
a suite.	**eine Suite.**
	eye-ne SWEET.
a penthouse.	**ein Penthhaus.**
	aihn PENT-house.
I would like a room ____	**Ich hätte gern ein Zimmer ____**
	Ee[ch] hat-teh ghern aihn tsimmer
	____
on the ground floor.	**im Erdgeschoß.**
	imm AIRD-gheh-shohhs.
near the elevator.	**in Aufzugnähe.**
	inn OUF-tsoogh-n[ae]h-he.
near the stairs.	**in der Nähe des**
	Treppenhauses.
	inn dher N[AE]-he dess TREP-
	penn-how-sess.
near the pool.	**in Poolnähe.**
	inn POOL-n[ae]h-he.
away from the street.	**das nicht in Richtung der**
	Straße liegt.
	dahs ni[ch]t inn RI[CH]-
	toonng der SHTRAH-se
	leeght.
I would like a corner room.	**Ich hätte gern ein Eckzimmer.**
	Ee[ch] hat-eh ghern aihn EKK-
	tsimmer.
Do you have ____	**Haben Sie ____?**
	Hah-ben zee ____?
a crib?	**ein Kinderbett?**
	aihn KIN-dehr-bet?

a foldout bed?	**ein ausklappbares Bett?**
	aihn OUS-klahpp-bah-rhes
	bet?

FOR GUESTS WITH SPECIAL NEEDS

I need a room with ____	**Ich benötige ein Zimmer mit ____**
	Ee[ch] beh-N[OE]-tiggeh aihn tsim-
	mer mitt ____

| wheelchair access. | **Zugang per Rollstuhl.** |
| | *TSOO-ghang pair ROLL-shtool.* |

| services for the | **Hilfe für Sehbehinderte.** |
| visually impaired. | *HILL-feh f[ue]r SEH-behin-derteh.* |

services for the hearing	**Hilfe für Hörgeschädigte.**
impaired.	*HILL-feh f[ue]r H[OE]R-gheh-*
	sh[ae]-digg-teh.

I am traveling with a	**Ich reise mit einem**
service dog.	**Blindenhund.**
	Ee[ch] RYE-seh mitt eye-nem
	BLIN-den-hoonnd.

MONEY MATTERS

I would like to make a	**Ich möchte reservieren.**
reservation.	*Ee[ch] m[oe][ch]-te reh-sehr-VEE-*
	renn.

How much per night?	**Wie viel pro Übernachtung?**
	Vee-feel proh [ue]behr-NA[CH]-
	toong?

| Do you have a ____ | **Bieten Sie ____** |
| | *BEE-ten zee ____* |

weekly / monthly rate?	**einen Wochentarif /**
	Monatstarif an?
	eye-nen VO-[ch]en-tah-reef /
	MO-nahts-tah-reef un?

a weekend rate?	**einen Wochenendtarif an?**
	eye-nen VO-[ch]enn-end-
	tah-reef un?

We will be staying for ____ days / weeks.	**Wir möchten ____ Tage / Wochen bleiben.** *Veer m[eo][ch]-ten ____ TAH-gheh / VO-[ch]enn blye-ben.*

For full coverage of number terms, see p7.

When is checkout time?	**Wann wird ausgecheckt?** *Vann vird OUS-gheh-checkt?*

For full coverage of time-related terms, see p11.

Do you accept credit cards / travelers checks?	**Akzeptieren Sie Kreditkarten / Reiseschecks?** *Acktsep-TEEREN zee cre-DEET-kahrr-ten / RYE-seh-shecks?*
May I see a room?	**Kann ich mir ein Zimmer ansehen?** *Kahnn ee[ch] mere aihn tsimmer UN-sehh-hen?*

Fenster
Licht
Bad
Spiegel
Decke
Lampe
Dusche Schreibtisch Vorhänge Fernseher
Wand
Badewanne
Waschbecken Kissen Stuhl Tisch
Toilette Bettdecke Bett Minibar
Boden

LODGING

How much are taxes?	**Wie viel Steuer muss ich bezahlen?**
	Vee feel shtoyer muss ee[ch] beh-TSAH-len?
Is there a service charge?	**Gibt es eine Servicegebühr?**
	Gheebt as eye-ne SER-vis-ghe-b[ue]hr?
I'd like to speak with the manager.	**Ich möchte den Manager sprechen.**
	Ee[ch] m[oe][ch]-te dehn MA-nager shpre-[ch]en.

IN-ROOM AMENITIES

I'd like ____	**Ich möchte ____**
	Ee[ch] m[oe][ch]-te ____
to place an international call.	**ein Auslandsgespräch führen.**
	aihn OUS-lahnds-gheh-shpr[ae][ch] f[ue]h-ren.
to place a long-distance call.	**ein Ferngespräch führen.**
	aihn FEHRN-gheh-shpr[ae][ch] f[ue]h-ren.
directory assistance in English.	**eine englischsprachige Telefonauskunft.**
	eye-ne ENG-lish-shprah[ch]igghe tehleh-PHON-ous-koonft.

Instructions for Dialing the Hotel Phone

Wählen Sie für einen Anruf auf einem anderen Zimmer die entsprechende Zimmernummer.	To call another room, dial the room number.
Wählen Sie für ein Ortsgespräch die 9 vor.	To make a local call, first dial 9.
Wählen Sie für einen Anruf bei der Vermittlung die 0.	To call the operator, dial 0.

room service.	**den Zimmerservice.**
	dehn TSIMMER-service.
maid service.	**den Raumpflegedienst.**
	dehn RAUHM-pfleh-ghe-
	deenst.
the front desk operator.	**die Vermittlung an der**
	Rezeption.
	dee fehr-MITT-loong un dehr
	reh-tsepp-tsee-OHN.
Do you have room service?	**Haben Sie Zimmerservice?**
	Hah-ben zee TSIMMER-service?
When is the kitchen open?	**Ab wann ist die Küche geöffnet?**
	Up vann isst dee k[ue][ch]e ghe-
	[OE]FF-net?
When is breakfast served?	**Wann wird das Frühstück serviert?**
	Vann vird dahs FR[UE]H-sht[ue]ck
	sehr-VEERT?

For full coverage of time-related terms, see p11.

Do you offer massages?	**Bieten Sie Massagen an?**
	Bee-ten zee ma-SSAH-shen un?
Do you have a lounge?	**Haben Sie ein Foyer?**
	Hah-ben zee aihn foy-YEH?
Do you have a business center?	**Haben Sie ein Geschäftscenter?**
	Hah-ben zee aihn gheh-SHAFTS-
	tsennt-senn-tehr?
Do you serve breakfast?	**Gibt es bei Ihnen Frühstück?**
	Gheebt as by eehnen FR[UE]H-
	sht[ue]ck?
Do you have Wi-Fi?	**Haben Sie Wi-Fi?**
	Hah-ben zee vee-fee?
May I have a newspaper in the morning?	**Kann ich morgens bitte eine Zeitung bekommen?**
	Khann ee[ch] MOR-ghens bit-eh eye-ne TSAI-toong beh-com-men?

Do you offer a tailor service?	**Haben Sie eine Schneiderei?**
	Hah-ben zee eye-ne shnai-de-RYE?
Do you offer laundry service?	**Haben Sie eine Wäscherei?**
	Hah-ben zee eye-neh v[ae]-sheh-RYE?
Do you offer dry cleaning?	**Haben Sie eine chemische Reinigung?**
	Hah-ben zee eye-ne KHE-mi-sheh RYE-nee-goong?
May we have ____	**Könnten wir bitte ____**
	K[oe]nn-ten veer bit-eh ____
clean sheets today?	**frische Bettwäsche bekommen?**
	frisheh BET-v[ae]sheh beh-com-men?
more towels?	**mehr Handtücher bekommen?**
	mehr HAHND-t[ue]-[ch]er beh-com-men?
more toilet paper?	**mehr Toilettenpapier bekommen?**
	mehr toi-LET-ten-pah-peer beh-com-men?
extra pillows?	**zusätzliche Kissen bekommen?**
	TSOO-sats-lee-[ch]e kissen beh-com-men?
Do you have an ice machine?	**Haben Sie eine Eismaschine?**
	Hah-ben zee eye-ne ICE-mah-shee-ne?
Did I receive any ____	**Haben Sie ____**
	Hah-ben zee
messages?	**Nachrichten für mich?**
	NA[CH]-ree[ch]ten f[ue]r mee[ch]?
mail?	**Post für mich?**
	POSST f[ue]r mee[ch]?

faxes?	**ein Fax für mich?**
	aihn FAHCKS f[ue]r mee[ch]?
A spare key, please.	**Geben Sie mir bitte einen Ersatzschlüssel.**
	Ghehben zee mere bit-eh eye-nen air-SAHTTS-SHL[UE]SS-ell.
More hangers please.	**Geben Sie mir bitte ein paar zusätzliche Kleiderbügel.**
	Ghehben zee mere bit-eh aihn par TSOO-sats-lee-[ch]e KLYE-dehr-b[ue]-ghell.
I am allergic to down pillows.	**Ich bin allergisch gegen Daunenkissen.**
	Ee[ch] bin ah-LERR-ghish gheghen DOW-nen-kissen.
I'd like a wake-up call.	**Ich hätte gern einen Weckruf.**
	Ee[ch] hat-teh ghern eye-nen VECK-roof.

For full coverage of time-related terms, see p11.

Do you have alarm clocks?	**Haben Sie Wecker?**
	Hah-ben zee VECK-ehr?
Is there a safe in the room?	**Verfügt das Zimmer über einen Tresor?**
	Fair-f[ue]ght dahs tsimmer [ue]h-ber eye-nen treh-SOHR?
Does the room have a hair dryer?	**Gibt es auf dem Zimmer einen Haartrockner?**
	Gheebt as ouf dehm tsimmer eye-nen HAAR-trocknehr?

HOTEL ROOM TROUBLE

May I speak with the manager?	**Könnte ich bitte den Manager sprechen?**
	K[oe]nn-teh ee[ch] bit-eh dehn MA-nager spre-[ch]en?

The _____ does not work.	**_____ funktioniert nicht.** *_____ funk-tsee-oh-NEERT ni[ch]t.*
television	**Der Fernseher** *Dehr FEHRN-sehh-her*
telephone	**Das Telefon** *Dahs tehleh-PHON*
air conditioning	**Die Klimaanlage** *Dee CLEE-mah-un-lahgheh*
Internet access	**Der Internetzugang** *Dehr IN-ternet-tsoo-gahng*
cable TV	**Das Kabelfernsehen** *Dahs KAH-bell-fehrn-sehhn*
There is no hot water.	**Es kommt kein warmes Wasser.** *As commt kyne varr-mes VAHSS-er.*
The toilet is over-flowing!	**Die Toilette läuft über!** *Dee toi-LET-teh loyft [ue]-ber!*
This room is _____	**Dieses Zimmer ist _____** *DEE-sess tsimmer isst _____*
too noisy.	**zu laut.** *tsoo lout.*
too cold.	**zu kalt.** *tsoo kahllt.*
too warm.	**zu warm.** *tsoo vaahrrm.*

This room has ____

bugs.

mice.

I'd like a different room.

Do you have a bigger room?

I locked myself out of my room.

Do you have any fans?

The sheets are not clean.

The towels are not clean.

The room is not clean.

The guests next door / above / below are being very loud.

In diesem Zimmer gibt es ____
In DEE-semm tsimmer gheebt as ____

Ungeziefer.
OOHN-gheh-tsee-fair.

Mäuse.
MOY-seh.

Ich möchte ein anderes Zimmer.
Ee[ch] m[oe][ch]-te aihn UN-deh-res tsimmer.

Haben Sie ein größeres Zimmer?
Hah-ben zee aihn GR[OE]-ceres tsimmer?

Ich habe mich aus meinem Zimmer ausgesperrt.
Ee[ch] hah-be mi[ch] ous my-nem TSIMMER ous-gheh-shperrt.

Haben Sie Ventilatoren?
Hah-ben zee venn-tee-lah-TOH-renn?

Die Bettwäsche ist schmutzig.
Dee BET-v[ae]sheh isst shmoottsig.

Die Handtücher sind schmutzig.
Dee HAHND-t[ue]-[ch]er sinnd shmoottsig.

Das Zimmer ist schmutzig.
Dahs tsimmer isst shmoottsig.

Die Gäste nebenan / über dem Zimmer / unter dem Zimmer sind sehr laut.
Dee guess-teh neh-ben-UN / [UE]-ber dehm tsimmer / OOHN-ter dehm tsimmer sinnd sehr lout.

CHECKING OUT

I think this charge is a mistake.

Ich glaube, diese Gebühr ist falsch.
Ee[ch] GLAU-be, dee-se ghe-B[UE]HR isst fahllsh.

Please explain this charge to me.

Könnten Sie mir diese Gebühr bitte erklären?
K[oe]nn-ten zee mere dee-se ghe-b[ue]hr bit-eh air-KL[AE]H-ren?

Thank you, we enjoyed our stay.

Vielen Dank, es war schön bei Ihnen.
Feel-en dunk, as vaar SH[OE]HN by eehnen.

The service was excellent.

Der Service war ausgezeichnet.
Dehr SER-vis vaar ous-gheh-TSAI[CH]-net.

The staff is very professional and courteous.

Das Personal ist sehr professionell und zuvorkommend.
Dahs pair-soh-NAAHL isst sehr proh-fess-yo-NELL oonnd tsoo-VOHR-comm-end.

Please call a cab for me.

Rufen Sie mir bitte ein Taxi.
Roo-fen zee mere bit-eh aihn TAHCK-zee.

Would someone please get my bags?

Könnte sich bitte jemand um mein Gepäck kümmern?
K[oe]nn-te si[ch] bit-eh YEH-mahnd oohmm mine ghe-P[AE]CK k[ue]mm-ern?

HAPPY CAMPING

I'd like a site for _____

Ich hätte gern einen Platz für _____
Ee[ch] hat-teh ghern eye-nen plahts f[ue]r _____

a tent.

ein Zelt.
aihn TSELLT.

a camper.	**einen Wohnwagen**
	eye-nen VOHN-vaah-ghenn.
Are there ____	**Gibt es hier ____**
	Gheebt as heer ____
bathrooms?	**Toiletten?**
	toi-LET-ten?
showers?	**Duschen?**
	DOO-shenn?
Is there running water?	**Gibt es fließend Wasser?**
	Gheebt es fleecent vahsser?
Is the water drinkable?	**Ist das Wasser trinkbar?**
	Isst dahs vahsser TRINK-bahr?
Where is the electrical hookup?	**Wo finde ich den Elektroanschluss?**
	Voh fin-deh ee[ch] dehn eh-LECK-troh-unshlooss?

HOTEL OVERVIEW

In general, Germany has one of the highest standards of innkeeping in the world. Even a €10 per night youth hostel is likely to be spotlessly clean, and a nicer hotel should positively gleam. However, many of the hotels in the former East Germany—once geared to tourism from the old Eastern Bloc countries—do not meet the same standard as those in the West. Hotels range from palaces of luxury and comfort to plain country inns and simple guesthouses (*Gasthäuser*), with a huge variation in rates. The cheapest accommodations are in pensions (*Fremdenheime*) or rooms in private homes (look for a sign saying ZIMMER FREI, meaning there's a room for rent). Hotels listed as *garni* provide no meals other than breakfast.

THE BEST LUXURY HOTELS

German efficiency and cleanliness are legendary, so it's little surprise that the top luxury hotels in Germany are among the world's best. If you can afford to stay, set your sights on the following hotels throughout the country. For more extensive listings, see Frommer's Germany.

Baden-Baden

Der Kleine Prinz One of the most romantic of Germany's many romantic hotels, Der Kleine Prinz occupies a century-old pair of neo-baroque houses in the heart of the elegant spa resort of Baden-Baden. Personalized and intimate, the rooms of Der Kleine Prinz each have a special feature: an open fireplace, a tower, a balcony, or a whirlpool bathtub. (© **0722/134-6600**; www.derkleineprinz.de).

Berlin

Grand Hotel Esplanade This strikingly contemporary hotel near hyper-modern Potsdamer Platz exudes quality and prestige. With its collection of modern art, its spacious and sun-flooded rooms overlooking the river, and its first-class service, it is a prime address for the luxury-minded. (© **413/241-2541**; www.esplanade.de).

Hotel Adlon   Berlin's most historic hotel is a phoenix belatedly risen from the ashes of the war. With an unbeatable location overlooking the Brandenburg Gate, it is permeated with the legends of a glamorous and tragic history. It reopened with a flourish in 1997, its grand public areas showcasing stained glass domes, Carrara marble, coffered ceilings, and lavish details. Well-appointed rooms feature state-of-the-art electronic extras. (© 800/426-3135 in the U.S.; www.hotel-adlon.de).

Celle

Fürstenhof Celle   This baroque manor house, enlarged with half-timbered wings, stands out even in a town legendary for its medieval and Renaissance buildings. There's a cozy bar in the medieval cellar and one of the best dining rooms in Lower Saxony. (© 05141/2010; www.fuerstenhof.de).

Hamburg

Raffles Vier Jahreszeiten   The Edwardian interior is warm and mellow, and as opulent as the 19th-century façade. The appeal is aristocratic, but with a hint of the saltwater zestiness that makes Hamburg such a great city. Expect a personalized touch to the service. (© 040/34940; www.hvj.de).

Munich

Bayerischer Hof & Palais Montgelas   Together, the Bayerischer Hof and the 17th-century Palais Montgelas form Munich's answer to New York's Waldorf Astoria. A royal favorite since the days when King Ludwig I used to come here to take a bath, the establishment has undergone lavish improvements of late. Room décor ranges from Bavarian provincial to British country-house chintz, and many beds are four-posters. (© 089/21200; www.bayerischerhof.de).

Kempinski Hotel Vier Jaherszeiten   This grand hotel is not only the most elegant in Munich, it's also Germany's most celebrated and one of the finest in the world. Rooms and suites combine the charm of days gone by with modern luxuries. The antique-style beds feature fine linens and sumptuous mattresses. (© 089/21250; www.kempinski-vierjahreszeiten.de)

Rothenburg ob der Tauber
Eisenhut (Iron Helmet)   Eisenhut is the most celebrated inn on the Romantic Road and one of the finest small hotels in Germany. It consists of four adjoining patrician houses with 16th-century walls and a valuable collection of antiques. Each room is unique—yours may feature hand-carved monumental pieces or a 1940s-style tufted satin headboard. (© 09861/7050; www.eisenhut.com).

Rüdesheim-Assmannshausen
Krone Assmannshausen   Sprawling along the banks of the Rhine in an oversized, gingerbread-laden fantasy, this hotel has witnessed the arrival of many important Germans, including Goethe and Kaiser Wilhelm II, in its 400-year history. It also contains one of the best traditional restaurants in town (© 06722/4030; www.hotel-krone.com).

Weimar
Hotel Elephant   In its 300 years, the Elephant has been the haunt of such luminaries as Schiller, Liszt, and Bach. Overlooking the old marketplace of Weimar, it weathered half a century of communist rule in East Germany with its elegant façade and distinctive terracotta roof intact. Bold Art Deco décor adds flair to the rooms. (© 03643/8020; www.arabellasheraton.com).

THE BEST SMALL INNS & HOTELS

These comfortable and atmospheric establishments offer some of the best values in Germany:

Berlin
Art'otel Berlin Ku'damm   This unique hotel is as chic as it is discreet. The swirling action of the Ku'damm lies right outside the door and the strictly minimalist décor inside includes touches by some of Europe's top designers. (© 030/240620; www.parkplaza.com).

Cologne

Antik-Hotel Bristol   In the heart of a cathedral city along the Rhine, this unique hotel is filled with antiques, both country-rustic and town-house elegant, making the atmosphere both authentic and inviting. (© 0221/120195; www.antik-hotel-bristol.de).

Hamburg

Hanseatic Hotel   This little hotel evokes the ambience of a prim and proper English gentleman's club. Rooms are one of a kind, many of them containing antiques. In summer, the owner may be out front tending the flower garden, getting ready to welcome his guests. (© 040/485772; www.hanseatic-hamburg.de).

Heidelberg

Parkhotel Atlantic Schlosshotel   This 24-room inn is on the wooded outskirts of Heidelberg, near the famous castle. Every room is comfortable and convenient, and in the afternoon you can go for long walks along the woodland trails surrounding the property. (© 06221/60420; www.parkhotel-atlantic.de).

Munich

Gästehaus Englischer Garten   This is an oasis of charm and tranquility, close to the English Garden where buffed Munich lies nude in the sun. The furnishings are in an old-fashioned Bavarian style, but the comfort level is first-rate. (© 089/3839410; www.hotelenglischergarten.de).

Passau

Altstadt-Hotel   This inexpensive hotel stands at the convergence of three rivers—the Danube, the Ilz, and the Inn. But the hotel offers more than river views—it's comfortably and traditionally furnished, and its regional cuisine and convivial pub attract the locals. (© 0851/3370; www.altstadt-hotel.de).

CHAPTER FOUR

DINING

This chapter includes a menu reader and the language you need to communicate in a range of dining establishments and food markets.

FINDING A RESTAURANT

Would you recommend a good ____ restaurant?	**Können Sie mir ein gutes ____ Restaurant empfehlen?** *K[oe]nn-en zee mere aihn goo-tess ____ ress-toh-ROHNG empfehlen?*
local	**örtliches** *[oe]rrt-li[ch]-es*
Italian	**italienisches** *ee-tahl-yeh-nee-shess*
French	**französisches** *frahnn-ts[oe]h-see-shess*
Turkish	**türkisches** *t[ue]rr-kee-shess*
Spanish	**spanisches** *spah-nee-shess*
Chinese	**chinesisches** *[ch]ee-nehh-see-shess*
Japanese	**japanisches** *yah-pah-nee-shess*
Asian	**asiatisches** *ah-see-ah-tish-es*
pizza	**Pizzeria** *Pittseh-REE-ah*
steakhouse	**Steakhaus** *STEAK-house*
family	**Familien-** *fah-mee-lee-en-*

seafood	**Fisch-** *fish*
vegetarian	**vegetarisches** *veh-gheh-TAH-ree-shess*
buffet-style	**Selbstbedienungs-** *sellbst-beh-dee-noongs-*
Greek	**griechisches** *gree-[ch]ish-ess*
budget	**günstiges** *gh[ue]nns-tee-ghess*

Which is the best restaurant in town?

Welches Restaurant ist das beste der Stadt?
Vell-[ch]ess ress-toh-rohng isst dahs BESS-teh dehr shtahtt?

Is there a late-night restaurant nearby?

Gibt es in der Nähe ein Restaurant, das auch noch spät geöffnet hat?
Gheebt as in dehr n[ae]h-heh aihn ress-toh-ROHNG, dahs ou[ch] noh[ch] SHP[AE]HT gheh-[oe]ff-net hut?

Is there a restaurant that serves breakfast nearby?

Gibt es in der Nähe ein Frühstückslokal?
Gheebt as in dehr n[ae]h-heh aihn FR[UE]H-sht[ue]cks-loh-kahl?

Is it very expensive?

Ist es dort teuer?
Isst as dohrrt TOY-ehr?

Do I need a reservation?

Benötige ich eine Reservierung?
Beh-n[oe]h-tiggeh ee[ch] eye-neh reh-sehr-VEE-roong?

Do I have to dress up?

Muss ich mich herausputzen?
Mooss ee[ch] mee[ch] heh-RAUS-put-senn?

Do they serve lunch?

Gibt es dort Mittagessen?
Gheebt as dohrrt MIT-tahg-ess-en?

What time do they open for dinner?	**Ab wann gibt es dort Abendessen?**
	Up vahnn gheebt as dohrrt AH-bent-ess-en?
For lunch?	**Mittagessen?**
	MIT-tahg-ess-en?
What time do they close?	**Wie lange ist dort geöffnet?**
	Vee lung-eh isst dohrrt gheh-[OE]FF-net?
Do you have a take out menu?	**Haben Sie Speisen zum Mitnehmen?**
	Hah-ben zee shpye-sen tsoom MIT-neh-men?
Do you have a bar?	**Haben Sie eine Bar?**
	Hah-ben zee eye-neh BAHR?
Is there a café nearby?	**Gibt es ein Café in der Nähe?**
	Gheebt as aihn kaff-EHH inn dehr n[ae]h-heh?

GETTING SEATED

Are you still serving?	**Haben Sie noch geöffnet?**
	Hah-ben zee noh[ch] gheh-[OE]FF-net?
How long is the wait?	**Wie lange muss ich warten? (sing.) / Wie lange müssen wir warten? (pl.)**
	Vee lung-eh mooss ee[ch] VAHRR-ten? / Vee lung-eh m[ue]ss-en veer VAHRR-ten?
Do you have a no-smoking section?	**Haben Sie einen Nichtraucherbereich?**
	Hah-ben zee eye-nen NI[CH]T-rauh-[ch]ehr-beh-rye[ch]?
A table for ____, please.	**Einen Tisch für ____ Personen, bitte.**
	Eye-nen TISH f[ue]hr ____ pehr-soh-nen, bit-eh.

For a full list of numbers, see p7.

Listen Up: Restaurant Lingo

Raucher oder Nichtraucher?
RAUH-[ch]ehr oh-der NI[CH]T-rauh-[ch]ehr?

Smoking or nonsmoking?

Sie benötigen eine Krawatte und ein Jackett.
Zee beh-n[oe]h-tiggen eye-neh krah-VAHTT-eh oonnd aihn shah-KETT.

You'll need a tie and jacket.

Es tut mir leid, aber kurze Hosen sind hier nicht erlaubt.
As toot mere LYDE, ah-behr koorrt-seh HOH-senn sinnd hear ni[ch]t air-LAUBT.

I'm sorry, no shorts are allowed.

Kann ich Ihnen etwas zu trinken bringen?
Khann ee[ch] eeh-nen at-vahs tsoo TRING-ken bring-en?

May I bring you something to drink?

Soll ich Ihnen die Weinkarte bringen?
Sohll ee[ch] eeh-nen dee VINE-kahrr-teh bring-en?

Would you like to see a wine list?

Darf ich Ihnen unsere Spezialitäten vorstellen?
Dharrf ee[ch] eeh-nen oonn-seh-reh shpeh-tsee-yahl-ee-T[AE]H-ten fohr-shtell-en?

Would you like to hear our specials?

Möchten Sie jetzt bestellen?
M[oe][ch]-ten zee yetst beh-SHTELL-en?

Are you ready to order?

Es tut mir leid, aber Ihre Kreditkarte wurde nicht akzeptiert.
As toot mere LYDE, ah-behr eeh-reh creh-DEET-kahrr-teh voorr-deh ni[ch]t ahcktsep-TEERT.

I'm sorry, but your credit card was declined.

Do you have a quiet table?	**Haben Sie einen ruhigen Tisch?**
	Hah-ben zee eye-nen ROO-hee-ghenn tish?
May we sit outside / inside please?	**Können wir draußen / drinnen sitzen?**
	K[oe]nn-en veer DROW-ssen / DRINN-en sitt-sen?
May we sit at the counter?	**Können wir an der Theke sitzen?**
	K[oe]nn-en veer un dehr TEH-keh sitt-sen?
The menu, please?	**Die Karte, bitte.**
	Dee KAHRR-teh, bit-eh.

ORDERING

Do you have a special tonight?	**Haben Sie heute Abend ein spezielles Angebot?**
	Hah-ben zee hoy-teh ah-bend aihn shpeh-tsee-ell-es UN-gheh-boht?
What do you recommend?	**Was können Sie empfehlen?**
	Vahs k[oe]nn-en zee em-PFEH-len?
May I see a wine list?	**Könnte ich bitte die Weinkarte haben?**
	K[oe]nn-teh ee[ch] bit-eh dee VINE-kahrr-teh hah-ben?
Do you serve wine by the glass?	**Servieren Sie Wein im Glas?**
	Serr-veer-en zee vine im GLAHSS?
May I see a drink list?	**Könnte ich bitte die Getränkekarte haben?**
	K[oe]nn-teh ee[ch] bit-eh dee gheh-TR[AE]NG-keh-kahrr-teh hah-ben?
I would like it cooked ____	**Ich hätte es gern ____**
	Ee[ch] hat-eh as ghern ____
rare.	**blutig.**
	BLOO-tigg.
medium rare.	**halb gar.**
	hahlbb GHAHR.

medium.	**medium.**
	MEH-dee-oomm.
medium well.	**halb durch.**
	hahlbb DOORR[CH].
well.	**gut durch.**
	goot DOORR[CH].
charred.	**verschmort.**
	fehr-SHMORRT.
Do you have a ___ menu?	**Haben Sie eine Karte mit ___ Speisen?**
	Hah-ben zee eye-neh kahrr-teh mit ___ shpye-sen?
diabetic	**diabetischen**
	dee-ah-BEH-tish-en
kosher	**kosheren**
	KOH-sheh-ren
vegetarian	**vegetarischen**
	veh-gheh-TAH-ree-shen
Do you have a children's menu?	**Haben Sie eine Karte für Kinder?**
	Hah-ben zee eye-neh kahrr-teh f[ue]hr KIN-dehr?
What is in this dish?	**Welche Zutaten enthält dieses Gericht?**
	Vell-[ch]eh TSOO-tah-ten ent-h[ae]llt dee-ses gheh-RI[CH]T?
How is it prepared?	**Wie wird es zubereitet?**
	Vee virrd ess TSOO-beh-rye-tet?
What kind of oil is that cooked in?	**In welchem Öl wird dieses Gericht zubereitet?**
	In vell-[ch]em [OE]HL virrd dee-ses gheh-ri[ch]t tsoo-beh-rye-tet?
Do you have any low-salt dishes?	**Haben Sie Gerichte mit wenig Salz?**
	Hah-ben zee ghe-ri[ch]-teh mit veh-nigg SAHLTTS?
On the side, please.	**Als Beilage, bitte.**
	Ahlls BYE-lah-gheh, bit-eh.

May I make a substitution?	**Kann ich die Zusammenstellung ändern?**
	Khann ee[ch] dee tsoo-SAHMM-en-shtell-oong [ae]nn-dehrn?
I'd like to try that.	**Das würde ich gern probieren.**
	Dahs v[ue]rr-deh ee[ch] ghern proh-BEE-ren.
Is that fresh?	**Ist das frisch?**
	Isst dahs FRISH?
Waiter!	**Bedienung!**
	Beh-DEE-noong!
Extra butter, please.	**Könnte ich bitte noch etwas Butter haben?**
	K[oe]nn-teh ee[ch] bit-eh noh[ch] at-vahs BOOTT-ehr hah-ben?
No butter, thanks.	**Keine Butter, danke.**
	Kye-neh BOOTT-ehr, dunk-eh.
No cream, thanks.	**Keine Sahne, danke.**
	Kye-neh SAH-neh, dunk-eh.
Dressing on the side, please.	**Dressing extra, bitte.**
	Dressing EKKS-trah, bit-eh.
No salt, please.	**Kein Salz, bitte.**
	Kyne SAHLTTS, bit-eh.
May I have some oil, please?	**Könnte ich bitte etwas Öl haben?**
	K[oe]nn-teh ee[ch] bit-eh at-vahs [OE]HL hah-ben?
More bread, please.	**Könnte ich bitte noch etwas Brot haben?**
	K[oe]nn-teh ee[ch] bit-eh noh[ch] at-vahs BROHT hah-ben?
I am lactose intolerant.	**Ich habe eine Laktoseunverträg-lichkeit.**
	Ee[ch] hah-beh eye-neh luck-TOH-seh-oon-fehr-tr[ae]g-li[ch]-kite.

Would you recommend something without milk?	**Könnten Sie mir bitte etwas ohne Milch empfehlen?**
	K[oe]nn-ten zee mere bit-eh at-vahs oh-neh MILL[CH] em-pfeh-len?
I am allergic to ____	**Ich bin allergisch gegen ____**
	Ee[ch] bin ah-LERR-ghish geh-ghenn ____
seafood.	**Meeresfrüchte.**
	mehh-res-fr[ue]ch-teh.
shellfish.	**Schalentiere.**
	shah-len-tee-reh.
nuts.	**Nüsse.**
	n[ue]ss-eh.
peanuts.	**Erdnüsse.**
	ehrrd-n[ue]ss-eh.
Water ____, please.	**Wasser ____, bitte.**
	Vahs-sehr ____, bit-eh.
with ice	**mit Eis,**
	mitt ICE
without ice	**ohne Eis,**
	ohh-ne ICE
I'm sorry, I don't think this is what I ordered.	**Verzeihung, aber ich glaube, das habe ich nicht bestellt.**
	Fehr-TSYE-oong, ah-behr ee[ch] GLAU-beh, dahs hah-beh ee[ch] ni[ch]t beh-SHTELLT.
My meat is a little over / under cooked.	**Mein Fleisch ist etwas zu stark / zu wenig durch.**
	Mine flye-sh isst at-vahs tsoo SHTARRK / tsoo VEH-nigg duhrr[ch].
My vegetables are a little over / under cooked.	**Mein Gemüse wurde etwas zu lang / zu kurz gekocht.**
	Mine gheh-m[ue]h-seh wurde at-vahs tsoo LUNG / tsoo KOORRTS gheh-ko[ch]t.

There's a bug in my food!	**Da ist ein Käfer in meinem Essen!**
	Dah isst aihn K[AE]H-fehr in my-nem ess-en!
May I have a refill?	**Würden Sie bitte nachschenken?**
	V[ue]rr-den zee bit-eh NAH[CH]-sheng-ken?
A dessert menu, please.	**Die Dessertkarte, bitte.**
	Dee dess-SEHR-kahrr-teh, bit-eh.

DRINKS

alcoholic	**Alkoholisch**
	ahll-koh-HOH-lish
neat / straight	**pur**
	poor
on the rocks	**auf Eis**
	ouf ICE
with (seltzer or soda) water	**mit (Selters- oder Soda-) Wasser**
	mitt (SELL-terrs oh-der SOH-dah) Vahs-sehr
beer	**Bier**
	beer
dark beer	**dunkles Bier**
	DOONNK-less beer
light beer	**helles Bier**
	HELL-ess bier
Kölsch	**Kölsch**
	K[OE]LL-sh
Weissbier	**Weißbier**
	VICE-beer
pilsner	**Pils**
	pillss
bock beer	**Bockbier**
	BOCK-beer
bottle	**Flasche**
	FLUSH-eh
glass	**Glas**
	glahss

wine	**Wein** *vine*
house wine	**Hauswein** *HOUSE-vine*
sweet wine	**lieblicher Wein** *LEEB-li[ch]-ehr vine*
dry white wine	**trockener Weißwein** *trokken-er VICE-vine*
Gewürztraminer	**Gewürztraminer** *Gheh-V[UE]RRTS-trah-mee-nehr*
Riesling	**Riesling** *REES-ling*
rosé	**Rosé** *roh-SEHH*
Scotch	**Scotch** *Scotch*
red wine	**Rotwein** *ROHT-vine*
Whiskey	**Whiskey** *Whiskey*
sparkling sweet wine	**Sekt** *SEKKT*
liqueur	**Likör** *lee-K[OE]HR*
brandy	**Brandy** *BRAN-dee*
cognac	**Kognak** *CON-yukk*
Kirschwasser (cherry-flavored liqueur)	**Kirschwasser** *KEERRSH-vahs-sehr*
gin	**Gin** *jinn*
vodka	**Wodka** *VODD-kah*
rum	**Rum** *roomm*

nonalcoholic	**alkoholfrei**
	ahll-koh-HOHL-frye
hot chocolate	**heiße Schokolade**
	hye-sseh shoh-koh-LAH-deh
lemonade	**Limonade**
	lee-moh-NAH-deh
radler / radlermass	**Radler (0,5 L) / Radlermaß (1 L)**
(beer mixed with lemonade or soda)	*RAHD-lehr / RAHD-lehr-mahss*
Apfelmost (hard cider)	**Apfelmost**
	UP-fell-mohsst
milkshake	**Milchshake**
	MILL[CH]-shake
milk	**Milch**
	mill[ch]
tea	**Tee**
	tehh
coffee	**Kaffee**
	kah-FEHH
cappuccino	**Cappuccino**
	kappoo-TSHEE-noh
espresso	**Espresso**
	ess-PRRESS-oh
iced coffee	**Eiskaffee**
	ICE-kahff-eh
fruit juice	**Fruchtsaft**
	FROO[CH]T-sufft

For a full list of fruits, see p103.

SETTLING UP

I'm stuffed.	**Ich bin voll.**
	Ee[ch] binn FOLL.
The meal was excellent.	**Das Essen war ausgezeichnet.**
	Dahs ess-en vaar ous-gheh-TSAI[CH]-net.

There's a problem with my bill.	**Es gibt da ein Problem mit meiner Rechnung.**
	As gheebt dah aihn proh-blehm mit minor RE[CH]-noong.
Is the tip included?	**Ist das inklusive Trinkgeld?**
	Isst dahs in-kloo-see-veh TRINK-gelld?
My compliments to the chef!	**Mein Kompliment an den Chefkoch!**
	Mine komm-plee-MEANT un dehn CHEFF-koh[ch]!
Check, please.	**Zahlen, bitte.**
	TSAH-len, bit-eh.

MENU READER

Each German-speaking country has its own regional and national specialties, but we've tried to make our list of classic dishes as broad as possible.

BREAKFAST

Eier: Eggs
EYE-ehr
Bread (Note: There are many kinds of bread in Germany. Following are some of the most common and delicious varieties.)

> **Roggenbrot:** rye bread
> **Toastbrot:** toast bread
> **Vollkornbrot:** whole-grain bread
> **Weizenbrot:** wheat bread
> **Weissbrot:** white bread
> **Mehrkornbrot:** multigrain bread
> **Roggenmischbrot:** rye-wheat bread
> **Zwiebelbrot:** onion bread
> **Semmel, Brötchen:** bread rolls

Sausage (Sausages can be bought at outdoor stalls throughout the year. They are eaten with a roll and some mustard.)

Weißwurst: Weisswurst
VICE-voorrst

Blutwurst: Blutwurst
BLOOT-voorrst

Kaffee: Coffee
KAHFF-eh

Sahne: Cream
SAH-ne

Butter: Butter
BOOTT-ehr

Zucker: Sugar
TSOOKK-ehr

Salz: Salt
sahllts

Pfeffer: Pepper
PFEHFF-ehr

Jogurt: Yogurt
YOH-ghoorrt

Quark: Quark (a creamy, savory dish eaten on bread)
kwarrk

Nutella: Nutella (a chocolate-hazelnut spread)
noo-TELL-ah

LUNCH / DINNER

German / Swiss / Austrian specialties

Following are special dishes from different German-speaking regions and countries. Although many are available in most regions in one form or another, the names can vary. The region or country is indicated in parentheses after the name of the dish.

Pfannkuchen: potato pancakes
PFAHNN-coo-[ch]en

Sauerbraten: marinated beef
SOUER-brah-ten

Rösti: fried potato dish (Switzerland)
R[OE]SS-tee

Wiener Schnitzel: breaded veal cutlets
vee-nair SHNITT-sell

Spätzle: heavy pasta served in place of potatoes (Southern Germany)
SHPATS-leh

Knödel: dumplings
KHN[OE]H-dell

Hasenpfeffer: rabbit stew
HAH-sen-pfeff-ehr

Jägerschnitzel: type of cutlet with mushrooms and peppers
Y[AE]H-ghair-shnitt-sell

Maultaschen: Swabian ravioli
MAUHL-tahshen

Nockerln: dumplings in Austria and Bavaria
NOCK-errln

Ochsenschwanzsuppe: Oxtail soup
OKKS-en-shvahnnts-soopp-eh

Schweinshaxe: pork hock
SHVINES-hahkks-eh

Sauerkraut
SOUER-kraut

Spanferkel: whole-roasted suckling pig
SHPAHN-fehrr-kell

Rote Grütze: red fruit pudding
roh-teh GR[UE]TT-seh

Menü: daily special
Meh-N[UE]H

Tagesgericht: dish of the day
TAH-ghess-gheh-ri[ch]t

DESSERT

Sacher Torte: Sacher Torte
SAH[CH]-ehr torr-teh

Käsekuchen: Cheese cake
K[AE]H-seh-coo-[ch]en

Apfelstrudel: Apple strudel
UP-fell-shtroo-dell

Schokolade: Chocolate
shoh-koh-LAH-deh

Stollen: Stollen (typically served at Christmas)
SHTOLL-en

Marzipan: Marzipan
MAHRR-tsee-pahn

Eiscreme: Ice cream
ICE-krehm

Kekse: Cookies / biscuits
KEHK-seh

MEAT

Rindfleisch: Beef
RINND-flye-sh

Schweinefleisch: Pork
SHVINE-eh-flye-sh

Würstchen: Sausage
V[UE]RRST-[ch]enn

Hähnchen: Chicken
H[AE]HN-[ch]en

Kalbfleisch: Veal
KAHLLB-flye-sh

Lammfleisch: Lamb
LAHMM-flye-sh

Hasenfleisch: Rabbit
HAH-senn-flye-sh

FISH AND SEAFOOD

Tunfisch: Tuna
TOON-fish

Lachs: Salmon
lahkks
Kabeljau: Cod
KAH-bell-yow
Hering: Herring
HEH-rring
Forelle: Trout
foh-RELL-eh
Buntbarsch: Tilapia
BOONNTT-bahrrsh
Karpfen: Carp
CAHRR-pfenn
Schwertfisch: Swordfish
SHVEHRRT-fish
Heilbutt: Halibut
HYLE-boott
Muscheln: Mussels
MOOSH-elln

PASTA

Spaghetti: Spaghetti
shpah-GET-ee
Pizza: Pizza
PIT-sah
Döner Kebab: meat sandwich with lettuce, onions and a cream sauce; invented by Turkish immigrants to Germany in Berlin in 1971.
d[oe]h-nehr KEH-bahpp
Currywurst: sausage seasoned with curry powder, usually served with French fries
CURRY-voorrsst

CHEESE

Blauschimmelkäse: Blue cheese
BLAUH-shimmel-k[ae]h-seh

Hüttenkäse: Cottage cheese
H[UE]TT-en-k[ae]h-seh

Frischkäse: Cream cheese
FRISH-k[ae]h-seh

Schweizer Käse: Swiss cheese
SHVYE-tsair k[ae]h-seh

Gorgonzola: Gorgonzola
gore-ghonn-TSOH-lah

Ziegenkäse: Goat cheese
TSEE-ghenn-k[ae]h-seh

UTENSILS

Gabel: Fork
GHAH-bell

Messer: Knife
MESS-ehr

Löffel: Spoon
L[OE]FF-ell

Suppenlöffel: Soup spoon
SOOPP-en-l[oe]ff-ell

Teelöffel: Teaspoon
TEHH-l[oe]ff-ell

Teller: Plate
TELL-ehr

Schüssel: Bowl
SH[UE]SS-ell

Topf: Pot
toppf

Pfanne: Pan
PFAHNN-eh

Serviette: Napkin
serr-vee-AT-eh

BUYING GROCERIES

Groceries can be purchased at supermarkets, neighborhood stores, or farmers' markets. Most cities and towns have farmers' markets that sell fruits, vegetables, cheeses, and other goods.

AT THE SUPERMARKET

Which aisle has _____ | **In welchem Regal finde ich _____**
 | *In vell-[ch]em reh-GAHL fin-deh ee[ch] _____*

spices?	**Gewürze?**
	gheh-V[UE]RR-tseh?
toiletries?	**Hygieneartikel?**
	h[ue]-GYEH-neh-arr-tee-kell?
paper plates and napkins?	**Papierteller und Servietten?**
	pah-PEER-tell-ehr oonnd serr-vee-AT-ten?
canned goods?	**Konserven?**
	con-SERR-ven?
snack food?	**Snacks?**
	snacks?
baby food?	**Babynahrung?**
	BEH-bee-nah-roong?
water?	**Wasser?**
	VAHS-ser?
juice?	**Säfte?**
	S[AE]FF-teh?
bread?	**Brot?**
	broht?
cheese?	**Käse?**
	K[AE]H-seh?
fruit?	**Obst?**
	Ohbsst?
cookies?	**Kekse?**
	KEHK-seh?

AT THE BUTCHER SHOP

Is the meat fresh?	**Ist das Fleisch frisch?**
	Isst dahs flye-sh FRISH?
Do you sell fresh ____	**Verkaufen Sie frisches ____**
	Fehr-cow-fen zee frish-ess ____
beef?	**Rindfleisch?**
	RINND-flye-sh?
pork?	**Schweinefleisch?**
	SHVINE-eh-flye-sh?
lamb?	**Lammfleisch?**
	LAHMM-flye-sh?
I would like a cut of ____	**Ich hätte gern ____**
	Ee[ch] HAT-eh ghern ____
tenderloin.	**ein Filetstück.**
	aihn fee-LEHH-sht[ue]ck.
T-bone.	**ein T-Bone-Steak.**
	aihn TEE-bone-steak.
brisket.	**ein Bruststück.**
	aihn BROOSSTT-sht[ue]ck.
rump roast.	**ein Rumpsteak.**
	aihn ROOMMP-steak.
chops.	**Koteletts.**
	kott-LETTS.
filet.	**ein Filet.**
	aihn fee-LEHH.
Thin / Thick cuts please.	**Dünne / Dicke Scheiben, bitte.**
	D[UE]NN-eh / DICK-eh shy-ben, bit-eh.
Please trim the fat.	**Entfernen Sie bitte das Fett.**
	Ent-fehr-nen zee bit-eh dahs FETT.
Do you have any sausage?	**Haben Sie Würstchen?**
	Hah-ben zee V[UE]RRST-[ch]enn?
Is the ____ fresh?	**____ frisch?**
	____ FRISH?

fish	**Ist der Fisch** *Isst dehr fish*
seafood	**Sind die Meeresfrüchte** *Sinnd dee mehh-res-fr[ue]ch-teh*
shrimp	**Sind die Garnelen** *Sinnd dee gharr-neh-len*
trout	**Ist die Forelle** *Isst dee foh-rell-eh*
flounder	**Ist die Flunder** *Isst dee floonn-dehr*
clams	**Sind die Muscheln** *Sinnd dee moosh-elln*
oysters	**Sind die Austern** *Sinnd dee ous-terrn*
May I smell it?	**Dürfte ich bitte daran riechen?** *D[ue]rf-teh ee[ch] bit-eh dah-rahn REE-[ch]en?*
Would you please ____	**Könnten Sie ____** *K[oe]nn-ten zee ____*
filet it?	**das bitte filetieren?** *dahs bit-eh fee-leh-TEE-ren?*
debone it?	**das bitte entbeinen?** *dahs bit-eh ent-BYE-nen?*
remove the head and tail?	**bitte Kopf und Schwanz entfernen?** *bit-eh copf oonnd SHVAHNNTS ent-fehr-nen?*

AT THE PRODUCE STAND / MARKET

Fruits

banana	**Banane** *bah-NAH-neh*
apple	**Apfel** *UP-fell*

grapes (green, red)	**Trauben**
	TRAUH-ben
orange	**Orange**
	oh-RUN-sheh
lime	**Limette**
	lee-METT-eh
lemon	**Zitrone**
	tsee-TROH-neh
mango	**Mango**
	MAHNG-goh
melon	**Melone**
	meh-LOH-neh
cantaloupe	**Cantaloupe-Melone**
	khann-tah-LOOP-meh-loh-neh
watermelon	**Wassermelone**
	VAHS-sehr-meh-loh-neh
honeydew	**Honigmelone**
	HOH-nigg-meh-loh-neh
cranberry	**Cranberry**
	CRAN-berry
cherry	**Kirsche**
	KEERR-sheh
peach	**Pfirsich**
	PFIRR-si[ch]
apricot	**Aprikose**
	up-ree-KOH-seh
strawberry	**Erdbeere**
	EHRRD-beh-reh
blueberry	**Heidelbeere**
	HYE-dell-beh-reh
kiwi	**Kiwi**
	KEE-vee
pineapple	**Ananas**
	ANNAH-nahss

blackberries	**Brombeeren**
	BROM-beh-ren
grapefruit	**Grapefruit**
	GRAPE-fruit
gooseberry	**Stachelbeere**
	SHTAH[CH]-ell-beh-reh
papaya	**Papaya**
	pah-PAHY-yah
tamarind	**Tamarinde**
	tah-mah-RINN-deh
tangerine	**Mandarine**
	mahnn-dah-REE-neh
plum	**Pflaume**
	PFLAUH-meh
pear	**Birne**
	BIRR-neh
Vegetables	
plantain	**Kochbanane**
	KOH[CH]-bah-nah-neh
regular	**normal**
	norr-MAHL
ripe	**reif**
	rye-ff
lettuce	**Kopfsalat**
	COPF-sah-laht
spinach	**Spinat**
	spee-NAHHT
avocado	**Avocado**
	ah-voh-KAH-doh
artichoke	**Artischocke**
	arr-tee-SHOCK-eh
olives	**Oliven**
	oh-LEE-ven
beans	**Bohnen**
	BOH-nen

green beans	**grüne Bohnen**
	gr[ue]h-neh BOH-nen
tomato	**Tomate**
	toh-MAH-teh
potato	**Kartoffel**
	karr-TOFF-ell
peppers	**Paprika**
	PAHPP-ree-kah
hot	**scharf**
	shahrrff
mild	**mild**
	milld
jalapeno	**Peperoni**
	pepp-eh-ROH-nee
onion	**Zwiebel**
	TSVEE-bell
celery	**Sellerie**
	SELL-eh-ree
broccoli	**Brokkoli**
	BROCK-oh-lee
cauliflower	**Blumenkohl**
	BLOOH-menn-kohl
carrot	**Karrotte**
	kah-ROTT-eh
corn	**Mais**
	mice
cucumber	**Gurke**
	GHOORR-keh
bean sprouts	**Sojasprossen**
	SOH-yah-shpross-en
sweet corn	**Mais**
	mice
eggplant	**Aubergine**
	oh-behr-SHEE-neh

sorrel	**Ampfer**
	UM-pfehr
yam	**Süßkartoffel**
	S[UE]HS-kahr-toff-ell
squash	**Kürbis**
	KYRR-biss

Fresh Herbs & Spices

cilantro / coriander	**Koriander**
	koh-ree-UNDER
black pepper	**schwarzer Pfeffer**
	shvahrrz-ehr PFEFF-ehr
salt	**Salz**
	sahltts
basil	**Basilikum**
	bah-SEE-lee-koom
parsley	**Petersilie**
	peh-tehr-SEAL-yeh
oregano	**Oregano**
	oh-REH-ghah-noh
sage	**Salbei**
	SAHLL-bye
thyme	**Thymian**
	T[UE]H-mee-ahn
cumin	**Kreuzkümmel**
	KRROYTS-k[ue]m-mell
paprika	**Paprika**
	PAHPP-ree-kah
garlic	**Knoblauch**
	KNOHB-lauh[ch]
clove	**Nelke**
	NELL-keh
allspice	**Piment**
	pee-MEANT
saffron	**Safran**
	SAHFF-rahn

rosemary	**Rosmarin**
	ROHS-mah-reen
anise	**Anis**
	AH-niss
sugar	**Zucker**
	TSOOKK-ehr
marjoram	**Majoran**
	MAH-yoh-rahn
dill	**Dill**
	dill
caraway	**Kümmel**
	K[UE]M-mell
bay leaf	**Lorbeer**
	LOHRR-behr
cacao	**Kakao**
	kah-COW
dried	**getrocknet**
	gheh-TROCK-net
fresh	**frisch**
	frish
seed	**Samen**
	SAH-men

AT THE DELI

What kind of salad is that?	**Was für ein Salat ist das?**
	Vahs f[ue]hr aihn sah-LAHT isst dahs?
What type of cheese is that?	**Was für ein Käse ist das?**
	Vahs f[ue]hr aihn K[AE]H-seh isst dahs?
What type of bread is that?	**Was für ein Brot ist das?**
	Vahs f[ue]hr aihn BROHT isst dahs?
Some of that, please.	**Geben Sie mir etwas davon, bitte.**
	Gheh-ben zee mere at-vahs DAH-fonn, bit-eh.

Is the salad fresh?	**Ist der Salat frisch?**
	Isst dehr sah-laht FRISH?
I'd like ____	**Ich hätte gern ____**
	Ee[ch] hat-eh ghern ____
a sandwich.	**ein Sandwich.**
	aihn SAND-which.
a salad.	**einen Salat.**
	eye-nen sah-LAHT.
tuna salad.	**einen Tunfischsalat.**
	eye-nen TOON-fish-sah-laht.
chicken salad.	**einen Geflügelsalat.**
	eye-nen gheh-FL[UE]H-ghell-sah-laht.
roast beef.	**ein Roastbeef.**
	aihn ROAST-beef.
ham.	**einen Schinken.**
	eye-nen SHING-ken.
that cheese.	**diesen Käse.**
	dee-sen K[AE]H-seh.
cole slaw.	**einen Krautsalat.**
	eye-nen KRAUT-sah-laht.
a package of tofu.	**eine Packung Tofu.**
	eye-neh pahkk-oong TOH-foo.
mustard.	**Senf.**
	sennff.
mayonaisse.	**Majonäse.**
	mah-yoh-N[AE]H-seh.
a pickle.	**eine Essiggurke.**
	eye-neh ESS-igg-ghoorr-keh.
Is that smoked?	**Ist das geräuchert?**
	Isst dahs gheh-ROY-[ch]errt?
a pound (0,5 kg)	**ein Pfund**
	ain PFOONND

a quarter-pound (0,125 kg)   **ein Viertelpfund**
                                ain FEER-tell-pfoonnd

a half-pound (0,25 kg)   **ein halbes Pfund**
                                ain HAHLL-bess pfoonnd

GERMAN FOOD

German cuisine offers more than just the robust charms of *wurst* (sausages), dumplings, pastries, and beer. Seasonal local vegetables such as *spargel* (white asparagus) in spring and *pfifferling* mushrooms in summer are often featured on restaurant menus, and light, healthy dishes increasingly abound. Those unsatisfied with the local fare can choose from a wide variety of international restaurants in major German cities, with especially good Middle Eastern and Italian food.

RESTAURANTS AND TIPPING

- Many restaurants expect guests to **seat themselves**.
- **Seating is often somewhat communal** at informal restaurants. Strangers who plunk themselves down next to you at a long shared table are not necessary trying to start a conversation with you.
- In traditional restaurants, address **waiters as Herr Ober and waitresses as Fräulein**.
- If a restaurant bill says *Bedienung*, that means a service charge has already been added, so just round up to the nearest euro. If not, add **10% to 15%**.
- **Tips in Germany are not left lying on the table**, but rather handed directly to the server when you pay.
- Many restaurants **do not accept credit cards**; always check ahead if you plan to pay by card.

REGIONAL SPECIALTIES

Baden-Württemberg Soups, stews and noodles: *Schneckensuppe* (snail soup), *Spätzle* (egg-based pasta), *Maultaschen* (ravioli stuffed with ground meat, spinach, and calves' brains), *Linsen mit Saiten* (lentil stew with sausages), *Gaisburger Marsch* (beef stew).

Bavaria Hearty fare: *Leberkäs* (chilled mold of minced pork, beef, and liver), *Knödel* (dumplings or soaked bread), *Haxen* (pork or veal trotters, usually served with sauerkraut), *Rostbratwürste* (small finger sausages), *Schweinwurst mit Kraut* (pork sausages with sauerkraut).

DINING

Berlin Comfort foods for cold nights: *Kohlsuppe* (cabbage soup), *Erbsensuppe* (pea soup), *Hase im Topf* (rabbit pâté), dark bread, spicy *Regensburger* pork sausage, *Currywurst* (sliced sausage with curry sauce; iconic Berlin street food).

Hessen & Westphalia Pork, and lots of it: hams, *Sulperknochen* (pigs' trotters, ears, and tail, served with peas pudding and pickled cabbage), *Tüttchen* (ragout of calves' heads and calves' brains), *Pickert* (sweet-potato cakes with raisins).

Lower Saxony & Schleswig-Holstein Maritime traditions: *Aalsuppe* (sweet-and-sour eel soup), *Labskaus* (medley of pork, salt herring, beef, potatoes, and beets), *Rollmops* (pickled herrings rolled in sour cream), *Finkenwerder Scholle* (plaice), oysters raw or baked with cheese.

Rhineland Quintessentially German dishes: *Saumagen* (stuffed pork belly with pickled cabbage), *Schweinepfeffer* (spicy pork ragout with pigs' blood), *Sauerbraten* (beef marinated in wine vinegar), *Reibekuchen* (potato pancakes with blueberries or applesauce).

Saxony & Thuringia Each city has its own popular dishes: *Rinderzunge in Rosinensauce* (calves' tongues in grape sauce), *Quarkkeulchen* (curd, boiled potatoes, flour, sugar, and raisins, baked and served with cinnamon and applesauce), *Leipziger Allerlei* (carrots, peas, asparagus, crayfish, ox tails, veal, dumplings).

BREAD

Germany's bakeries produce a wondrous variety of breads. *Vollkornbrot* is heavy whole-wheat, *Roggenbrot* is rye, *Schwarzbrot* is dense and dark, and *Bauernbrot* is a light, slightly sour loaf. *Brötchen* (rolls) range from standard white rolls to hearty *Kürbiskernbrötchen* topped with pumpkin seeds. Perhaps the most distinctive of all German breads is *Brezel*, the South German soft pretzel. German bread does not contain preservatives and will go stale the day after you buy it; Germans typically visit the bakery every day. Bread is usually sold as a whole loaf, but you can also ask for a half loaf.

CAKES AND DESSERTS

Cakes

Germans traditionally eat cakes not after dinner but with coffee in a special meal, *Kaffee* und *Kuchen*, served around 4pm. Typical cakes include:

Apfelkuchen Similar to a deep-dish apple pie.

Käsekuchen (cheesecake) and **Kugelhupf** (coffeecake) Especially good in Berlin.

Schwarwalder Kirschtorte (Black Forest cake) A southern German specialty.

Sachertorte An elegant chocolate torte of Austrian origin.

Desserts

Sweets served as **desserts** are often mushier in nature, such as eggy chocolate mousses, **Rote Grütze** (a medley of red berries served with cream), and **Griesbrei** (sweetened farina pudding).

BEER GUIDE

Home to the world's oldest brewery, Germany is unequaled for the quality and variety of beer it produces. Each region guards its own centuries-old beer-making tradition and its own special brews. Here are a few:

Alt (Düsseldorf, Frankfurt): dark, top-fermented barley malt beer.

Berliner Weiße (Berlin): light wheat beer, often served with a shot of raspberry syrup.

Bockbier & Doppelbock (Bavaria, Einbeck): potent, extra dark beer with numerous seasonal variations; doppelbock beers have names ending in "-ator."

Dampfbier (Bayreuth): fruity "steam beer."

Dortmunder (Dortmund): mild, bottom-fermented blond lager.

Dunkles Lagerbier (Bavaria): strong, malty, mahogany-brown all-barley lager.

Gose (Leipzig): pale, sour, saline-tasting pale wheat beer.

Hefeweizen (Bavaria): yeasty wheat beer, often drunk with a squeeze of lemon.

Kölsch (Cologne): pale ale, local brew of the city of Cologne.

Märzen (Bavaria): amber colored lager, brewed in the month of March.

Pils /Pilsner (Northern Germany): light and hoppy lager, originally Czech.

Rauchbier (Bamberg): dark "smoked" beer.

SELECTING GERMAN WINES

Germany has produced excellent wines for centuries—but it has more recently been the butt of jokes for churning out cheap, cloyingly sweet table wines such as the much-ridiculed *Liebfraumilch*. The better German wines earn praise for their natural lightness, and the slow maturing of grapes in the Rhine and Mosel valleys gives German wines a fresh, fruity acidity. Here are some tips for finding a German wine that will please your palate:

- Germany does produce red wine, but as a rule it's **better to stick to white**.
- *Trocken* (dry) or *halbtrocken* (semidry) are often listed on labels: look for them if you want to avoid anything sweet.
- A wine label should name the grape variety. **Riesling** ranges from fruity to spicy; **Weissburgender** grapes are used to make dry wines, often with a melon or pear aroma; and **Scheurebe** grapes produce high-quality wine with the aroma of red currant.
- The **level of ripeness** will also appear on the label. German law distinguishes between *Tafelwein* (table wine) and *Qualitätswein* (quality wine). A higher level of distinction, *Qualitätswein mit Prädikat*, distinguishes wine that carries one of six special attributes. These six, in ascending order of price, are *Kabinett, Spätlese, Auslese, Beerenauslese* (BA), *Eiswein*, and *Trockenbeerenauslese* (TBA).
- *Kabinett* wines go well with light snacks or veal. *Auslese* are mildly sweet and fruity, and the full-bodied *Spätlese* are well suited to rich dishes such as duck, smoked fowl, and oysters.
- The **rarest vintages**, those sweet wines carrying the BA or TBA designation, are best left for anything oily or pungent in flavor, such as goose liver pâté or rich cheeses. They are also wonderful with cheeses.

CHAPTER FIVE
SOCIALIZING

Whether you're meeting people in a bar or a park, you'll find the language you need, in this chapter, to make new friends.

GREETINGS

Hello.	**Hallo.**
	Hah-LOH.
How are you?	**Wie geht es Ihnen?**
	Vee GHEHHT as eehnen?
Fine, thanks.	**Gut, danke.**
	Goot, DUNK-eh.
And you?	**Und Ihnen?**
	Oonnd EEH-nen?
I'm exhausted from the trip.	**Ich bin erschöpft von der Reise.**
	Ee[ch] bin air-SH[OE]PFT fonn dehr RYE-seh.
I have a headache.	**Ich habe Kopfschmerzen.**
	Ee[ch] hah-beh COPF-shmairtsenn.
I'm terrible.	**Ich fühle mich schlecht.**
	Ee[ch] f[ue]hl-eh mi[ch] SHLE[CH]T.
I have a cold.	**Ich habe eine Erkältung.**
	Ee[ch] hah-beh eye-ne air-KELL-toong.
Good morning.	**Guten Morgen.**
	Goo-ten MOR-ghenn.
Good evening.	**Guten Abend.**
	Goo-ten AHH-bend.
Good afternoon.	**Guten Tag.**
	Goo-ten TAHHG.
Good night.	**Gute Nacht.**
	Goo-teh NA[CH]T.

Listen Up: Common Greetings

Freut mich. *FROYT mee[ch].*	It's a pleasure.
Sehr erfreut. *Sehhr ehr-FROYT.*	Delighted.
Zu Ihren Diensten. / Ganz wie Sie wünschen. *Tsooh eehren DEENS-ten. / Gahnnts vee zee V[UE]N-shenn.*	At your service. / As you wish.
Guten Tag. *Goo-ten TAHGG.*	Good day.
Hallo. *Hah-LOH.*	Hello.
Wie geht's? *Vee GHETS?*	How's it going?
Was gibt's? *Vahs GHEEBTS?*	What's up?
Was ist los? *Vahs isst LOHHS?*	What's going on?
Tschüss! *Tsh[ue]ss!*	Bye!
Auf Wiedersehen. *Ouf VEE-dehr-seh-hen.*	Goodbye.
Bis später. *Biss SHP[AE]-tehr.*	See you later.

OVERCOMING THE LANGUAGE BARRIER

I don't understand.	**Ich verstehe Sie nicht.**
	Ee[ch] fair-STEH-heh zee ni[ch]t.
Please speak more slowly.	**Könnten Sie bitte etwas langsamer sprechen?**
	K[oe]nn-ten zee bit-eh atvahs LAHNG-summer shpre-[ch]en?
Please speak louder.	**Könnten Sie bitte etwas lauter sprechen?**
	K[oe]nn-ten zee bit-eh atvahs LOU-tehr shpre-[ch]en?

Curse Words

Here are some common curse words used across German-speaking countries.

Scheiße	shit
SHYE-sseh	
Drecksau	son of a bitch (literally, dirty sow)
DREKK-saoo	
Vollidiot	jerk
FOLL-eedeeoht	
Verdammt!	damn
Fehr-DAHMMT!	
Arsch	ass
arrsh	
durchgeknallt	screwed up
DUHR[CH]-gheh-knallt	
Arschloch	bastard
ARRSH-lo[ch]	
abgewichst	fucked up
UP-gheh-vixt	
ficken	to fuck
fikken	
See p20, 21 for conjugation.	

Do you speak English?	**Sprechen Sie Englisch?**
	Shpre-[ch]en zee ENG-lish?
I speak ____ better than German.	**Ich spreche besser ____ als Deutsch.**
	Ee[ch] shpre-[ch]eh bess-er ____ ahlls DOYTSH.
Please spell that.	**Könnten Sie das bitte buchstabieren?**
	K[oe]nn-ten zee dahs bit-eh bu[ch]-shtah-BEE-ren?
Please repeat that?	**Könnten Sie das bitte wiederholen?**
	K[oe]nn-ten zee dahs bit-eh vee-dair-HOH-len?
How do you say ____?	**Wie sagt man ____?**
	Vee sahggt man ____?
Would you show me that in this dictionary?	**Könnten Sie mir das bitte in diesem Wörterbuch zeigen?**
	K[oe]nn-ten zee mere dahs bit-eh in dee-sem V[OE]R-tehr-boo[ch] tsai-ghen?

GETTING PERSONAL

People in German-speaking countries are generally friendly, but more formal than Americans. Remember to use the *Sie* form of address until given permission to employ the more familiar *Du*.

INTRODUCTIONS

What is your name?	**Wie heißen Sie?**
	Vee HYE-ssenn zee?
My name is ____.	**Ich heiße ____.**
	Ee[ch] HYE-sseh ____.
I'm very pleased to meet you.	**Freut mich, Sie kennen zu lernen.**
	Freud mi[ch], zee CANON tsoo lehr-nen.

May I introduce my _____ | **Darf ich Sie meinem (male) / meiner (female) / meinen (plural) _____ bekannt machen?**
Dahrrff ee[ch] zee mitt my-nem / minor/my-nen _____ beh-KAHNNT ma[ch]en?

How is your _____ | **Wie geht es Ihrem (male) / Ihrer (female) / Ihren (plural) _____**
Vee ghehht as eehrehr (eeh-rem / eeh-ren) _____

wife? | **Frau?**
frow?

husband? | **Mann?**
mahnn?

child? | **Kind?**
kin-d?

friends? | **Freunden?**
FROYN-denn?

boyfriend / girlfriend? | **Freund / Freundin?**
froynd / froyn-din?

family? | **Familie?**
fah-MEE-lee-eh?

mother? | **Mutter?**
MOOT-tehr?

father? | **Vater?**
FAH-tehr?

brother / sister? | **Bruder / Schwester?**
broo-dehr / shvesstehr?

friend? | **Freund / Freundin?**
froynd / froyn-din?

neighbor? | **Nachbarn / Nachbarin?**
nah[ch]-bar / nah[ch]-bah-rinn?

boss? | **Chef?**
sheff?

cousin? | **Cousin / Cousine?**
coo-SAH / coo-SEE-neh?

aunt / uncle?	**Tante / Onkel?**
	tahnn-teh / ong-kell?
fiancée / fiancé?	**Verlobten?**
	fehr-LOHB-ten?
partner?	**Partner / Partnerin?**
	PARRT-ner / PARRT-neh-rin?
niece / nephew?	**Nichte / Neffen?**
	NI[CH]-teh / NEFF-en?
parents?	**Eltern?**
	ELL-tern?
grandparents?	**Großeltern?**
	GROHS-ell-tern?
Are you married / single?	**Sind Sie verheiratet / ledig?**
	Sinnd zee fehr-HAI-rah-tet / LEH-dig?
I'm married.	**Ich bin verheiratet.**
	Ee[ch] bin fehr-HAI-rah-tet.
I'm single.	**Ich bin ledig.**
	Ee[ch] bin LEH-dig.
I'm divorced.	**Ich bin geschieden.**
	Ee[ch] bin gheh-SHEE-den.
I'm a widow / widower.	**Ich bin Witwe / Witwer.**
	Ee[ch] bin VIT-veh / VIT-vehr.
We're separated.	**Wir leben getrennt.**
	Veer leh-ben gheh-TRENNT.
I live with my boyfriend / girlfriend.	**Ich wohne mit meinem Freund / meiner Freundin zusammen.**
	Ee[ch] VOH-neh mit my-nem FROYND / minor FROYN-din tsoo-sahmmen.
How old are you?	**Wie alt sind Sie?**
	Vee AHLLT sinnd zee?
How old are your children?	**Wie alt sind Ihre Kinder?**
	Vee ahllt sinnd eehreh KIN-dehr?

Wow! That's very young.

Wow! Noch so jung?
Wow! Noh[ch] SOH yoonng?

No you're not! You're much younger.

Das kann nicht stimmen! Sie sind doch viel jünger.
Dahs kahnn ni[ch]t shtimmen! Zee sinnd doh[ch] FEEL y[ue]hngh-ehr.

Your wife / daughter is beautiful.

Sie haben eine hübsche Frau / Tochter.
Zee hah-ben eye-neh H[UE]B-sheh frow / to[ch]-tehr.

Your husband / son is handsome.

Sie haben einen gutaussehenden Mann / Sohn.
Zee hah-ben eye-nen GOOT-ous-seh-hen-denn mahnn / sohn.

What a beautiful baby!

Was für ein bezauberndes Baby!
Vahs f[ue]hr aihn beh-TSOW-behrn-dess baby!

Are you here on business?

Sind Sie geschäftlich hier?
Sinnd zee ge-SHAFT-li[ch] heer?

I am vacationing.

Ich mache Urlaub.
Ee[ch] ma[ch]-eh OOHR-loub.

I'm attending a conference.

Ich nehme an einer Konferenz teil.
Ee[ch] neh-meh un eye-nehr kon-feh-RENTS tile.

How long are you staying?

Wie lange bleiben Sie?
Vee lahng-he BLYE-ben zee?

What are you studying?

Was studieren Sie?
Vahs shtoo-DEE-ren zee?

I'm a student.

Ich bin Student.
Ee[ch] bin shtoo-DENT.

Where are you from?

Woher kommen Sie?
Voh-hair COM-mehnn zee?

PERSONAL DESCRIPTIONS

blond(e)	**blond**
	blonnd
brunette	**brünett**
	br[ue]h-nett
redhead	**rothaarig**
	ROHT-haah-rig
straight hair	**glattes Haar**
	GLAHT-tes haahr
curly hair	**gelocktes Haar**
	gheh-LOCK-tess haahr
kinky hair	**krauses Haar**
	KROUH-sess haahr
long hair	**lange Haare**
	LAHNG-he haah-reh
short hair	**kurze Haare**
	KUHRT-seh haah-reh
tanned	**braungebrannt**
	brown-gheh-brahnnt
pale	**blass**
	blahss
mocha-skinned	**dunkelhäutig**
	DOONG-kell-hoy-tig
black	**schwarz**
	shvahrrz

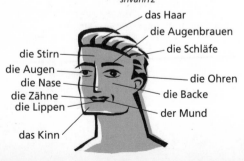

das Haar
die Augenbrauen
die Schläfe
die Stirn
die Augen
die Nase
die Zähne
die Lippen
das Kinn
die Ohren
die Backe
der Mund

white	**weiß**	
	vice	
Asian	**asiatisch**	
	ah-see-AH-tish	
African-American	**afro-amerikanisch**	
	ah-froh-ah-merry-KAH-nish	
caucasian	**weiß**	
	vice	
tall	**groß**	
	grohss	
short	**klein**	
	klyne	
thin	**dünn**	
	d[ue]nn	
fat	**dick**	
	dick	
blue eyes	**blaue Augen**	
	blou-eh ou-ghenn	
brown eyes	**braune Augen**	
	brown-eh ou-ghenn	
green eyes	**grüne Augen**	
	gr[ue]h-neh ou-ghenn	
hazel eyes	**braune Augen**	
	brown-eh ou-ghenn	
eyebrows	**Augenbrauen**	
	OU-ghenn-brown	
eyelashes	**Wimpern**	
	whimpern	
freckles	**Sommersprossen**	
	SOHMMER-shprossen	
moles	**Muttermale**	
	MUHTT-ehr-mah-leh	
face	**Gesicht**	
	gheh-SI[CH]T	

Listen Up: Nationalities

Ich bin Deutscher (m) / Deutsche (f).   I'm German.
Ee[ch] bin DOY-tsher / DOY-tsheh.

Ich bin Österreicher (m) / Österreicherin (f).   I'm Austrian.
Ee[ch] bin [OE]HS-tehr-rye-[ch]ehr / [OE]HS-tehr-rye-[ch]ehr-in.

Ich bin Türke (m) / Türkin (f).   I'm Turkish.
Ee[ch] bin T[UE]RR-keh / T[UE]RR-kin.

Ich bin Schweizer (m) / Schweizerin (f).   I'm Swiss.
Ee[ch] bin SHVYE-tsehr / SHVYE-tsehr-in.

Ich bin Italiener (m) / Italienerin (f).   I'm Italian.
Ee[ch] bin eetal-YEH-nehr / eetal-YEH-nehr-in.

Ich bin Franzose (m) / Französin (f).   I'm French.
Ee[ch] bin frahnn-TSOH-seh / frahnn-TS[OE]H-sinn.

Ich bin Pole (m) / Polin (f).   I'm Polish.
Ee[ch] bin POH-leh / POH-lin.

Ich bin Tscheche (m) / Tschechin (f).   I'm Czech.
Ee[ch] bin TSHE[CH]-eh / TSHE[CH]-in.

Ich bin Spanier (m) / Spanierin (f).   I'm Spanish.
Ee[ch] bin SHPAH-nee-her / SHPAH-nee-her-in.

Ich bin Portugiese (m) / Portugiesin (f).   I'm Portuguese.
Ee[ch] bin porr-too-GHEE-seh / porr-too-GHEE-sin.

Ich bin Grieche (m) / Griechin (f).   I'm Greek.
Ee[ch] bin GREE-[ch]eh / GREE-[ch]inn.

Ich bin Niederländer (m) / Niederländerin (f).   I'm Dutch.
Ee[ch] bin NEE-dair-lenn-dehr / NEE-dair-lenn-dehr-in.

Ich bin Belgier (m) / Belgierin (f).   I'm Belgian.
Ee[ch] bin BELL-ghee-her / BELL-ghee-her-in.

Ich bin Däne (m) / Dänin (f).   I'm Danish.
Ee[ch] bin D[AE]H-neh / D[AE]H-nin.

Ich bin Vietnamese (m) / Vietnamesin (f). *Ee[ch] bin vee-at-nah-MEH-seh / vee-at-nah-MEH-sin*	I'm Vietnamese.
Ich bin Nordafrikaner (m) / Nordafrikanerin (f). *Ee[ch] bin norrd-uff-ree-KAH-nehr / norrd-uff-ree-KAH-nehr-in*	I'm North African.
Ich bin Iraner (m) / Ich bin Iranerin (f). *Ee[ch] bin eeh-RAH-nehr / eeh-RAH-nehr-in.*	I'm Iranian.
Ich bin Japaner (m) / Japanerin (f). *Ee[ch] bin yah-PAH-nehr / yah-PAH-nehr.*	I'm Japanese.
Ich bin Schwede (m) / Schwedin (f). *Ee[ch] bin SHVEH-deh / SHVEH-dinn.*	I'm Swedish.
Ich bin Norweger (m) / Norwegerin (f). *Ee[ch] bin NORR-veh-gher / NORR-veh-gher-in.*	I'm Norwegian.
Ich bin Amerikaner (m) / Amerikanerin (f). *Ee[ch] bin ah-meh-rhee-KAH-nehr / ah-meh-rhee-KAH-nehr-in.*	I'm American.
Ich bin Russe (m) / Russin (f). *Ee[ch] bin RUUSS-eh / RUSS-in.*	I'm Russian.

For a full list of nationalities, see English / German dictionary.

DISPOSITIONS AND MOODS

sad	**traurig** *TROU-rig*
happy	**fröhlich** *FR[OE]H-li[ch]*
angry	**verärgert** *fehr-AIR-ghert*
tired	**müde** *M[UE]H-deh*
anxious	**besorgt** *beh-SORGHT*
confused	**verwirrt** *fehr-VIRRT*
enthusiastic	**begeistert** *beh-GYSE-tehrt*

PROFESSIONS

What do you do for a living?	**Was machen Sie beruflich?**
	Vaahs mah[ch]en zee beh-ROOF-li[ch]?
Here is my business card.	**Hier ist meine Karte.**
	Heer isst my-neh KAHRR-teh.
I am ____	**Ich bin ____**
	ee[ch] bin ____
a doctor.	**Arzt / Ärztin.**
	artst / airts-tin.
an engineer.	**Ingenieur / -in.**
	in-genn- / IEUR / -in.
a lawyer.	**Anwalt / Anwältin.**
	UN-wallt / un-VELL-tin.
a salesperson.	**Verkäufer / -in.**
	fehr-KOY-fehr / -in.
a writer.	**Autor / Autorin.**
	OU-tohr / ou-TOH-rin.
an editor.	**Redakteur / -in.**
	reh-duck-T[OE]HR / -in.
a designer.	**Designer / -in.**
	designer / -in.
an educator.	**Erzieher / -in.**
	air-TSEE-hair / -in.
an artist.	**Künstler / -in.**
	K[UE]NNST-lair / -in.
a craftsperson.	**Handwerker / -in.**
	HAHNND-verr-kerr / -in.
a homemaker.	**Hausfrau / Hausmann.**
	HOUSE-frow / HOUSE-mahnn.
an accountant.	**Buchhalter / -in.**
	BOOH[CH]-hall-tehr / -in.
a nurse.	**Krankenpfleger / -in.**
	KRAHNG-ken-pfleh-gher / -in.
a musician.	**Musiker / -in.**
	MOO-sicker / -in.

a military professional.	**beim Militär.**
	byme milli-TEHR.
a government employee.	**Regierungsangestellter.**
	reh-GHEE-roongs-un-gheh-shtell-tehr.

DOING BUSINESS

I'd like an appointment.	**Ich hätte gern einen Termin.**
	Ee[ch] HAT-eh ghern eye-nen tair-MEAN.
I'm here to see ____.	**Ich habe einen Termin bei ____.**
	Ee[ch] hah-beh eye-nen tair-MEAN bye ____.
May I photocopy this?	**Kann ich das bitte kopieren?**
	Khann ee[ch] dahs bit-eh koh-PEE-ren?
May I use a computer here?	**Kann ich hier einen Computer benutzen?**
	Khann ee[ch] heer eye-nen compu-ter beh-NOOTT-sen?
What's the password?	**Wie lautet das Kennwort?**
	Vee loutet dahs KENN-vohrt?
May I access the Internet?	**Dürfte ich bitte auf das Internet zugreifen?**
	D[ue]rf-teh ee[ch] bit-eh ouf dahs internet TSOO-grye-fenn?
May I send a fax?	**Dürfte ich bitte das Faxgerät benutzen?**
	D[ue]rf-teh ee[ch] bit-eh dahs FAHXX-gheh-r[ae]ht beh-NOOTT-sen?
May I use the phone?	**Dürfte ich bitte das Telefon benutzen?**
	D[ue]rf-teh ee[ch] bit-eh dahs teh-leh-PHON beh-NOOTT-sen?

PARTING WAYS

Keep in touch.	**Lassen Sie uns in Verbindung bleiben.**
	Lahssen zee oons in fair-BIN-doong blye-ben.
Please write or email.	**Schicken Sie mir einen Brief oder eine E-Mail.**
	CHIC-en zee mere eye-nen BRIEF oh-dehr eye-neh E-Mail.
Here's my phone number.	**Hier ist meine Telefonnummer.**
	Heer isst my-neh tehleh-PHON-noommer.
Call me.	**Rufen Sie mich an.**
	Roo-fenn zee mi[ch] UN.
May I have your phone number / e-mail please?	**Könnten Sie mir bitte Ihre Telefonnummer / E-Mail-Adresse geben?**
	K[oe]nn-ten zee mere bit-eh eeh-reh tehleh-PHON-noommer / E-mail-ah-dress-eh gheh-ben?
May I have your card?	**Geben Sie mir Ihre Visitenkarte?**
	Gheh-ben zee mere eehre vee-SEE-ten-kahrr-teh?
Give me your address and I'll write you.	**Wenn Sie mir Ihre Adresse geben, schreibe ich Ihnen.**
	Venn zee mere eehre ah-DRESS-eh ghehben, shryebeh ee[ch] eehnen.

TOPICS OF CONVERSATION

As in the United States or Europe, the weather and current affairs are common conversation topics.

THE WEATHER

It's so ____	**Es ist so ____** *As isst soh ____*
Is it always so ____	**Ist es immer so ____** *Isst as IM-mehr soh ____*
sunny?	**sonnig?** *sonic?*
rainy?	**regnerisch?** *REHG-nehrish?*
cloudy?	**bewölkt?** *beh-W[OE]LLKT?*
humid?	**feucht?** *foy[ch]t?*
warm?	**warm?** *vahrrm?*
cool?	**kalt?** *kahllt?*
windy?	**windig?** *VINN-digg?*
Do you know the weather forecast for tomorrow?	**Wissen Sie, wie morgen das Wetter wird?** *Vissen zee, vee MOR-ghen dahs vetter virrd?*

THE ISSUES

What do you think about ____	**Was denken Sie über ____** *Vahs dengh-kenn zee [ue]ber ____*
democracy?	**Demokratie?** *deh-moh-krah-TEE?*
socialism?	**Sozialismus?** *soh-tsee-ah-LISS-mooss?*
American Democrats?	**die Demokraten in Amerika?** *dee deh-moh-KRAH-ten in ah-MEH-ree-kah?*

American Republicans?	**die Republikaner in Amerika?**
	dee reh-puh-blee-KAH-nehr in ah-MEH-ree-kah?
monarchy?	**die Monarchie?**
	dee moh-nahr-[CH]EE?
the environment?	**die Umwelt?**
	dee OOHM-vellt?
climate change?	**den Klimawandel?**
	dehn KLEEH-mah-wunn-dell?
the economy?	**die Wirtschaft?**
	dee VIRRT-shafft?
What political party do you belong to?	**Welcher Partei gehören Sie an?**
	Vell-[ch]er pahrr-TYE gheh-h[oe]ren zee un?
What did you think of the election in ___?	**Was halten Sie von den Wahlen in ___?**
	Vahs hull-ten zee vonn dehn vah-len in ___?
What do you think of the war in ___?	**Was denken Sie über den Krieg in ___?**
	Vahs dengh-kenn zee [ue]ber dehn kreegg in ___?

RELIGION

Do you go to church / temple / mosque?	**Gehen Sie in die Kirche / den Tempel / die Moschee?**
	Ghe-hen zee in dee KIRR-[ch]eh / dehn TEM-pell / dee moh-SHEHH?
Are you religious?	**Sind Sie religiös?**
	Sinnd zee reli-GY[OE]SS?
I'm ___ / I was raised ___	**Ich bin ___ / Ich wurde ___ erzogen.**
	Ee[ch] bin ___ / Ee[ch] vurr-deh ___ ehr-TSOH-ghenn.

Protestant.	**protestantisch.**
	proh-tess-TANN-tish.
Catholic.	**katholisch.**
	kah-TOH-lish.
Jewish.	**jüdisch.**
	Y[UE]H-dish.
Muslim.	**muslimisch.**
	mooss-LEE-mish.
Buddhist.	**buddhistisch.**
	boo-DISS-tish.
Greek Orthodox.	**griechisch-orthodox.**
	GREE-[ch]ish-ortodox.
Hindu.	**hinduistisch.**
	hin-doo-ISS-tish.
agnostic.	**agnostisch.**
	ahgg-NOSS-tish.
atheist.	**atheistisch.**
	ah-teh-ISS-tish.

I'm spiritual but I don't attend services.

Ich bin gläubig, gehe aber nicht zu Gottesdiensten.
Ee[ch] bin GLOY-big, gheh-he ah-behr ni[ch]t tsoo GOT-tess-deensten.

I don't believe in that.

Ich bin nicht gläubig.
Ee[ch] bin ni[ch]t GLOY-big.

That's against my beliefs.

Das ist gegen meinen Glauben.
Dahs isst GHEH-gen my-nen GLOU-ben.

I'd rather not talk about it.

Darüber möchte ich eigentlich nicht sprechen.
DAH-r[ue]h-behr m[oe][ch]-te ee[ch] eye-ghent-li[ch] ni[ch]t sprechen.

GETTING TO KNOW SOMEONE

Following are some conversation starters.

MUSICAL TASTES

What kind of music do you like?	**Welche Art von Musik mögen Sie?**
	Vell-[ch]eh ahrt fonn moo-SEEK m[oe]-ghenn zee?
I like _____	**Ich mag _____**
	Ee[ch] mahgg _____
rock 'n' roll.	**Rock'n'Roll.**
	Rock'n'Roll.
hip hop.	**Hiphop.**
	Hip hop.
techno.	**Techno.**
	Tekkno.
Soul.	**Soul.**
	soul.
classical.	**Klassik.**
	KLASSick.
jazz.	**Jazz.**
	Jazz.
country and western.	**Country-Musik.**
	Country-moo-SEEK.
reggae.	**Reggae.**
	Reggae.
calypso.	**Calypso.**
	Kah-LYPP-soh.
opera.	**Opern.**
	OH-pehrrn.
show-tunes / musicals.	**Shows / Musicals.**
	Shows / Musicals.
New Age.	**New Age.**
	New Age.
pop.	**Pop.**
	Pop.

HOBBIES

What do you like to do in your spare time?	**Was machen Sie in Ihrer Freizeit?**
	Vahs mah-[ch]en zee inn eehrer FRYE-tsait?
I like ____	**Ich ____**
	Ee[ch] ____
playing guitar.	**spiele gern Gitarre.**
	spee-leh ghern ghee-TARR-eh.
piano.	**spiele gern Klavier.**
	spee-leh ghern klah-VEER.

For other instruments, see the English / German dictionary.

painting.	**male gern.**
	MAH-leh ghern.
drawing.	**zeichne gern.**
	TSAI[CH]-neh ghern.
dancing.	**tanze gern.**
	TAHNN-tseh ghern.
reading.	**lese gern.**
	LEH-seh ghern.
watching TV.	**sehe gern fern.**
	seh-heh ghern FEHRN.
shopping.	**gehe gern einkaufen.**
	ghe-heh ghern AIHN-cow-fenn.
going to the movies.	**gehe gern ins Kino.**
	geh-heh ghern inns KEE-noh.
hiking.	**gehe gern wandern.**
	geh-heh ghern VANN-dehrn.
camping.	**gehe gern campen.**
	geh-heh ghern KAM-penn.
hanging out.	**treffe mich gern mit Freunden.**
	treff-eh mee[ch] ghern mitt FROYN-denn.
traveling.	**reise gern.**
	RYE-seh ghern.

eating out.	**esse gern auswärts.**
	ESS-eh ghern OUS-v[ae]rts.
cooking.	**koche gern.**
	KO[CH]-eh ghern.
sewing.	**nähe gern.**
	N[AE]H-heh ghern.
sports.	**interessiere mich für Sport.**
	interess-EE-reh mi[ch] f[ue]hr SHPOHRRT.
Do you like to dance?	**Möchten Sie tanzen?**
	M[oe][ch]-ten zee TAHNN-tsenn?
Would you like to go out?	**Würden Sie gern ausgehen?**
	V[ue]rr-denn zee ghern OUS-gheh-hen?
May I buy you dinner sometime?	**Darf ich Sie vielleicht mal zum Essen einladen?**
	Daahrf ee[ch] zee feel-lai[ch]t mahl tsoomm ESS-en aihn-lah-denn?
What kind of food do you like?	**Welche Art von Essen mögen Sie?**
	Vell-[ch]eh ahrt fonn essen M[OE]-ghenn zee?

For a full list of food types, see Dining in Chapter 4.

Would you like to go ____	**Würden Sie gern ____**
	V[ue]rr-denn zee ghern ____
to a movie?	**ins Kino gehen?**
	inns KEE-noh ghe-hen?
to a concert?	**zu einem Konzert gehen?**
	tsooh eye-nem konn-TSEHRRT ghe-hen?
to the zoo?	**in den Zoo gehen?**
	inn dehn TSOHH ghe-hen?
to the beach?	**an den Strand gehen?**
	un dehn SHTRAHND ghe-hen?
to a museum?	**ein Museum besuchen?**
	aihn moo-SEHH-oom beh-SOO-[ch]enn?

for a walk in the park?	**im Park spazieren gehen?** *imm PARRK shpah-TSEE-ren gheh-hen?*
dancing?	**tanzen gehen?** *TAHNN-tseh gheh-hen?*
Would you like to get ____	**Hätten Sie Lust auf ____** *Hat-ten zee LOOSST ouf ____*
lunch?	**ein Mittagessen?** *aihn MIT-tahg-essen?*
coffee?	**einen Kaffee?** *eye-nen kah-FEHH?*
dinner?	**ein Abendessen?** *aihn AH-bend-essen?*
What kind of books do you like to read?	**Welche Art von Büchern lesen Sie gern?** *Vell-[ch]eh ahrt fonn B[UE]-[ch]ern leh-senn zee ghern?*
I like ____	**Ich mag ____** *Ee[ch] mahgg ____*
mysteries.	**Mystery-Romane.** *Mystery-roh-MAH-neh.*
Westerns.	**Westernromane.** *Western-roh-MAH-neh.*
dramas.	**Dramen.** *DRAH-men.*
novels.	**Romane.** *roh-MAH-neh.*
biographies.	**Biografien.** *bee-oh-gra-FEE-hen.*
auto-biographies.	**Autobiografien.** *ou-toh-bee-oh-gra-FEE-hen.*
romance.	**Liebesgeschichten.** *LEE-bess-gheh-shi[ch]-ten.*
history.	**historische Romane.** *his-TOH-ree-sheh roh-MAH-neh.*

For dating terms, see Nightlife in Chapter 10.

ETIQUETTE & CUSTOMS

German Reserve   Although Germans can seem reserved or even unfriendly, most are polite and pleasant if you approach them. Germans consider speaking directly to be an important form of honesty, and tend to voice their opinions very frankly. Many Germans are wary of enthusiastic chumminess, and Americans are sometimes viewed as overly friendly and therefore disingenuous.

Greetings   Etiquette in Germany is far more relaxed than it used to be, but visitors should still be careful to use the formal *Sie* with strangers, especially with older people and in rural areas. The informal *du* is always appropriate with friends and children. All women (except waitresses in traditional restaurants) should be addressed as Frau rather than Fräulein.

Public Order   The German love of civic order is not just a stereotype. Petty offenses such as jaywalking or littering can earn you a hefty fine or an angry scolding from a concerned passerby. Be aware that walking or standing in the bicycle lane is also strictly forbidden and can arouse the fury of cyclists.

Punctuality   It's no accident that there are so many clocks in public places in Germany: punctuality is very important to Germans. If an appointment is at eight, feel free to arrive anytime between 7:59 and 8:01. This goes for both business and social situations. Even arriving five minutes after the scheduled time is considered unacceptably late.

GERMAN FESTIVALS AND EVENTS

Along with the major events listed below, smaller traditional festivals abound throughout the year, especially in the villages of southern Germany,

January

New Year's Day International Ski Jumping, Garmisch-Partenkirchen   One of Europe's major winter sporting events. *Jan. 1.*

February

Berlinale International Film Festival, Berlin This festival lasts for ten days and showcases the work of international film directors as well as the latest German films. Tickets can be purchased at any box office. www.berlinale.de. *Ten days in early February.*

Fasching Germany's take on Carnival (Mardi Gras) is a boisterous one, with masks, costumes, parades, and free-flowing beer. Many of the traditions of this pre-Lenten party date to the Middle Ages. Carnivals dot the country, but the ones in Munich and Cologne are especially famous. *Week before Ash Wednesday.*

April

Walpurgisnacht, Harz Mountains Derived from old pagan fertility rites, Walpurgisnacht is a festival that celebrates the arrival of spring with massive bonfires and youthful pranks on the eve of May Day. *Night of April 30 to May 1.*

May

International May Festival, Wiesbaden This city near Frankfurt, renowned for its spas, hosts a premier cultural event—a series of top-notch theater, opera, dance, and musical performances lasting a full month. www.wiesbaden.de. *Late April to late May.*

June

Floodlighting of the Castle, Heidelberg Dramatic floodlights, fireworks, and concerts enliven the castle perched above this historical university city. www.cvb-heidelberg.de. *June, July, and September.*

Mozart Festival, Würzburg Mozart fans flock to this major cultural event in the baroque city of Würzburg, with world-class musicians and a full month-long roster of concerts in illuminated gardens. www.mozartfest-wuerzburg.de. *Throughout June.*

July

Freiburg Wine Tasting, Freiburg   Local residents and visitors enjoy the first vintages from grapes grown in the Black Forest district. *Early July*.

Richard Wagner Festival, Bayreuth   One of Europe's top opera events, this festival has taken place every summer since 1876 in the Festspielhaus Wagner built for his "music of the future." *Late July to late August*.

Love Parade, Berlin/Essen   The world's largest techno party originated in Berlin in 1989, a few months before the Wall came down, and the annual parade now features over 200 DJs. To be held in cities in the Ruhr area until 2011. *July or August*.

August

Red Wine Festival, Rüdesheim/Assmannshausen   Early harvest festival held in the Rhine village most famous for red wines. *Late August to early September*.

September

Oktoberfest, Munich   Millions throng to Munich for Germany's most famous festival, and hotels fill up months in advance. Most festivities take place at Theresienwiese, where local breweries sponsor massive tents that can hold up to 6,000 beer drinkers. *Mid-September to mid-October*.

November

Jazz-Fest Berlin   This annual festival staged at the Philharmonie attracts some of the world's finest jazz artists, ranging from traditional to experimental. *Early November*.

Winter Dom, Hamburg   Family-friendly annual amusement fair at the Heiligengeistfeld is part traditional Christmas fair, part modern amusement park. *Early November to early December*.

December

Christmas Fair, Mainz   This city on the Rhine stages its Christmas fair for the four weeks preceding Christmas. Throughout Advent, the fair's lights blaze on the historic market square against the backdrop of the city's thousand-year-old cathedral. *Four weeks before Christmas*.

HOLIDAYS

Public holidays are:

- **January 1** (New Year's Day)
- **Easter** (Good Friday and Easter Monday)
- **May 1** (Labor Day)
- **Ascension Day** (10 days before Pentecost/Whitsunday, the seventh Sunday after Easter)
- **Whitmonday** (day after Pentecost/Whitsunday)
- **October 3** (Day of German Unity)
- **November 17** (Day of Prayer and Repentance)
- **December 25 and 26** (Christmas)
- In addition, the following holidays are observed in German states with large Catholic populations: **January 6** (Epiphany), **Corpus Christi** (10 days after Pentecost), **August 15** (Assumption), and **November 1** (All Saints' Day).

MEET THE GERMANS

Servas supports global goodwill by arranging free home stays of up to 2 nights for travelers. Single-day visits, including a meal and sightseeing, can also be arranged. For more information, visit www.servas.org. **Friendship Force International** (✆ 800/554-6715; www.friendshipforce.org) also supports home stays around the world. A less formal home stay network, increasingly popular with young people in Germany, is Internet-based **Couch Surfing** (www.couchsurfing.com).

LANGUAGE SCHOOLS

The largest and best-reputed school is the **Goethe-Institut**, which runs German language programs in 16 German cities and abroad. Goethe is, however, one of the most expensive language schools: expect to pay about €750 without accommodation for a 2-week intensive language and culture course (www.goethe.de). Other language schools, known as *Sprachschulen*, abound in major cities, and many of these are significantly cheaper—around €200-400 for a two-week intensive course—but the quality of instruction varies widely. For other language programs located around Germany, contact the **American Institute for Foreign Study** (✆ 800/727-AIFS; www.aifs.org).

CHAPTER SIX
MONEY & COMMUNICATIONS

This chapter covers money, the mail, phone, Internet service, and other tools you need to connect with the outside world.

MONEY

Do you accept ____	**Akzeptieren Sie ____**
	Ahcktsep-TEEREN zee ____
Visa / MasterCard / Discover / American Express / Diners' Club? credit cards?	**Visa / MasterCard / Discover / American Express / Diners' Club? Kreditkarten?**
	Creh-DEET-kahrr-ten?
bills?	**Scheine?**
	SHY-neh?
coins?	**Münzen?**
	M[UE]NN-tsen?
checks?	**Schecks?**
	Shecks?
travelers checks?	**Reiseschecks?**
	RYE-seh-shecks?
money transfer?	**Überweisungen?**
	[Ue]h-behr-VYE-soong-en?
May I wire transfer funds here?	**Kann ich hier Überweisungen vornehmen?**
	Khann ee[ch] hear [Ue]h-behr-VYE-soong-en FOHR-neh-men?
Would you please tell me where to find ____	**Wo finde ich hier ____**
	Voh FIN-deh ee[ch] hear ____
a bank?	**eine Bank?**
	eye-neh BAHNNK?
a credit bureau?	**ein Kreditinstitut?**
	aihn creh-DEET-ins-tee-toot?

an ATM?	**einen Geldautomaten?** *eye-nen GELLD-auh-toh-* *MAH-ten?*
a currency exchange?	**eine Geldwechselstube?** *eye-neh GELLD-whecksel-* *shtoobeh?*
A receipt, please.	**Geben Sie mir bitte eine Quittung.** *Gheh-ben zee mere bit-eh eye-neh* *QUIT-toong.*
Would you tell me ____	**Sagen Sie mir bitte ____** *Sah-ghenn zee mere bit-eh ____*
the exchange rate for dollars to ____?	**den Wechselkurs von Dollar** **in ____?** *dehn VECK-sell-koorrs fonn* *dollar in ____?*
the exchange rate for pounds to ____?	**den Wechselkurs von Pfund** **in ____?** *dehn veck-sell-koorrs fonn* *PFOONND in ____?*
Is there a service charge?	**Gibt es eine Servicegebühr?** *Gheebt as eye-ne SIR-viss-ghe-* *b[ue]hr?*
May I have a cash advance on my credit card?	**Könnte ich bitte eine** **Barauszahlung über meine** **Kreditkarte bekommen?** *K[oe]nn-teh ee[ch] bit-eh eye-neh* *BAHR-ous-tsah-loonng [ue]h-behr* *my-neh creh-DEET-kahrr-teh beh-* *com-men?*
Will you accept a credit card?	**Akzeptieren Sie eine Kreditkarte?** *Ahcktsep-teeren zee eye-neh creh-* *DEET-kahrr-teh?*
May I have smaller bills, please.	**Könnte ich bitte kleinere Scheine** **bekommen?** *K[oe]nn-teh ee[ch] bit-eh klye-neh-* *reh SHY-neh beh-com-men?*

Listen Up: Bank Lingo

Unterschreiben Sie bitte hier. *Oonn-tehr-shrye-ben zee bit-eh HEAR.*	Please sign here.
Hier ist Ihre Quittung. *Hear isst eeh-reh QUIT-toong.*	Here is your receipt.
Zeigen Sie mir bitte Ihren Ausweis. *Tsye-ghenn zee mere bit-eh eeh-ren OUS-vise.*	May I see your ID, please?
Wir akzeptieren Reiseschecks. *Veer ahcktsep-teeren RYE-seh-shecks.*	We accept travelers checks.
Nur gegen bar. *Noor gheh-ghen BAR.*	Cash only.

Can you make change?	**Können Sie wechseln?** *K[oe]nn-en zee VECK-selln?*
I only have bills.	**Ich habe nur Scheine.** *Ee[ch] hah-beh noor SHY-neh.*
Some coins, please.	**Geben Sie mir bitte ein paar Münzen.** *Gheh-ben zee mere bit-eh aihn paahr M[UE]NN-tsen.*

PHONE SERVICE

Where can I buy or rent a cell phone?	**Wo kann ich ein Mobiltelefon kaufen oder mieten?** *Voh khann ee[ch] aihn moh-BEEL-tehleh-fohn COW-fenn oh-dehr MEE-ten?*

ATM Machine

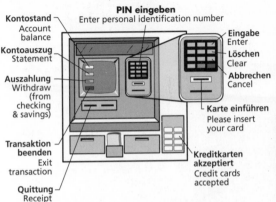

PIN eingeben
Enter personal identification number

Kontostand
Account balance

Kontoauszug
Statement

Auszahlung
Withdraw
(from checking & savings)

Transaktion beenden
Exit transaction

Quittung
Receipt

Eingabe
Enter

Löschen
Clear

Abbrechen
Cancel

Karte einführen
Please insert your card

Kreditkarten akzeptiert
Credit cards accepted

What rate plans do you have?	**Welche Tarife bieten Sie an?** *Vell-[ch]eh tah-REEF-eh beaten zee un?*
Is this good throughout the country?	**Funktioniert das im ganzen Land?** *Foonk-tsee-yoh-neert dahs im GHAHNN-tsenn lahnnd?*
May I have a prepaid phone?	**Könnte ich bitte ein Prepaid-Telefon haben?** *K[oe]nn-teh ee[ch] bit-eh aihn PRE-paid-tehleh-fohn hah-ben?*
Where can I buy a phone card?	**Wo kann ich eine Telefonkarte kaufen?** *Voh khann ee[ch] eye-neh tehleh-FOHN-kahrr-teh cow-fehn?*
May I add more minutes to my phone card?	**Kann ich meine Telefonkarte auf-laden?** *Khann ee[ch] my-neh tehleh-FOHN-kahrr-teh ouf-lah-denn?*

MAKING A CALL

May I dial direct?

Kann ich direkt wählen?
Khann ee[ch] dee-RECKT v[ae]h-lenn?

Operator please.

Die Vermittlung, bitte.
Dee Fehr-MITT-loong, bit-eh.

I'd like to make an international call.

Ich möchte ein Auslandsgespräch führen.
Ee[ch] m[oe][ch]-te aihn OUS-lahnds-geh-shpr[ae][ch] f[ue]h-ren.

I'd like to make a collect call.

Ich möchte ein R-Gespräch führen.
Ee[ch] m[oe][ch]-te aihn ERR-geh-shpr[ae][ch] f[ue]h-ren.

I'd like to use a calling card.

Ich möchte eine Telefonkarte verwenden.
Ee[ch] m[oe][ch]-te eye-neh teh-leh-FOHN-kahrr-teh fehr-venn-denn.

Bill my credit card.

Belasten Sie meine Kreditkarte.
Beh-LUSS-ten zee my-neh creh-DEET-kahrr-teh.

May I bill the charges to my room?

Kann ich die Kosten über mein Zimmer abrechnen?
Khann ee[ch] dee coss-ten [ue]h-behr mine TSIMMER up-re[ch]-nen?

May I bill the charges to my home phone?

Kann ich die Kosten über meine Telefonrechnung abrechnen?
Khann ee[ch] dee coss-ten [ue]h-behr my-neh tehleh-FOHN-re[ch]-noonng up-re[ch]-nen?

Information, please.

Die Auskunft, bitte.
Dee OUS-koonnft, bit-eh.

Listen Up: Telephone Lingo

Hallo?
HAH-loh?

Hello?

Welche Nummer?
Vell-[ch]eh NOOMMER?

What number?

**Es tut mir leid, die
Leitung ist besetzt.**
*As toot mere lyde, dee
lye-toong isst beh-
SETTST.*

I'm sorry, the line
is busy.

**Legen Sie bitte auf,
und wählen Sie erneut.**
*Leh-ghen zee bit-eh
OUF, oonnd v[ae]h-len
zee air-NOYT.*

Please, hang up and redial.

**Leider nimmt niemand
ab.**
*Lye-dehr nimmt nee-
mahnd UP.*

I'm sorry, nobody is answering.

**Auf Ihrer Karte sind
noch zehn Minuten
übrig.**
*Ouf eeh-rehr kahrr-teh
sinnd noh[ch] TSEHN
mee-nooh-ten [ue]h-
brigg.*

Your card has ten minutes left.

I'd like the number for ___.	**Ich hätte gern die Nummer von ___.**
	Ee[ch] hat-eh ghern dee noommer fonn ___.
I just got disconnected.	**Die Verbindung wurde gerade unterbrochen.**
	Dee fehr-BIN-doonng vuhr-deh gheh-rah-deh oontehr-BRO[CH]-enn.
The line is busy.	**Die Leitung ist belegt.**
	Dee lye-toonng isst beh-LEHGT.
I lost the connection.	**Die Verbindung wurde unterbrochen.**
	Dee fehr-BIN-doonng vuhr-deh oontehr-BRO[CH]-enn.

INTERNET ACCESS

Where is an Internet café?	**Wo finde ich ein Internetcafé?**
	Voh fin-deh ee[ch] aihn INternet-kaff-ehh?
Is there a wireless hub nearby?	**Gibt es in der Nähe einen Wireless-Hub?**
	Gheebt as in der n[ae]h-heh eye-nen WIREless-hub?

How much do you charge per minute / hour?	**Wie viel kostet das pro Minute / Stunde?**
	Vee-feel coss-tet dahs proh mee-NOO-teh / SHTOONN-deh?
Can I print here?	**Kann ich hier etwas ausdrucken?**
	Khann ee[ch] hear at-vahs OUS-drookk-kenn?
Can I burn a CD?	**Kann ich eine CD brennen?**
	Khann ee[ch] eye-neh tseh-DEH brenn-en?
Would you please help me change the language preference to English?	**Könnten Sie mir bitte die Sprache auf Englisch umstellen?**
	K[oe]nn-ten zee mere bit-eh dee shprah-[ch]eh ouf ENG-lish oomm-shtell-en?
May I scan something?	**Kann ich etwas einscannen?**
	Khann ee[ch] at-vahs AIHN-scan-nen?
Can I upload photos?	**Kann ich Fotos hochladen?**
	Khann ee[ch] FOH-tohs ho[ch]-lah-denn?
Do you have a USB port so I can download music?	**Gibt es hier einen USB-Anschluss, damit ich Musik herunterladen kann?**
	Gheebt as hear eye-nen ooh-ess-BEH-un-shlooss, dah-mitt ee[ch] moo-SEEK hehrunn-tehr lah-denn khann?
Do you have a machine compatible with iTunes?	**Haben Sie einen iTunes-kompatiblen Computer?**
	Hah-ben zee eye-nen iTUNES-comm-pah-teeblen computer?

Do you have a Mac?	**Haben Sie einen Mac?**
	Hah-ben zee eye-nen MAC?
Do you have a PC?	**Haben Sie einen PC?**
	Hah-ben zee eye-nen peh-TSEH?
Do you have a newer version of this software?	**Haben Sie eine neuere Version dieser Software?**
	Hah-ben zee eye-neh noy-eh-reh verr-SYOHN dee-sehr software?
Do you have broadband?	**Haben Sie einen Breitbandzugang?**
	Hah-ben zee eye-nen BRITE-bund-tsoo-gung?
How fast is your connection speed here?	**Wie hoch ist hier die Verbindungsgeschwindigkeit?**
	Vee hoh[ch] isst hear dee fehr-BIN-doonngs-ghe-shvinn-digg-kite?

GETTING MAIL

Where is the post office?	**Wo finde ich das Postamt?**
	Voh fin-deh ee[ch] dahs POSST-ahmmt?
May I send an international package?	**Kann ich ein Paket ins Ausland versenden?**
	Khann ee[ch] aihn pah-KEHHT inns OUS-lahnd fehr-senn-den?
Do I need a customs form?	**Benötige ich ein Zollformular?**
	Beh-n[oe]h-tiggeh ee[ch] aihn TSOLL-forr-moo-lahr?
Do you sell insurance for packages?	**Bieten Sie Paketversicherungen an?**
	Beaten zee pah-KEHHT-fehr-si[ch]e-roong-en un?

Please, mark it fragile.	**Kennzeichnen Sie das Paket bitte als zerbrechlich.** *Kenn-tsye[ch]-nen zee dahs pah-kehht bit-eh ahlls tsaihr-BRE[CH]-li[ch].*
Please, handle with care.	**Behandeln Sie es bitte vorsichtig.** *Beh-hun-delln zee as bit-eh FOHR-si[ch]-tigg.*
Do you have twine?	**Haben Sie Paketschnur?** *Hah-ben zee pah-KEHHT-shnoor?*
Where is a DHL office?	**Wo finde ich eine DHL-Niederlassung?** *Voh fin-deh ee[ch] eye-neh deh-hah-ELL nee-dehr-lass-oong?*
Do you sell stamps?	**Verkaufen Sie Briefmarken?** *Fehr-cow-fenn zee BREEF-marr-ken?*
Do you sell postcards?	**Verkaufen Sie Postkarten?** *Fehr-cow-fenn zee POSST-kahrr-ten?*
May I send that first class?	**Kann ich das erster Klasse versenden?** *Khann ee[ch] dahs airs-tehr KLASS-eh fehr-senn-den?*
How much to send that express / air mail?	**Wie viel kostet der Expressversand / Luftpostversand?** *Vee feel coss-tet dehr ex-PRESS-fehr-sannd / LOOFFT-pohsst-fehr-sannd?*
Do you offer overnight delivery?	**Bieten Sie einen Übernachtversand an?** *Beaten zee eye-nen [ue]h-behr-NAH[CH]T-fehr-sannd un?*

Listen Up: Postal Lingo

Der Nächste, bitte! *Dehr N[AE][CH]S-teh, bit-eh!*	Next!
Stellen Sie das bitte hier ab. *Shtell-en zee dahs bit-eh HEAR up.*	Please, set it here.
Welche Klasse? *Vell-[ch]eh KLAHSS-eh?*	Which class?
Welchen Service möchten Sie? *Vell-[ch]en SIR-viss m[oe][ch]-ten zee?*	What kind of service would you like?
Was kann ich für Sie tun? *Vahss khann ee[ch] f[ue]hr zee TOON?*	How can I help you?
Abgabeschalter *UP-ghah-beh-shull-tehr*	dropoff window
Abholschalter *UP-hohl-shull-tehr*	pickup window

How long will it take to reach the United States?	**Wie lange dauert der Versand in die USA?** *Vee lung-eh dowert dehr fehr-sannd inn dee ohh ess AH?*
I'd like to buy an envelope.	**Ich möchte ein Kuvert kaufen.** *Ee[ch] m[oe][ch]-teh aihn coo-VEHR cow-fen.*

May I send it airmail?	**Kann ich das per Luftpost senden?** *Khann ee[ch] dahs pair LOOFFT-posst senn-den?*
I'd like to send it certified / registered mail.	**Ich möchte das als Einschreiben senden.** *Ee[ch] m[oe][ch]-teh dahs ahlls AIHN-shrye-ben senn-den.*

MONEY

Moneysaving Tips

- The major cities of Germany are some of the world's most expensive; your euros will stretch farther if you cut short your time in Munich or Frankfurt and concentrate on interesting regional capitals such as Freiburg in the Black Forest.
- A rail pass can yield significant savings, and German Rail (www.bahn.de) offers a variety of rather complicated deals, such as the Schönes-Wochenende-Ticket, which allows up to five people unlimited travel on regional trains during any 24-hour period over the weekend for a total of €33.
- The cost of skiing in Germany can be astronomical, but if you avoid chic Garmisch-Partenkirchen, you'll find winter fun nearby at more moderate costs. Some less fashionable spots in the Bavarian Alps, such as Ramsau and Oberammergau, offer excellent value for your money. Prices in a village next to a resort are often 30% lower than in the resort itself,
- Many prices for children are considerably lower than for adults, and fees for children under 6 are often waived entirely. Students and retired people also get discounts at many attractions. Always ask about discounts.

Getting Cash

An ATM, known as a *geldautomat*, is the easiest and best way to get cash from home. Even the smallest village should have at least one ATM, although they tend to be fewer and farther between in German cities than in American cities. Most ATMs are linked to the Cirrus and Plus networks; look at the back of your bank card to see which network you're on. Do keep in mind the following stipulations:

- Your bank will probably charge a fee for using a different bank's ATM, and international fees can be much higher than those at home—often about $5 per ATM withdrawal.

The bank whose ATM you're using may charge its own fee.

- Find out what your daily withdrawal limit is before you leave home. Many German ATMs have a one-time withdrawal limit of €500.
- If you use a PIN to withdraw money from your credit card, keep in mind that interest accrues from the day of your withdrawal, even if you pay your monthly bill on time.
- German ATMs take only four-digit PINs (Personal Identification Numbers), so if you have a six-digit PIN, contact your bank to change it before you leave home.

Traveler's Checks

These are not nearly as convenient to use, and the exchange rate you get at an ATM is likely to be much better. On the plus side: If you plan to burn through a lot of cash, traveler's checks could be cheaper to use, given that most ATM withdrawals are limited to a few hundred euros, and banks charge for each withdrawal. If you pay a hotel or other establishment with traveler's checks, you'll get the worst possible exchange rate.

If you decide to purchase traveler's checks, contact **American Express** (© 800/721-9768 in the U.S. and Canada; www. americanexpress.com); **Thomas Cook** (© 800/223-7373 in the U.S. and Canada; www.thomascook.com); **Visa** (© 800/227-6811 in the U.S. and Canada; www.visa.com); or **Citicorp** (© 800/645-6556 in the U.S. and Canada; www.citicorp.com).

Credit Cards

Credit cards are a safe way to carry money, provide a convenient record of all your expenses, and generally offer decent exchange rates. You can also withdraw cash advances from your credit card at banks or ATMs, provided you know your PIN. Keep in mind that when you use your credit card abroad, most banks assess a 2% fee above the 1% fee charged by Visa, MasterCard, or American Express. In Germany, MasterCard and Visa predominate, and American Express and Diners Club are also widely accepted. Keep in mind that while almost all major hotels accept credit cards, restaurants and shops that only take cash are more prevalent in Germany than in the U.S.

STAYING CONNECTED

Telephone Matters

The country code for Germany is 49. **To call Germany from the United States or Canada**, dial the international access code 011, then 49, then the city code, then the regular phone number. If there is a 0 listed at the beginning of the city code, leave this out when dialing from abroad.

To dial internationally from Germany   Dial 00, then the country code, then the area code, then the number. The country code for the U.S. and Canada is 1.

To call one city from another within Germany   Dial the city code (including the initial 0), then the regular phone number. When making a local call from a landline, leave out the city code. When calling a German landline from a German cell phone, you will always have to include the city code.

Many public telephone booths require a **prepaid telephone card** from **Deutsche Telekom**, the German telephone company. These phone cards are sold at post offices and newsstands, and cost between €6 and €25.

Telephone calls made through hotel switchboards can double, triple, or even quadruple the regular charge; try not to use the phone in your hotel room.

German phone numbers are not standardized. In some places, numbers have as few as three digits. One number may have five digits while the phone next door has nine digits.

Cell Phones

If your cell phone is on a GSM network (Global System for Mobiles) and you have a world-capable multiband phone, you can make and receive phone calls in Germany (and much of the rest of the world). Just call your wireless operator and ask to have "international roaming" activated. Unfortunately, per minute charges can be steep—usually at least $2. You'll get much better rates if you have a cheap, prepaid SIM card—widely available at electronics shops—installed in your phone in Germany. If your phone is "locked," however, you won't be able to take out the SIM card.

Internet

You'll find Internet cafes in almost all German cities and towns; many libraries, youth hostels, and hotels also provide Internet access. If you're traveling with your laptop, you'll likely be pleased with the plentiful Wi-Fi access in Germany. Most upscale hotels, and even many youth hostels, now provide guests with Wi-Fi, known in German as WLAN (pronounced VAY-lahn). Restaurants and cafes that provide wireless Internet will be marked with a sticker in the window that says "WLAN."

Mail

The German postal system is generally quick and efficient, but you should still allow a week for a letter or postcard to cross the Atlantic. It costs €1.70 to send an airmail letter of up to 20gr (about 0.7oz) to the U.S. or Canada, €1 for a postcard. www.deutschepost.de.

COMMUNICATIONS

CHAPTER SEVEN

CULTURE

CINEMA

Is there a movie theater nearby?	**Gibt es hier in der Nähe ein Kino?** *Gheebt as hear in dehr n[ae]h-heh aihn KEE-noh?*
What's playing tonight?	**Was läuft heute Abend?** *Vahhs LOYFT hoy-teh ah-bend?*
Is that in English or German?	**Ist das auf Englisch oder auf Deutsch?** *Isst dahs ouf ENG-lish oh-dehr ouf doytsh?*
Are there English subtitles?	**Gibt es englische Untertitel?** *Gheebt as eng-lisheh OONN-tehr-tee-tell?*
Is the theater air conditioned?	**Ist das Kino klimatisiert?** *Isst dahs kee-noh klee-mah-tee-SEERT?*
How much is a ticket?	**Wie viel kostet eine Karte?** *Vee feel coss-tet eye-neh KAHRR-teh?*
Do you have a ____ discount?	**Gibt es einen Rabatt für ____?** *Gheebt as eye-nen rah-BAHTT f[ue]hr ____?*
senior	**Senioren** *sehn-YOH-ren*
student	**Studenten** *shtoo-DENN-ten*
children's	**Kinder** *KIN-dehr*
What time is the movie showing?	**Wann läuft der Film?** *Vahnn LOYFT dehr fillm?*

How long is the movie?	**Wie lang dauert der Film?**
	Vee lahng DOW-ert dehr fillm?
May I buy tickets in advance?	**Kann ich schon vorher Karten kaufen?**
	Khann ee[ch] shohn FOHR-hair kahrr-ten cow-fen?
Is it sold out?	**Ist die Vorstellung ausverkauft?**
	Isst dee fohr-shtelloong OUS-fehr-cowft?
When does it begin?	**Wann beginnt die Vorstellung?**
	Vahnn beh-GHINNT dee fohr-shtel-loong?

PERFORMANCES

Do you have ballroom dancing?	**Gibt es hier Gesellschaftstanz?**
	Gheebt as hear gheh-SELL-shahfts-tunnts?
Are there any plays showing right now?	**Finden derzeit irgendwelche Aufführungen statt?**
	Fin-den dehr-tsyte irr-ghennd-vell-[ch]eh OUF-f[ue]h-roong-en shtahtt?
Is there a dinner theater?	**Gibt es hier ein Theater mit angeschlossener Gastronomie?**
	Gheebt as hear aihn teh-AH-tehr mitt un-gheh-shloss-ehn-er gahss-troh-noh-MEE?
Where can I buy tickets?	**Wo kann ich Karten kaufen?**
	Voh khann ee[ch] KAHRR-ten cow-fen?
Are there student discounts?	**Gibt es einen Studentenrabatt?**
	Gheebt as eye-nen shtoo-DENN-ten-rah-bahtt?
I need ____ seats.	**Ich benötige ____ Plätze.**
	Ee[ch] beh-n[oe]-tiggeh ____ PL[AE]TT-seh.

For a full list of numbers, see p7.

CULTURE

Listen Up: Box Office Lingo

Was möchten Sie gern sehen?	What would you like to see?
Vahs m[oe][ch]-ten zee ghern SEHH-hen?	
Wie viele?	How many?
Vee FEE-leh?	
Für zwei Erwachsene?	For two adults?
F[ue]hr tsvaih air-VUCK-seh-neh?	
Mit Butter? Gesalzen?	With butter? Salt?
Mitt BOOT-ehr? Ghe-SAHLL-tsenn?	
Darf's sonst noch was sein?	Would you like anything else?
Dharrfs SONNST noh[ch] vahs syne?	

An aisle seat.	**Einen Gangplatz, bitte.**
	Eye-nen GAHNG-plahts, bit-eh.
Orchestra seat, please.	**Einen Orchesterplatz, bitte.**
	Eye-nen orr-KESS-tehr-plahts, bit-eh.
What time does the play start?	**Wann beginnt die Vorstellung?**
	Vahnn beh-GHINNT dee fohr-shtel-loong?
Is there an intermission?	**Gibt es eine Pause?**
	Gheebt as eye-neh POW-seh?
Do you have an opera house?	**Gibt es hier ein Opernhaus?**
	Gheebt as hear aihn OH-pehrrn-house?
Is there a local symphony?	**Gibt es hier ein örtliches Symphonieorchester?**
	Gheebt as hear aihn [oe]rrt-li[ch]-ess sym-foh-NEE-orr-kess-tehr?

May I purchase tickets over the phone?

Kann ich die Karten telefonisch bestellen?

Khann ee[ch] dee kahrr-ten teh-leh-FOH-nish beh-shtellen?

What time is the box office open?

Welche Öffnungszeiten hat der Kartenschalter?

Vell-[ch]eh [OE]FF-noongs-tsye-ten hut dehr kahrr-ten-shahll-tehr?

I need space for a wheelchair, please.

Ich benötige einen Platz für einen Rollstuhl.

Ee[ch] beh-n[oe]-tiggeh eye-nen plahts f[ue]hr eye-nen ROLL-shtool.

Do you have private boxes available?

Verfügen Sie über Privatlogen?

Fehr-f[ue]h-ghenn zee [ue]h-behr pree-VAHT-loh-shen?

Is there a church that gives concerts?

Gibt es hier eine Kirche, in der Konzerte gegeben werden?

Gheebt as hear eye-neh kirr-[ch]eh, inn dehr con-TSERR-teh gheh-gheh-ben vehr-denn?

A program, please.

Ein Programm, bitte.

Aihn proh-GRAHMM, bit-eh.

Please show us to our seats.

Zeigen Sie uns bitte unsere Plätze.

Tsye-ghenn zee oonns bit-eh oonn-seh-reh PL[AE]TT-seh.

MUSEUMS, GALLERIES & SIGHTS

Do you have a museum guide?

Haben Sie einen Museumsführer?

Hah-ben zee eye-nen moo-SEHH-ooms-f[ue]h-rehr?

Do you have guided tours?

Bieten Sie Fremdenführungen an?

Beaten zee FREMM-denn-f[ue]h-roongen un?

What are the museum hours?

Wann hat das Museum geöffnet?
Vahnn hut dahs moo-sehh-oom gheh-[OE]FF-net?

Do I need an appointment?

Benötige ich einen Termin?
Beh-n[oe]-tiggeh ee[ch] eye-nen tehr-MEEN?

What is the admission fee?

Wie hoch ist der Eintrittspreis?
Vee hoh[ch] isst dehr AIHN-tritts-pryes?

Do you have ____

Haben Sie ____?
Hah-ben zee ____?

  student discounts?

  Studentenrabatte?
  shtoo-DENN-ten-rah-bahtt-eh?

  senior discounts?

  Seniorenrabatte?
  senn-YOH-ren-rah-bahtt-eh?

Do you have services for the hearing impaired?

Haben Sie Angebote für Hörgeschädigte?
Hah-ben zee UN-gheh-boh-teh f[ue]r H[OE]R-gheh-sh[ae]h-digg-teh?

Do you have audio tours in English?

Werden Audioführungen in englischer Sprache angeboten?
Vehr-denn OW-dee-ohh-f[ue]h-roongen in eng-lisher SHPRAH-[ch]eh un-gheh-boh-ten?

GERMANY FOR JEWISH VISITORS

The Jewish community in Germany is growing. Immigration from Eastern Europe, especially the former Soviet Union, has largely fueled this growth, and in some cities, 70% of Jews are native Russian speakers. Berlin, with the largest Jewish population, is served by several kosher restaurants, a Jewish high school, the new Mendelssohn Center at nearby Potsdam University, and both weekly and monthly papers.

Anti-Semitism has not disappeared completely, but postwar Germany as a whole has worked hard to confront its past. German high schools include Holocaust studies in their curriculum, over 30 museums deal with Jewish issues, and the sites of concentration camps are preserved for visitors as sobering reminders of the past. Neo-Nazi and extreme-right groups count about 65,000 total members nationwide, a tiny minority in a country of more than 80 million people.

Berlin has the highest concentration of places of interest to Jewish visitors. The **Memorial to the Murdered Jews of Europe**, designed by American architect Peter Eisenman, occupies a full city block in the center of Berlin. The city's **Jewish Museum** (Jüdisches Museum Berlin) presents an exhaustive thousand-year history of German Jewry, and the **Jüdischer Friedhof** at Weissensee, once Europe's largest Jewish cemetery, contains 110,000 graves and a memorial to victims of the Nazis. A darker sight is the chillingly elegant **Wannsee Villa**, where the details of the "Final Solution" were hammered out in 1942; more hopeful is the newly renovated **Oranienburger Strasse Synagogue**, a glorious Moorish-style structure that now operates as a memorial and museum.

BEST MUSEUMS

Prosperity, artistic flair, and intellectual curiosity have made Germany home to some of the world's best museums:

Gemäldegalerie (Picture Gallery), Berlin   This is one of Europe's leading art museums, with a celebrated collection of paintings that ranges from the 13th to 18th centuries, from Botticelli and Brueghel to Vermeer and Velázquez. © **030/2090-5555**; www.smb.spk-berlin.de/gg.

Pergamon Museum, Berlin   Built in 1930 on an island in the Spree River, this astonishing museum contains entirely reconstructed

CULTURE

temples from ancient Assyria, Greece, Rome, and Sumer. Don't miss the sprawling exhibition devoted to the ancient art of the Islamic world and the Far East. ✆ 030/2090-5301.

Zwinger, Dresden Pavilions, heroic statues, galleries, and formal gardens flank a vast rectangular esplanade. Designed for the 17th-century king Augustus the Strong, the Zwinger was destroyed in the final days of World War II; its postwar reconstruction was a great triumph for the East German government. The treasures amassed inside include paintings, 18th-century Dresden porcelain, and antique weapons. www.skd-dresden.de.

Deutsches Museum, Munich Since 1925, this museum has been a preeminent showcase of science and technology. Occupying an island in the Isar River, it features plenty of hands-on exhibits: there are hundreds of buttons to push, levers to crank, and gears to turn. ✆ 089/21791; www.deutsches-museum.de.

Dachau Concentration Camp Memorial Site, near Munich Heinrich Himmler first organized Dachau as a concentration camp for enemies of the Reich in 1933. An escaped inmate, Joseph Rovan, described it as "implacable, perverted, an organization that was totally murderous, a marvelous machine for the debasement and dehumanization of man." Today, it's one of the most poignant museums in the world. ✆ 08131/669970; www.kz-gedenkstaette-dachau.de.

Stadtische Galerie im Lenbachhaus, Munich Housed in the former villa of portrait painter Franz von Lenbach, this museum has a stunning and internationally renowned collection of modern art, including the Blauer Reiter (Blue Rider) period best represented by Kandinsky. It also has a rich collection of Gothic artwork. ✆ 089/2333-2000.

Gutenberg Museum, Mainz This museum is one of the most comprehensive tributes to printing and publishing anywhere in the world. The bulky presses on which Johannes Gutenberg used movable type and two of the earliest Bibles ever printed are the primary displays here. ✆ 06131/1226-4042.

Museum Ludwig, Cologne This is the home of one of the world's largest collections of work by Pablo Picasso. The collection was beefed up when Irene Ludwig, widow of the late German art patron Peter Ludwig, donated 774 Picasso works to the museum. ✆ 0221/2212-6165.

Kunsthalle, Hamburg With some 3,000 paintings and around 400 sculptures in its treasure trove, the Kunsthalle is the leading art museum in northern Germany. Rare treasures dating to the 14th century include works by Bertram, the leading German master of that time. One section of the gallery also displays modern works, including art by Andy Warhol, Josef Beuys, and Pablo Picasso. ℗ 040/4281-31200; www.hamburger-kunsthalle.de.

BEST CASTLES AND PALACES

The first castles in what is now Germany were fortifications built to protect the territory of feudal lords in the Middle Ages. As the centuries passed, hostilities among principalities died down and architects began to design castles for prestige and comfort rather than defense. Thanks to this slow evolution, Germany is now full of castles (*Burg*) and palaces (*Schloss*) of all shapes, sizes, and styles.

Sans Souci Palace, Potsdam   Frederick the Great's retreat is Germany's most successful blend of landscape and architecture, dubbed the "Prussian Versailles." The more than 296 acres of intricately landscaped gardens have enough pavilions, orangeries, and heroic statues to keep a visitor intrigued for days. ℗ 0331/969-4190.

Schloss Wartburg, Eisenach   Built between the 11th and 16th centuries, this castle on a rocky hilltop was a center of patronage for troubadours and a place of refuge for Martin Luther, who completed his translation of the Bible within its massive walls. Wagner used it as inspiration for the setting of Tannhäuser, and Bach and Goethe visited. ℗ 03691/2500; www.wartburg-eisenach.de.

Residenz, Würzburg   Built between 1720 and 1744 as the official residence of the powerful bishops of Würzburg, this is one of the most massive baroque palaces in Germany. It combines a chapel with gardens, a gallery of paintings, frescoes by Italian master Tiepolo, and enough decorations to satisfy the most demanding taste for ornamentation. Also within its showrooms are Greco-Roman artifacts and valuable paintings from the 14th to the 19th centuries. ℗ 0931/355-170.

Neuschwanstein, near Füssen   When the creators of California's Disneyland needed an inspiration for their fairy-tale castle, this is the model they picked. Neuschwanstein is the most lavishly romantic (and impractical) castle in the German-speaking world. A 19th-century theatrical set designer drew it up in a neofeudal style. The man who ordered its construction was (who else?) "Mad" King Ludwig of Bavaria. ℗ 08362/938-523.

CULTURE

Hohenschwangau Castle, near Füssen   It was completed in 1836 and built on the ruins of a 12th-century fortress at the behest of the youthful prince regent, Maximilian II of Bavaria, who used it to indulge his taste for "troubadour romanticism" and the life of the English country manor. © 08362/930-830.

Schloss Nymphenburg, Munich   It was originally constructed between 1664 and 1674 as an Italian-inspired summer home for Bavarian monarchs. Subsequent kings added on to its structure until around 1780, by which time the building and its lavish park closely resembled the French palace at Versailles. A highlight of the interior is the green, gold, and white banqueting hall, whose frescoes and ornate stucco are among the most memorable in Bavaria. © 089/17-908-668.

THE BEST CATHEDRALS

Kaiserdom (Imperial Cathedral), Speyer   This Romanesque massive church from 1030 has four bell towers, a cornerstone laid by one of Germany's earliest kings, Konrad II, and an undeniable sense of the (anonymous) architect's aesthetic links with the traditions of ancient Rome. © 06232/1020.

Dom St. Peter, Worms   This church is a grand example of High Romanesque style, its oldest section dating from 1132. The Diet of Worms, held here in 1521, condemned the beliefs of the young Martin Luther and banished him to the far boundaries of the Holy Roman Empire. © 06241/6151.

Cologne Cathedral, Cologne   Based on French Gothic models in Paris and Amiens, this cathedral was envisioned as one of the largest religious buildings in Christendom. It required 600 years to finish—work stopped for about 300 years until the neo-Gothic fervor of the romantic age fueled its completion. In 1880, it was inaugurated with appropriate pomp and circumstance in the presence of the German Kaiser. Today, its rust-colored bulk towers above Cologne, instantly recognizable from miles away. © 0221/92584731.

Dom (Cathedral), Aachen   Its size and the stonework dating from 1414 are deeply impressive, but even more so is the cathedral's association with the earliest of German emperors, Charlemagne. He was crowned in an older building on this site on Christmas Day, AD 800. The cathedral's treasury contains gem-encrusted Christian artifacts from the 10th century whose heft and barbaric glitter evoke pre-Christian Germania. © 0241/47709127.

CHAPTER EIGHT

This chapter covers the phrases you'll need to shop in a variety of settings, from the mall to the town square artisan market. We also threw in the terminology you'll need to visit the barber or hairdresser.

For coverage of food and grocery shopping, see p101.

GENERAL SHOPPING TERMS

Please tell me ____	**Könnten Sie mir bitte sagen, ____** *K[oe]nn-ten zee mere bit-eh SAH-ghenn, ____*
how to get to a mall?	**wie ich zu einem Einkaufszentrum komme?** *ee[ch] tsoo eye-nem AIHN-cowfs-tsenn-troom kom-meh?*
the best place for shopping?	**wo man hier am besten Shoppen kann?** *voh mahn hear um bess-ten SHOPPEN khann?*
how to get downtown?	**wie ich in die Stadt komme?** *vee ee[ch] inn dee SHTAHTT kom-meh?*
Where can I find a ____	**Wo finde ich ____** *Voh fin-deh ee[ch] ____*
shoe store?	**ein Schuhgeschäft?** *aihn SHOO-gheh-sh[ae]fft?*
men's / women's / children's clothing store?	**ein Bekleidungsgeschäft für Herren / Damen / Kinder?** *aihn beh-KLYE-doongs-gheh-sh[ae]fft f[ue]hr HERR-en / DAH-menn / KIN-dehr?*

designer fashion shop?	**ein Geschäft mit Designermode?** *aihn gheh-SH[AE]FFT mitt designer-moh-deh?*
vintage clothing store?	**ein Second-Hand-Geschäft?** *aihn second-HAND-geh-sh[ae]fft?*
jewelry store?	**einen Juwelier?** *eye-nen you-vehll-LEER?*
bookstore?	**eine Buchhandlung?** *eye-neh BOO[CH]-hahnd loong?*
toy store?	**ein Spielwarengeschäft?** *aihn SHPEEL-vah-ren-gheh-sh[ae]fft?*
stationery store?	**eine Schreibwarenhandlung?** *eye-neh SHRYEB-vah-ren-hahndloong?*
antique shop?	**einen Antiquitätenhändler?** *eye-nen ahnnti-quee-T[AE]H-ten-hen-dlehr?*
cigar shop?	**einen Tabakladen?** *eye-nen TAH-buck-lah-denn?*
souvenir shop?	**ein Souvenirgeschäft?** *aihn souveNIR-gheh-sh[ae]fft?*
Where can I find a flea market?	**Wo finde ich einen Flohmarkt?** *Voh finn-deh ee[ch] eye-nen FLOHH-marrkt?*

CLOTHES SHOPPING

I'd like to buy ____	**Ich möchte ____ kaufen.** *Ee[ch] m[oe][ch]-teh ____ cow-fen.*
men's shirts.	**Herrenhemden** *HERR-en-hem-denn*

women's shoes.	**Damenschuhe**
	DAH-menn-shoo-heh
children's clothes.	**Kinderbekleidung**
	KIN-dehr-beh-klye-doong
toys.	**Spielwaren**
	SHPEEL-vah-ren

For a full list of numbers, see p7.

I'm looking for a size ____	**Ich suche etwas in Größe ____**
	Ee[ch] SOO-[ch]eh at-vahs inn
	gr[oe]sseh ____
small.	**S.**
	ess.
medium.	**M.**
	emm.
large.	**L.**
	ell.
extra-large.	**XL.**
	ICKS ell.
I'm looking for ____	**Ich suche ____**
	Ee[ch] SOO-[ch]eh ____
a silk blouse.	**eine Seidenbluse.**
	eye-neh SYE-denn-bloo-seh.
cotton pants.	**eine Baumwollhose.**
	BOWM-voll-hoh-seh.
a hat.	**einen Hut.**
	eye-nen HOOT.
sunglasses.	**eine Sonnenbrille.**
	eye-neh SONN-en-brrill-eh.
underwear.	**Unterwäsche.**
	OONN-tehr-v[ae]sh-eh.
cashmere.	**nach etwas aus Kaschmir.**
	nah[ch] at-vahs ous KHASH-
	mere.
socks.	**nach Socken.**
	nah[ch] SOKKEN.
sweaters.	**nach Pullovern.**
	nah[ch] pull-OH-vehrn.

Ohrringe
Halskette
Armbanduhr
Kleid

Hemd
Krawatte
Jackett
Gürtel
Hose
Schuhe

a coat.	**eine Jacke.** *eye-ne YAKK-eh.*
a swimsuit.	**einen Badeanzug.** *eye-nen BAH-deh-un-tsoog.*
May I try it on?	**Kann ich das anprobieren?** *Khann ee[ch] dahs UN-proh-bee-ren?*
Do you have fitting rooms?	**Haben Sie Umkleidekabinen?** *Hah-ben zee OOMM-klye-deh-kah-bee-nen?*
This is _____	**Das ist _____** *Dahs isst _____*
too tight.	**zu eng.** *tsoo ENNG.*
too loose.	**zu weit.** *tsoo VYTE.*
too long.	**zu lang.** *tsoo LAHNGG.*
too short.	**zu kurz.** *tsoo KOORRTS.*

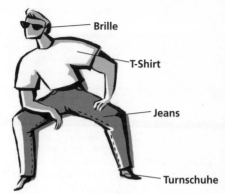

Brille

T-Shirt

Jeans

Turnschuhe

This fits great!	**Das passt gut!**
	Dahs pahsst GOOT!
Thanks, I'll take it.	**Danke, das nehme ich.**
	Dunk-eh, dahs NEH-meh ee[ch].
Do you have that in ____	**Haben Sie das ____**
	Hah-ben zee dahs ____
a smaller / larger size?	**kleiner / größer?**
	KLYE-nehr / GR[OE]-ssehr?
a different color?	**in einer anderen Farbe?**
	inn eye-nehr un-deh-ren FARR-beh?
How much is it?	**Wie viel kostet das?**
	Vee feel COSS-tet dahs?

ARTISAN MARKET SHOPPING

Is there a craft / artisan market?	**Gibt es hier einen Handwerksmarkt / Künstlermarkt?**
	Gheebt as hear eye-nen HAHNND-vehrrks-marrkt / K[UE]NNST-lehr-marrkt?

That's beautiful. May I look at it?

Das ist wunderschön. Darf ich mir das näher ansehen?

Dahs isst voohn-dehr-SH[OE]HN. Dharrf ee[ch] mere dahs N[AE]-hehr un-seh-hen?

When is the farmers' market open?

Wann hat der Bauernmarkt geöffnet?

Vahnn hut dehr BOW-errn-marrkt gheh-[OE]FF-net?

Is that open every day of the week?

Ist das die ganze Woche über geöffnet?

Isst dahs dee GHANN-tseh voh-[ch]eh [ue]h-behr ghe-[oe]ff-net?

How much does that cost?

Wie viel kostet das?

Vee feel COSS-tet dahs?

That's too expensive.

Das ist zu teuer.

Dahs isst tsoo TOY-ehr.

How much for two?

Wie viel für zwei Stück?

Vee feel f[ue]hr TSVAIH sht[ue]ck?

Do I get a discount if I buy two or more?

Bekomme ich einen Nachlass, wenn ich zwei oder mehr kaufe?

Beh-com-meh ee[ch] eye-nen NA[CH]-lahss, venn ee[ch] tsvaih oder mehrr cow-feh?

Do I get a discount if I pay in cash?

Bekomme ich einen Nachlass bei Barzahlung?

Beh-com-meh ee[ch] eye-nen na[ch]-lahss bye BAAR-tsah-loong?

No thanks, maybe I'll come back.

Nein, danke. Vielleicht komme ich später nochmal vorbei.

Nine, dunk-eh, feel-lye[ch]t kom-meh ee[ch] SHP[AE]-tehr noh[ch]-mahl fohr-bye.

Listen Up: Market Lingo

Wenden Sie sich bei Fragen zu den Artikeln an das Personal. *Venn-denn zee see[ch] by FRAH-ghenn tsoo dehn arr-TEE-kelln un dahs perr-soh-NAHL.*	Please ask for help before handling goods.
Hier ist Ihr Wechselgeld. *Hear isst eehr VECK-sell-gelld.*	Here is your change.
Zwei für vierzig, der Herr. *Tsvaih f[ue]hr FEER-tsigg, dehr herr.*	Two for forty, sir.

Would you take €____?	**Sagen wir ____ Euro?** *Sah-ghen veer ___ OY-roh?*
For a full list of numbers, see p7.	
That's a deal!	**Abgemacht!** *UP-gheh-mah[ch]t!*
Do you have a less expensive one?	**Haben Sie eine günstigere Ausführung?** *Hah-ben zee eye-neh GH[UE]NS-tee-gheh-reh ous-f[ue]h-roong?*
Is there tax?	**Fällt Steuer an?** *F[ae]llt SHTOYER un?*
May I have the VAT forms? (Europe only)	**Könnte ich bitte die Formulare für die Mehrwertsteuer haben?** *K[oe]nn-teh ee[ch] bit-eh dee fohr-moo-LAAH-reh f[ue]hr dee MEHHR-vehrt-shtoyer hah-ben?*

BOOKSTORE / NEWSSTAND SHOPPING

Is there a ____ nearby?	**Gibt es in der Nähe ____ ?**
	Gheebt as inn dehr n[ae]h-heh ____?
a bookstore	**eine Buchhandlung**
	eye-neh BOO[CH]-hahnd loong
a newsstand	**einen Zeitungsstand**
	eye-nen TSITE-oongs-shtahnd
Do you have ____ in English?	**Haben Sie ____ in englischer Sprache?**
	Hah-ben zee ____ in eng-lisher SHPRAH-[ch]eh?
books	**Bücher**
	B[ue]h-[ch]ehr
newspapers	**Zeitungen**
	Tsite-oong-en
magazines	**Zeitschriften**
	Tsite-shriff-ten
books about local history	**Bücher zur örtlichen Geschichte**
	B[ue]h-[ch]ehr tsoor [oe]rrt-li[ch]-en gheh-SHI[CH]-teh
picture books	**Bilderbücher**
	BILL-dehr-b[ue]h-[ch]ehr

SHOPPING FOR ELECTRONICS

With some exceptions, shopping for electronic goods in Germany, Switzerland or Austria is generally not recommended. Many DVDs, CDs, and other products contain different signal coding from that used in the United States or Canada, to help deter piracy. In addition, electronic goods are generally more expensive than in the United States or Canada. They can be even more epensive if the exchange rate is high.

Can I play this in the United States / United Kingdom?

Lässt sich das in den USA abspielen?

L[ae]sst zee[ch] dahs inn dehn ohh ess AH up-shpee-len?

Will this game work on my game console in the United States / United Kingdom?

Funktioniert dieses Spiel auf meiner Spielekonsole in den USA?

Foonnk-tsee-yoh-NEERT dee-sehs shpeel ouf minor SHPEE-leh-con-soh-leh inn dehn ohh ess AH?

Do you have this in a U.S. / U.K. market format?

Haben Sie das in einem US-kompatiblen Format?

Hah-ben zee dahs in eye-nem ohh ESS-com-pah-tee-blenn forr-MAHT?

Can you convert this to a U.S. market format?

Können Sie das in ein US-kompatibles Format umwandeln?

K[oe]n-nen zee dahs inn aihn ohh ESS-com-pah-tee-bles forr-maht OOMM-vahnn-delln?

Will this work with a 110 VAC adapter?

Funktioniert das mit einem 110-Volt-Adapter?

Foonnk-tsee-yoh-NEERT dahs mit eye-nem hoon-dehrt-tsehn-VOLLT ah-dahpp-tehr?

Do you have an adapter plug for 110 to 220?

Haben Sie einen Adapterstecker von 110 auf 220 Volt?

Hah-ben zee eye-nen ah-DAHPP-tehr-shteck-ehr fonn hoon-dehrt-TSEHN ouf tsvaih-honn-dehrt-TSVANN-tsigg vollt?

Do you sell electronics adapters here?

Gibt es hier Elektronikadapter?

Gheebt as hear ehlec-TROH-nick-ah-dahpp-tehr?

Is it safe to use my laptop with this adapter?	**Kann ich mein Notebook mit diesem Adapter betreiben?**
	Khann ee[ch] mine NOTE-book mitt dee-sem ah-dahpp-tehr beh-TRYE-ben?
If it doesn't work, may I return it?	**Kann ich den Artikel zurückgeben, wenn er nicht funktioniert?**
	Khann ee[ch] dehn arr-tee-kell tsoo-R[UE]CK-gheh-ben, venn air ni[ch]t foonnk-tsee-yoh-NEERT?
May I try it here in the store?	**Kann ich den Artikel hier im Laden ausprobieren?**
	Khann ee[ch] dehn arr-tee-kell hear im lah-denn OUS-proh-bee-ren?

AT THE BARBER / HAIRDRESSER

Do you have a style guide?	**Haben Sie einen Frisurenkatalog?**
	Hah-ben zee eye-nen frree-SOO-ren-kah-tah-lohg?
A trim, please.	**Schneiden, bitte.**
	SHNYE-denn, bit-eh.
I'd like it bleached.	**Ich hätte mein Haar gern blondiert.**
	Ee[ch] hat-teh mine haahr ghern blonn-DEERT.
Would you make the color ____	**Könnten Sie die Farbe bitte ____**
	K[oe]nn-ten zee dee fahrr-beh bit-eh ____
darker?	**dunkler machen?**
	DOONNK-lehr mah[ch]-en?
lighter?	**heller machen?**
	HELL-ehr mah[ch]-en?

Would you just touch it up a little?

Könnten Sie es bitte nur ein wenig nachschneiden?

K[oe]nn-ten zee as bit-eh noohr aihn veh-nigg NAH[CH]-shnye-denn?

I'd like it curled.

Ich hätte mein Haar gern gelockt.

Ee[ch] hat-teh mine haahr ghern gheh-LOCKT.

Do I need an appointment?

Benötige ich einen Termin?

Beh-n[oe]-tiggeh ee[ch] eye-nen tehr-MEEN?

Wash, dry, and set.

Waschen, Trocknen und Legen.

VAHSH-en, TROKK-nen oonnd LEH-ghenn.

Do you do permanents?

Kann ich bei Ihnen eine Dauerwelle bekommen?

Khann ee[ch] by eeh-nen eye-neh DOWER-vell-eh beh-com-men?

May I make an appointment?

Ich hätte gern einen Termin.

Ee[ch] hat-eh ghern eye-nen tehr-MEEN.

Please use low heat.

Bitte nicht zu heiß.

Bit-eh ni[ch]t tsoo HYE-ss.

Please don't blow dry it.

Bitte nicht trockenföhnen.

Bit-eh ni[ch]t TROKK-en-f[oe]h-nen.

Please dry it curly / straight.

Föhnen Sie die Haare bitte lockig / glatt.

F[oe]h-nen zee dee haah-reh bit-eh LOCK-igg / GLAHTT.

Would you fix my braids?

Könnten Sie sich bitte um meinen Zopf kümmern?

K[oe]nn-ten zee see[ch] bit-eh oomm my-nen TSOPF k[ue]m-mehrn?

Would you fix my highlights?	**Könnten Sie sich bitte um meinen Strähnen kümmern?** *K[oe]nn-ten zee see[ch] bit-eh oomm my-neh SHTR[AE]H-nen k[ue]m-mehrn?*
Do you wax?	**Bieten Sie Enthaarungen an?** *Beaten zee ent-HAAH-roongen un?*
Please wax my ___	**Bitte enthaaren Sie meine ___** *Bit-eh ent-haah-ren zee my-neh*
legs.	**Beine.** *BY-neh.*
bikini line.	**Bikinilinie.** *bee-KEE-nee-lee-nee-eh.*
eyebrows.	**Augenbrauen.** *OW-ghenn-brown.*
under my nose.	**Oberlippe.** *OH-behr-lipp-eh.*
Please trim my beard.	**Trimmen Sie bitte meinen Bart.** *Trimmen zee bit-eh my-nen BAHRRT.*
A shave, please.	**Rasieren, bitte.** *Rah-SEE-ren, bit-eh.*
Use a fresh blade please.	**Verwenden Sie bitte eine neue Klinge.** *Fair-venn-denn zee bit-eh eye-neh noy-eh KLING-eh.*
Sure, cut it all off.	**Klar, schneiden Sie ruhig alles ab.** *Klahr, shnye-denn zee ROO-higg ull-es up.*

SHOPPING GUIDE

Germany is neither a shopper's paradise nor a bargain basement, and shopping here is best approached as a part of your overall experience rather than an end unto itself. That said, here are a few German products especially worth taking home and the best places to find them:

Toys

From traditional wood figures to stuffed animals to high-tech toys, Germany produces high-quality playthings with a whimsical flair. Imaginative toys can be found throughout the country, but **Nürnberg** has been a toy production center for centuries. Try **Obletter**, a massive toy store near the town center, or look for handcrafted toys at the **Handwerkhof**, a crafts market in a medieval castle. In case you'd rather look than buy, Nürnberg is also home to a toy museum. Another must-see among German toyshops is the **Münchner Poupenstuben und Zinnfiguren Kabinette** in **Munich**, an emporium of all things miniature: tiny houses, furniture, birdcages, and people are all cunningly crafted from pewter or carved wood.

Porcelain

Many German porcelain manufacturers date back hundreds of years—as does their reputation for excellence. **Berlin's KPM** (www.kpm-berlin.de) produces exquisite hand-painted items based on 18th and 19th century patterns, and will ship virtually anywhere in the world. The longstanding archrival of KPM, **Meissener Porzellan** (www.meisenusa.com), is based near Dresden in the town of Meissen, and made its name with the production of "Dresden china," once a carefully guarded secret of Dresden princes. Both companies have shops in Berlin, and both offer factory tours.

Sweets

The bad news is that German pastries probably won't survive the journey home—the good news is that candy will. The northern city of **Lübeck** is famed for its **marzipan**: according to legend,

Lübeckers ran out of flour during a long-ago siege of the city and began grinding almonds to make bread—the results were so delightful that they haven't looked back since. **J.G. Niederegger** has been the king of Lübecker marzipan since 1806, and the specialty of the Niederegger shop in Lübeck is a nut torte resting under a huge slab of fresh marzipan. Germany also gave the world the **gummy bear**, known in German as *Gummibärchen*. **Bärenland**, a national chain, specializes in high-quality gummy candies of all shapes and flavors, including distinctively German flavors such as *Sanddorn* and *rote Grütze*.

Woodcarvings

The town of **Oberammergau** in the Bavarian Alps produces much-sought-after **woodcarvings**. Most subjects are religious, deriving strictly from 14th-century originals. **Baur Anton** offers Oberammergau's most sophisticated inventory of carvings. The shop employs carvers who work from their homes, crafting intricate pieces from maple, pine, and linden.

Cuckoo Clocks

Corny they may be, but carved **Black Forest cuckoo clocks** remain an enduring favorite. An especially memorable place to find one is the **House of 1,000 Clocks** (Haus der 1000 Uhren) (www.hausder1000uhren.de) along the B33 between **Triberg** and **Hornberg**. You'll recognize the shop by the giant cuckoo clock and water wheel out front. A painter of clock faces, Josef Weisser, launched the business in 1824; today, his great-great-grandson owns the place. Cuckoo, grandfather, wall, and table clocks are on offer.

CHRISTMAS MARKETS

Germans go all-out for Christmas, and the Christmas Markets (*Christkindlmärkte*) to be found on almost every town square during the four weeks of Advent make December an especially enjoyable time to shop in Germany. At a typical Christmas market, you can expect a fragrant and cheerfully lit warren of stalls where artisans peddle handicrafts and vendors offer mulled wine, gingerbread, and regional foods and drinks. The following cities and town host exemplary Christmas markets:

Cologne Come December, just about the entire city center of Cologne seems to be given over to Christmas markets, including markets on boats moored in the Rhine. Local treats that abound at the Cologne markets include *Spekulatius*, a spiced butter cookie, and *Reibekuchen*, deep-fried potato pancakes served with applesauce.

Dresden Germany's oldest Christmas market has been a Dresden tradition since 1434. On the old town square, stunning blown-glass tree ornaments are sold alongside *Christstollen*, the city's famous fruitcake. The market culminates each year in Stollenfest: A giant *Christstollen* rolls through the city to the square, where a girl crowned the Stollenmädchen cuts the four-ton fruitcake with the traditional "Dresdener Stollen Knife" and distributes pieces to the waiting crowd.

Munich The sprawling market on Munich's Marienplatz focuses on stocking-stuffers rather than sausages and *Glühwein*. It's a great place to buy tree ornaments, candles, and wooden toys.

Nürnberg The most famous Christmas market in Germany is strictly traditional: bans on plastic trees, fairground rides, and recorded music keep the tackiness at bay. Instead, you'll find live carolers and lots of local food specialties, such as *Nürnberger Rostbratwurst*, miniature sausages served with sauerkraut. Tourist crowds can make for long lines here.

Quedlinburg This medieval town survived World War II intact and the city center is now a UNESCO World Heritage Site. The fairytale town makes a perfect backdrop for a Christmas market.

UNDERSTANDING VAT

As a member of the European Union, Germany imposes on most goods and services a tax called value-added tax (VAT) or, in German, *Mehrwertsteuer* (marked on receipts as MwSt). Nearly everything is taxed at 19%. Food and books are taxed at 7%.

VAT is built into prices of restaurants, hotels, and goods for sale in shops, rather than added on to the bill. Stores that display a tax-free sticker will issue you a Tax-Free Shopping Check at the time of purchase. When leaving the country, have the check stamped by the German Customs Service as your proof of legal export. You can then get a cash refund at one of the Tax-free Shopping Service offices in major airports and many train stations. Otherwise, you must mail the checks to Tax-Free Shopping Service, Mengstrasse 19, D-23552 Lübeck, Germany.

WHAT YOU CAN BRING HOME

Returning U.S. citizens who have been away for at least 48 hours can bring back, once every 30 days, $800 worth of merchandise duty-free. You'll be charged a flat rate of 4% on the next $1,000 worth of purchases. Be sure to have your receipts handy. On mailed gifts, the duty-free limit is $200. With some exceptions, you cannot bring fresh fruit or vegetables into the U.S. For specifics on what you can bring back, download the invaluable pamphlet Know Before You Go online at www.cbp.gov or contact the United States Customs & Border Protection (CBP), 1300 Pennsylvania Ave. NW, Washington, DC 20229; © 877/287-8667.

Canada allows its citizens a C$750 exemption. You're allowed to bring back duty-free one carton of cigarettes, one can of tobacco, 40 imperial ounces of liquor, and 50 cigars. In addition, you're allowed to mail gifts to Canada valued at less than C$60, if they're unsolicited and don't contain alcohol or tobacco. The $750 exemption can only be used once a year and only after an absence of seven days. For a clear summary of Canadian rules, write for the booklet I Declare, issued by the **Canada Border Services Agency** (© 800/461-9999 in Canada, or © 204/983-3500; www.cbsa-asfc.gc.ca).

CHAPTER NINE

SPORTS & FITNESS

GETTING FIT

Is there a gym nearby?	**Gibt es ein Fitnessstudio in der Nähe?** *Gheebt as aihn FIT-ness-shtoo-dee-oh inn dehr n[ae]h-heh?*
Do you have free weights?	**Haben Sie Hanteln und Gewichte?** *Hah-ben zee HAHN-teln oond gheh-WI[CH]-teh?*
I'd like to go for a swim.	**Ich möchte gern schwimmen gehen.** *Ee[ch] m[oe][ch]-teh ghern SHVIMM-en gheh-hen.*
Do I have to be a member?	**Muss ich Mitglied sein?** *Mooss ee[ch] MITT-gleed syne?*
May I come here for one day?	**Kann ich Ihr Angebot an einem einzelnen Tag nutzen?** *Khann ee[ch] eehr un-gheh-boht un eye-nem AIHN-tsell-nen tahgg noott-senn?*

How much does a membership cost?	**Wie viel kostet die Mitgliedschaft?**
	Vee feel coss-tet dee MITT-gleed-shufft?
I need to get a locker please.	**Ich hätte gern einen Spind.**
	Ee[ch] hat-eh ghern eye-nen SHPINNT.
Do you have a lock?	**Haben Sie ein Schloss?**
	Hah-ben zee aihn SHLOSS?
Do you have a treadmill?	**Haben Sie ein Laufband?**
	Hah-ben zee aihn LOUF-bund?
Do you have a stationary bike?	**Haben Sie ein Trainingsrad?**
	Hah-ben zee aihn TRAI-nings-rahd?
Do you have squash / American handball courts?	**Haben Sie einen Squashplatz / Platz für American Handball?**
	Hah-ben zee eye-nen SQUASH-plahts / plahts f[ue]hr american HAND-ball?
Are they indoors?	**In der Halle?**
	Inn dehr HULL-eh?
I'd like to play tennis.	**Ich würde gern Tennis spielen.**
	Ee[ch] v[ue]rr-deh ghern TEN-nis shpee-len.
Would you like to play?	**Möchten Sie gern spielen?**
	M[oe][ch]-ten zee ghern SHPEE-len?
I'd like to rent a racquet.	**Ich würde gern einen Schläger mieten.**
	Ee[ch] v[ue]rr-deh ghern eye-nen SHL[AE]h-gher meeten.
I need to buy some ____	**Ich benötige ____**
	Ee[ch] beh-n[oe]-tiggeh ____
new balls.	**neue Bälle.**
	noy-eh B[AE]LL-eh.
safety glasses.	**eine Schutzbrille.**
	eye-neh SHOOTTS-brill-eh.

May I rent a court for tomorrow?

Kann ich für morgen einen Platz mieten?

Khann ee[ch] f[ue]r morr-ghenn eye-nen PLAHTS meeten?

May I have clean towels?

Könnte ich bitte saubere Handtücher bekommen?

K[oe]nn-teh ee[ch] bit-eh sow-beh-reh HAHND-t[ue]h-[ch]ehr beh-com-men?

Where are the showers / locker-rooms?

Wo finde ich die Duschen / Umkleiden?

Voh fin-deh ee[ch] dee DOO-shenn / OOMM-klye-denn?

Do you have a workout room for women only?

Haben Sie einen Trainingsraum für Frauen?

Hah-ben zee eye-nen trainings-roum f[ue]hr FROW-en?

Do you have aerobics classes?

Bieten Sie Aerobic-Kurse an?

Bee-ten zee aeRObic-koorr-seh un?

Do you have a women's pool?

Haben Sie einen Pool für Frauen?

Hah-ben zee eye-nen pool f[ue]hr FROW-en?

Let's go for a jog.

Gehen wir eine Runde joggen.

Gheh-hen veer eye-neh roonn-deh JOG-en.

That was a great workout.

Das war ein großartiges Training.

Dahs vahr aihn GROHS-arr-tee-ghess training.

CATCHING A GAME

Where is the stadium?

Wo finde ich das Stadion?
Voh fin-deh ee[ch] dahs SHTAH-dee-on?

Who is your favorite player?

Wer ist Ihr Lieblingsspieler?
Vehr isst eehr LEEB-links-shpeel-er?

Who is the best goalie?

Wer ist der beste Torwart?
Vehr isst dehr bess-teh TOHR-wahrrt?

Where can I watch a soccer game?

Wo kann ich ein Fußballspiel sehen?
Voh khann ee[ch] aihn FOOSS-bahl-speel seh-en?

Where can I see a volleyball game?

Wo kann ich ein Volleyballspiel sehen
Voh khann ee[ch] aihn VOL-ley-bahl-speel seh-en?

Are there any women's teams?

Gibt es Frauenteams?
Gheebt as FROW-en-teams?

Do you have any amateur / professional teams?

Gibt es hier Amateurteams / Profiteams?
Gheebt as hear ama-TEUR-teams / PROH-fee-teams?

Is there a game I could play in?	**Gibt es ein Spiel, bei dem ich mit-spielen kann?**
	Gheebt as aihn shpeel, by dehm ee[ch] MITT-shpee-len khann?
Which is the best team?	**Welches Team ist das beste?**
	Vell-[ch]ess team isst dahs BESS-teh?
Will the game be on television?	**Wird das Spiel im Fernsehen über-tragen?**
	Virrd dahs shpeel im FEHRN-sehh-hen [ue]h-behr-trah-ghenn?
Where can I buy tickets?	**Wo kann ich Karten kaufen?**
	Voh khann ee[ch] KAHRR-ten cow-fen?
The best seats, please.	**Die besten Plätze, bitte.**
	Dee bess-ten PL[AE]TT-seh, bit-eh.
The cheapest seats, please.	**Die billigsten Plätze, bitte.**
	Dee bill-igg-sten PL[AE]TT-seh, bit-eh.
How close are these seats?	**Wie nah sind diese Plätze?**
	Vee NAH sinnd dee-seh pl[ae]tt-seh?
May I have box seats?	**Könnte ich bitte Logenplätze haben?**
	K[oe]nn-teh ee[ch] bit-eh LOH-shen-pl[ae]tt-seh hah-ben?
Wow! What a game!	**Wow! Was für ein Spiel!**
	Wow! VAHS f[ue]hr aihn shpeel!
Go Go Go!	**Los, los, los!**
	LOHS, LOHS, LOHS!
Oh No!	**Oh nein!**
	Oh NINE!
Give it to them!	**Gebt ihnen Saures!**
	Ghehbt eeh-nen SOW-ress!

Go for it!	**Auf geht's!**
	OUF ghehts!
Score!	**Tor!**
	TOHHR!
What's the score?	**Wie lautet der Spielstand?**
	Vee loutet dehr SHPEEL-shtahnd?
Who's winning?	**Wer gewinnt?**
	Vehr gheh-VINNT?

HIKING

Where can I find a guide to hiking trails?	**Wo finde ich einen Führer für Wandertouren?**
	Voh fin-deh ee[ch] eye-nen f[ue]h-rehr f[ue]hr VAHNN-dehr-touren?
Do we need to hire a guide?	**Benötigen wir einen Führer?**
	Beh-n[oe]-tiggen veer eye-nen F[UE]H-rehr?
Where can I rent equipment?	**Wo kann ich Ausrüstung mieten?**
	Voh khann ee[ch] OUS-r[ue]ss-toong meeten?
Do they have rock climbing there?	**Gibt es hier eine Möglichkeit zum Felsenklettern?**
	Gheebt as hear eye-neh m[oe]g-lee[ch]-kite tsoom FELL-senn-klet-tern?

We need more ropes and carabiners.

Wir benötigen mehr Seile und Karabiner.

Veer beh-n[oe]-tiggen mehhr SYE-leh oonnd kah-rah-BEE-nehr.

Where can we go mountain climbing?

Wo können wir hier bergsteigen?

Voh k[oe]n-nen veer hear BEHRRG-shtye-ghenn?

Are the routes ____

Sind die Routen ____

Sinnd dee roo-ten ____

well marked?

gut gekennzeichnet?

goot gheh-KENN-tsye[ch]-net?

in good condition?

in gutem Zustand?

inn goo-tem TSOO-shtahnd?

What is the altitude there?

Wie hoch ist es dort?

Vee HOH[CH] isst as dohrrt?

How long will it take?

Wie lange dauert die Tour?

Vee lahng-eh DOWERT dee tour?

Is it very difficult?

Ist die Tour sehr schwierig?

Isst dee tour sehr SHVEE-rigg?

I'd like a challenging climb but I don't want to take oxygen.

Ich möchte eine herausfordernde Tour unternehmen, aber keine Sauerstoffflaschen mitnehmen.

Ee[ch] m[oe][ch]-teh eye-neh heh-ROUS-forr-derrn-deh tour oonntehr-neh-men, ah-behr kye-neh SOUER-shtoff-flahshenn mitt-neh-men.

I want to hire someone to carry my excess gear.

Ich möchte einen Träger für meine Zusatzausrüstung engagieren.

Ee[ch] m[oe][ch]-teh eye-nen tr[ae]-ghehr f[ue]hr my-ne TSOO-sutts-ous-r[ue]ss-toong ong-ghah-SHEE-ren.

We don't have time for a long route.	**Wir haben nicht genügend Zeit für eine lange Tour.**
	Veer hah-ben ni[ch]t gheh-n[ue]h-ghennd TSITE f[ue]hr eye-ne lahng-eh tour.
I don't think it's safe to proceed.	**Ich denke, wir sollten aus Sicherheitsgründen nicht weitergehen.**
	Ee[ch] dehng-keh, veer soll-ten ous SI[CH]-ehr-hytes-gr[ue]nn-den nee[ch]t VYE-tehr-gheh-hen.
Do we have a backup plan?	**Haben wir einen Notfallplan?**
	Hah-ben veer eye-nen NOHT-fahll-plahn?
If we're not back by tomorrow, send a search party.	**Sollten wir bis morgen nicht zurück sein, schicken Sie einen Suchtrupp.**
	Soll-ten veer biss morr-ghenn nee[ch]t tsoo-R[UE]CK syne, shick-en zee eye-nehn SOO[CH]-troopp.
Are the campsites marked?	**Sind die Zeltplätze gekennzeich-net?**
	Sinnd dee tsellt-pl[ae]tt-seh gheh-KENN-tsye[ch]-net?
Can we camp off the trail?	**Können wir abseits der Strecke campieren?**
	K[oe]nn-en veer UP-sites dehr shtrek-keh cumpeeren?
Is it okay to build fires here?	**Ist hier Feuermachen erlaubt?**
	Isst hear foyer-mah-[ch]en air-LOUBT?
Do we need permits?	**Benötigen wir eine Genehmigung?**
	Beh-n[oe]-tiggen veer eye-ne gheh-NEH-mee-goong?

For more camping terms, see p78.
For more camping terms, see p78.

BOATING OR FISHING

When do we sail?

Wann legen wir ab?
Vahnn leh-ghenn veer UP?

Where are the life preservers?

Wo befinden sich die Schwimmwesten?
Voh beh-fin-den si[ch] dee SHVIMM-vess-ten?

Can I purchase bait?

Kann ich Köder kaufen?
Khann ee[ch] K[OE]H-dehr cow-fen?

Can I rent a pole?

Kann ich eine Angel leihen?
Khann ee[ch] eye-neh UNG-ell lye-hen?

How long is the voyage?

Wie lang dauert die Reise?
Vee lahng DOW-ert dee rye-seh?

Are we going up river or down?

Fahren wir flussauf- oder flussabwärts?
Fah-ren veer flooss-OUF oh-dehr flooss-UP-v[ae]rrts?

How far are we going?

Wie weit fahren wir?
Vee vite FAH-ren veer?

How fast are we going?

Wie schnell fahren wir?
Vee SHNELL fah-ren veer?

How deep is the water here?

Wie tief ist das Wasser hier?
Vee teef isst dah VAHS-ser hear?

I got one!	**Ich hab einen!**
	Ee[ch] HUB eye-nen!
I can't swim.	**Ich kann nicht schwimmen.**
	Ee[ch] khann nee[ch]t SHVIMM-men.
Can we go ashore?	**Können wir an Land gehen?**
	K[oe]nn-en veer un LAHNND gheh-hen?

For more boating terms, see p58.

DIVING

I'd like to go snorkeling.	**Ich würde gern schnorcheln gehen.**
	Ee[ch] v[ue]rr-deh ghern SHNORR-[ch]elln gheh-hen.
I'd like to go scuba diving.	**Ich würde gern mit Atemgerät tauchen gehen.**
	Ee[ch] v[ue]rr-deh ghern mitt AH-tehm-gheh-r[ae]ht TOU-[ch]enn gheh-hen.
I have a NAUI / PADI certification.	**Ich habe ein NAUI / PADI-Zertifikat.**
	Ee[ch] hah-beh aihn NAUI / PADI-tserr-tee-fee-KAHT.
I need to rent gear.	**Ich muss Ausrüstung mieten.**
	Ee[ch] mooss OUS-r[ue]ss-toong meeten.
We'd like to see some shipwrecks if we can.	**Wir würden gern ein paar Wracks sehen.**
	Veer v[ue]rr-den ghern aihn paahr VRRAHCKS seh-hen.
Are there any good reef dives?	**Gibt es hier schöne Riffe zum Tauchen?**
	Gheebt as hear sh[oe]h-neh riff-eh tsoomm TOU-[ch]en?

I'd like to see a lot of sea-life.	**Ich möchte gern viel von der Unterwasserwelt sehen.**
	Ee[ch] m[oe][ch]-teh ghern feel fonn dehr oonter-VAHS-sehr-vellt seh-hen.
Are the currents strong?	**Ist die Strömung stark?**
	Isst dee shtr[oe]h-moonng SHTARRK?
How clear is the water?	**Wie klar ist das Wasser?**
	Vee klaar isst dahs VAHS-sehr?
I want / don't want to go with a group.	**Ich möchte gern / nicht mit einer Gruppe tauchen.**
	Ee[ch] m[oe][ch]-teh ghern / nee[ch]t mitt eye-ner GROOPP-eh tou-[ch]en.
Can we charter our own boat?	**Können wir ein eigenes Boot chartern?**
	K[oe]nn-en veer aihn EYE-ghenn-es boht chartehrn?

SURFING

I'd like to go surfing.	**Ich würde gern surfen gehen.**
	Ee[ch] v[ue]rr-deh ghern SUR-fen gheh-hen.
Are there any good beaches?	**Gibt es hier schöne Strände?**
	Gheebt as hear sh[oe]h-neh SHTR[AE]N-deh?
Can I rent a board?	**Kann ich ein Surfbrett leihen?**
	Khann ee[ch] aihn SURF-brrett lye-hen?
How are the currents?	**Wie ist die Strömung?**
	Vee isst dee SHTR[OE]H-moonng?

How high are the waves?

Wie hoch sind die Wellen?
Vee hoh[ch] sinnd dee VELL-ehn?

Is it usually crowded?

Sind viele Menschen dort?
Sinnd FEE-leh menn-shenn dohrrt?

Are there facilities on that beach?

Gibt es Einrichtungen an diesem Strand?
Gheebt as AIHN-ri[ch]-toong-en un dee-sem shtrahnd?

Is there wind surfing there also?

Ist dort auch Windsurfing möglich?
Isst dohrrt ouh[ch] WIND-surfing m[oe]h-gli[ch]?

GOLFING

I'd like to reserve a tee-time, please.

Ich möchte eine Tee-Time reservieren.
Ee[ch] m[oe][ch]-teh eye-neh TEE-time reh-sehr-vee-renn.

Do we need to be members to play?

Müssen wir Mitglied sein, um spielen zu dürfen?
M[ue]ss-ehn veer MITT-gleed syne, oomm shpee-len tsoo d[ue]rr-fen?

How many holes is your course?

Wie viele Löcher hat Ihr Platz?
Vee fee-leh l[oe][ch]-ehr hut eehr PLAHTS?

What is par for the course?	**Wie hoch ist das Par auf diesem Platz?**
	Vee hoh[ch] isst dahs PAAR ouf dee-sem plahts?
I need to rent clubs.	**Ich möchte Schläger mieten.**
	Ee[ch] m[oe][ch]-teh SHL[AE]H-ghehr meeten.
I need to purchase a sleeve of balls.	**Ich möchte Golfbälle kaufen.**
	Ee[ch] m[oe][ch]-teh GOLLF-b[ae]ll-eh cow-fen.
I need a glove.	**Ich benötige einen Handschuh.**
	Ee[ch] beh-n[oe]h-tiggeh eye-nen HAHND-shoo.
I need a new hat.	**Ich brauche einen neuen Hut.**
	Ee[ch] brow-[ch]eh eye-nen noy-en HOOT.
Do you require soft spikes?	**Muss ich weiche Spikes tragen?**
	Mooss ee[ch] VYE-[ch]eh spikes trah-ghenn?
Do you have carts?	**Haben Sie Golfwägen?**
	Hah-ben zee GOLLF-v[ae]h-ghenn?
I'd like to hire a caddy.	**Ich würde gern einen Caddy mieten.**
	Ee[ch] v[ue]rr-deh ghern eye-nen CADDY meeten.
Do you have a driving range?	**Haben Sie eine Driving Range?**
	Hah-ben zee eye-neh DRIving Range?
How much are the greens fees?	**Wie hoch ist die Green Fee?**
	Vee hoh[ch] isst dee GREEN fee?
Can I book a lesson with the pro?	**Kann ich eine Unterrichtseinheit mit dem Profi buchen?**
	Khann ee[ch] eye-neh oon-tehr-ri[ch]ts-aihn-hyte mitt dehm PRO-fee boo-[ch]enn?

I need to have a club repaired.

Ich benötige eine Schlägerreparatur.
Ee[ch] beh-n[oe]h-tiggeh eye-neh SHL[AE]H-ghehr-reh-pah-rah-tour.

Is the course dry?

Ist der Platz trocken?
Isst dehr plahts TROKK-en?

Are there any wildlife hazards?

Besteht eine Gefahr durch wilde-bende Tiere?
Beh-shteht eye-neh gheh-fahr doohr[ch] villd-leh-benn-deh TEE-reh?

How many meters is the course?

Wie groß ist der Platz in Metern?
Vee grohs isst dehr plahts inn MEH-terrn?

Is it very hilly?

Ist der Platz sehr hügelig?
Isst dehr plahts sehr H[UE]H-gheh-lligg?

THE BEST ACTIVE SPORTS

Cycling

Most German cities are bike-friendly, but urban cyclists will especially enjoy **Munich**, where you'll be in the company of plenty of bike-riding locals. If you'd like to join the fun, pick up a copy of the pamphlet *Rad-Touren für unsere Gäste* (Bicycling for Our Guests) at the tourist office. It outlines itineraries for touring Munich by bike.

In **Lake Constance**, rent a bike at the train station in the former imperial town of Lindau and set out in any direction to enjoy spectacular lake views. The Lindau tourist office will provide a map and suggestions for the best routes to follow.

The well-marked **Neckar Valley Cycle Path** follows the Neckar River, beginning at its source in Villingen-Schwenningen and going all the way to the confluence with the Rhine at Mannheim. Along the way, you'll pass castles, manor houses, vineyards, country inns, and ancient towns. Many visitors pick up a bicycle in Heidelberg and cycle along the riverbanks until they find a good spot for a picnic.

The wild **Lüneburg Heath** in northern Germany is one of the country's major natural attractions—some of the greatest German poets have waxed rhapsodic about its heather-covered expanse, which is most beautiful in August and September. Rent a bike and pick up a map at the Lüneburg tourist office.

Potsdam, the onetime summer home of Prussian monarchs, is also great for cycling. This town near Berlin is dotted with stunning palaces such as the famed Sans Souci. The palaces are too far apart from one another to be seen easily on foot, but are in a park setting that limits car access to them, making cycling the most convenient solution. You can rent a bike at the Potsdam train station.

The truly ambitious cyclist can follow the 630km (391mi) **bike path that connects Berlin with Copenhagen, Denmark**. This popular long-distance bike path, which takes about 15 days at a moderate pace, passes Hanseatic towns, seaside cliffs, forests, and the unspoiled lake district countryside of Brandenburg—plus it's a flat ride the whole way.

Bike Tours   For over 20 years, **Classic Adventures** (© 800/777-8090; www.classicadventures.com) has offered bike tours of such areas as the Romantic Road. **Euro-Bike and Walking Tours** (© 800/321-6060; www.eurobike.com) has a full range of bicycling and walking tours in Bavaria, as well as a 9-day biking tour of Germany, France, and Switzerland.

Golf

Most German golf courses welcome visiting players who are members of courses at home. Weekday greens fees are usually around €45, rising to as much as €85 on Saturday and Sunday. For information about the various golf courses, contact the **Deutscher Golf-Verband**, Viktoriastrasse 16, 65189 Wiesbaden (© 0611/990200; www.golf.de/dgv). The Swabian region of Allgäu has several good courses. **Golf Club Oberstaufen und Steibis**, at Oberstaufen, is an 18-hole course close to a forest and nature park (www.golf-oberstaufen.de). Ofterschwang, a small, peaceful resort on the lovely Tiefenberger Moor, has the **Golf Club Sonnenalp** (www.sonnenalp.de). A good 18-hole golf course is found at **Golf Club Bodensee** (© 08389/89190; www.gcbw.de) on Lake Constance in southern Germany. Farther north, the city of Augsburg has an 18-hole course at **Golf Augsburg** (© 08234/5621; www.golfclub-augsburg.de).

Hiking and Mountain Climbing

Hiking and mountain climbing are popular in the German uplands. It's estimated that Germany has more than 80,000 marked hiking and mountain-walking tracks. The **Deutscher Wanderverband**, Wilhelmshöher Allee 157-159, 34121 Kassel (© 0561/938730; www.wanderverband.de) services the trails and offers information about trails, huts, and regional hiking associations. The **Deutscher Alpverein (DAV)**, Von-Kahr-Strasse 2-4, 80997 Munich (© 089/140030; www.alpenverein.de), owns and operates 50 huts in and around the Alps that are open to all mountaineers. This association also maintains a 15,000km (9,300mi) network of alpine trails.

The best alpine hiking is in the **Bavarian Alps**, especially the 1,240km (4,067ft) Eckbauer, on the southern fringe of

Partenkirchen. The tourist office will supply hiking maps and details. Another great place for hiking is **Berchtesgaden National Park**, Maximilianstrasse 1, Berchtesgaden (© **08652/64343**; www.nationalpark-berchtesgaden.de), bordering the Austrian province of Salzburg. This park offers the best-organized hikes and will hook you up with various groups offering hikes.

Walks

The Royal Castle Walks   For grand alpine vistas, hike up to the Marienbrücke, the bridge that spans the Pöllat Gorge behind Neuschwanstein Castle. From there, you can continue uphill for about an hour for an amazing view of "Mad" Kind Ludwig's fantasy castle.

Partnachklamm   One of the most dramatic walks in all of the Bavarian Alps departs from the great winter sports resort of Garmisch-Partenkirchen. A signposted trail leads to the dramatic Partnachklamm Gorge. Carved from solid rock, the route passes two panoramic bottlenecks amid the thunder of falling water and clouds of spray.

Mainau Island   A walk across the footbridge to Mainau, in Lake Constance, is like a visit to a tropical country. Mainau blossoms with exotic plants collected by the Baden princes and members of the Royal House of Sweden. Tropical brushwood and other botanical wonders still thrive in this mild climate.

Cochem Reichsburg Castle   Towering over the little town of Cochem, it can be reached on foot in about 15 minutes from the town's Marktplatz, or market square. This walk is one of the most rewarding you'll find in Germany, with panoramas in all directions.

Winter Sports

More than 300 winter sports resorts operate in the German Alps and in wooded hill terrain such as the Harz Mountains and the Black Forest. In addition to outstanding ski slopes, trails, lifts, jumps, toboggan slides, and skating rinks, many larger resorts also offer ice hockey, ice boating, and bobsledding. Curling is popular as well, especially in upper Bavaria. The Olympic sports facilities like Garmisch-Partenkirchen enjoy international renown, as do the ski jumps of Oberstdorf and the artificial-ice speed-skating rink at Inzell. More than 250 ski lifts are found in the German Alps, the Black Forest, and the Harz Mountains. Information on winter-sports facilities is available from local tourist bureaus and the offices of the German National Tourist Board (www.germany-tourism.de).

Garmisch-Partenkirchen is Germany's most famous winter sports center. Set amidst beautiful alpine scenery, this picturesque resort is close to Zugspitze, Germany's highest mountain. A mountain railway and a cable car can take you to the peak. In the town is the Olympic Ice Stadium, built in 1936, and the Ski Stadium, which has two jumps and a slalom course. Skiers of every level will be satisfied on the mountain slopes above the town. For information, contact the Tourist Office on Richard-Strauss-Platz (✆ **08821/180700**).

NATIONAL PARKS

The national parks of Germany are rich in attractions for hikers, skiers, and beachgoers alike. Despite their beauty and amenities, many national parks remain largely undiscovered by international visitors. The best parks are:

Bayerischer Wald National Park   Palaces, churches, and castles are tucked into the velvet-green folds of mountains in the Bavarian Forest.

Berchtesgaden National Park   Bavaria's natural treasure offers snowy mountain peaks, serene glacial lakes, and the fairytale "Magic Forest" (*Zauberwald*).

Hainich National Park   This rich beech forest in Thuringia is home to wildcats, bats, and wild boars, as well as a spa town.

Jasmund National Park   On Rügen Island, Jasmund rewards cyclists and hikers with dramatic landscapes: White chalk cliffs plunge into the Baltic Sea, while springs, moors, and ancient graveyards adorn the inland areas of the park.

Wattenmeer National Park   With invigorating salty sea breezes, wide beaches, and miles of mud flats, this park in Schleswig-Holstein attracts hikers, beachgoers, and birdwatchers.

CHAPTER TEN

For coverage of movies and cultural events, see Chapter Seven, "Culture."

CLUB HOPPING

Where can I find ___	**Wo finde ich ___**
	Voh fin-deh ee[ch] ___
a good nightclub?	**einen guten Nachtclub?**
	eye-nen gooten NAH[CH]T-cloopp?
a club with a live band?	**einen Club mit Liveband?**
	eye-nen cloopp mitt LIVE-band?
a reggae club?	**einen Reggaeclub?**
	eye-nen REGGAE-cloopp?
a hip hop club?	**einen Hiphop-Club?**
	eye-nen HIP-hop-cloopp?
a techno club?	**einen Technoclub?**
	eye-nen TEKK-noh-cloopp?
a jazz club?	**einen Jazzclub?**
	eye-nen JAZZ-cloopp?
a country-western club?	**einen Country-und-Western-Club?**
	eye-nen country oonnd WESS-tern cloopp?
a gay / lesbian club?	**einen Schwulen- / Lesbenclub?**
	eye-nen SHVOO-len / LESS-ben-cloopp?
a club where I can dance?	**einen Tanzclub?**
	eye-nen TUNNTS-cloopp?

a club with Salsa music?	**einen Club mit Salsa-Musik?**
	eye-nen CLOOPP mitt SAL-sa moo-SEEK?
the most popular club in town?	**den beliebtesten Club der Stadt?**
	dehn beh-LEEB-tess-ten cloopp dehr shtahtt?
a singles bar?	**eine Singlebar?**
	eye-ne SINGLE-bahr?
a piano bar?	**eine Pianobar?**
	eye-ne pee-AH-noh-bahr?
the most upscale club?	**den exklusivsten Club?**
	dehn ekks-cloo-SEEVS-ten cloopp?
What's the hottest bar these days?	**Welcher Club ist zurzeit besonders angesagt?**
	Vell-[ch]ehr cloopp isst tsoor-tsite beh-SONN-dehrs un-gheh-sahggt?
What's the cover charge?	**Wie viel kostet der Eintritt?**
	Vee feel coss-tet dehr AIHN-tritt?
Do they have a dress code?	**Ist eine bestimmte Kleidung vorge-schrieben?**
	Isst eye-ne beh-shtimm-teh KLYE-doong fohr-gheh-shree-ben?
Is it expensive?	**Ist es dort teuer?**
	Isst as dohrrt TOY-ehr?
What's the best time to go?	**Wann geht man dort am besten hin?**
	Vahnn gheht mahnn dohrrt um bess-ten HINN?
What kind of music do they play there?	**Welche Art von Musik wird dort gespielt?**
	Vell-[ch]eh arrt fonn moo-SEEK virrd dohrrt gheh-shpeelt?

Is it smoking?	**Darf geraucht werden?**
	Dahrrf gheh-RAU[CH]T vehr-denn?
Is it nonsmoking?	**Ist das Rauchen dort verboten?**
	Isst dahs rauh-[ch]en dohrrt fehr-BOH-ten?
I'm looking for ____	**Ich suche ____**
	Ee[ch] SOO-[ch]eh ____
a good cigar shop.	**ein gutes Zigarrengeschäft.**
	aihn goo-tess tsee-GHARR-en-gheh-sh[ae]fft.
a pack of cigarettes.	**eine Packung Zigaretten.**
	eye-neh pahkk-oong tsee-ghah-RET-ten.
I'd like ____	**Ich hätte gern ____**
	Ee[ch] hat-eh ghern ____
a drink please.	**etwas zu trinken.**
	at-vahs tsoo TRING-ken.
a bottle of beer please.	**ein Bier aus der Flasche.**
	aihn beer ous dehr FLUSH-eh.

NIGHTLIFE

Do You Mind If I Smoke?

Haben Sie eine Zigarette?	Do you have a cigarette?
Hah-ben zee eye-neh tsee-ghah-RETT-eh?	
Haben Sie Feuer?	Do you have a light?
Hah-ben zee FOY-ehr?	
Darf ich Ihnen Feuer geben?	May I offer you a light?
Dharrf ee[ch] eeh-nen FOY-ehr gheh-ben?	
Rauchen verboten.	Smoking not permitted.
Rauh-[ch]en fair-BOH-ten.	

A beer on tap please.	**ein Bier vom Fass.**
	aihn beer fomm FAHSS.
a shot of ____ please.	**einen ____.**
	eye-nen ____.

For a full list of drinks, see p92.

Make it a double please!	**Einen Doppelten, bitte!**
	Eye-nen DOPP-ell-ten, bit-eh!
With ice, please.	**Mit Eis, bitte.**
	Mitt ICE, bit-eh.
And one for the lady / the gentleman!	**Und einen für die Dame / den Herrn!**
	Oonnd eye-nen f[ue]hr dee DAH-meh / dehn HERRN.
How much for a bottle / glass of beer?	**Wie viel kostet eine Flasche / ein Glas Bier?**
	Vee feel coss-tet eye-neh FLUSH-eh/aihn GLAHS beer?
I'd like to buy a drink for that woman / man over there.	**ch würde der Dame / dem Herrn da drüben gern einen Drink spendieren.**
	Ee[ch] v[ue]rr-deh dehr DAH-meh / dem HEHRRN dah dr[ue]h-ben ghern eye-nen DRINK shpenn-dee-ren.
A pack of cigarettes, please.	**Eine Packung Zigaretten, bitte.**
	Eye-neh pahkk-oong tsee-ghah-RET-ten, bit-eh.
Do you have a lighter or matches?	**Hast du Feuer?**
	Hahsst doo FOY-ehr?
Do you smoke?	**Rauchst du?**
	RAU[CH]ST doo?
Would you like a cigarette?	**Darf ich dir eine Zigarette anbieten?**
	Dharrf ee[ch] deer eye-ne tsee-ghah-RETT-eh un-bee-ten?

May I run a tab?	**Kann ich die Getränke bezahlen, wenn ich gehe?**
	Khann ee[ch] dee ghe-trank-eh beh-tsah-len, venn ee[ch] GHEH-heh?
What's the cover?	**Was kostet der Eintritt?**
	Vahs coss-tet dehr AIHN-tritt?

ACROSS A CROWDED ROOM

Excuse me, may I buy you a drink?	**Verzeihung. Darf ich dich auf einen Drink einladen?**
	Fehr-TSYE-oong. Dharrf ee[ch] di[ch] ouf eye-nen DRINK aihn-lah-den?
You look amazing.	**Du siehst umwerfend aus.**
	Doo seehst OOMM-vehrr-fennd ous.
You look like the most interesting person in the room.	**Du bist mit Abstand die interessanteste Person im Raum.**
	Doo bisst mitt up-shtahnnd dee in-teh-ress-UN-tess-teh pehr-sohn imm rowm.

Would you like to dance?	**Möchtest du gern tanzen?**
	M[oe][ch]-test doo ghern TUNN-tsenn?
Do you like to dance fast or slow?	**Tanzt du lieber schnell oder lang-sam?**
	Tunntst doo lee-behr SHNELL oh-der LUNG-sahm?
Give me your hand.	**Gib mir deine Hand.**
	Gheeb mere dye-neh HAHND.
What would you like to drink?	**Was möchtest du trinken?**
	Vahs m[oe][ch]-test doo TRING-kenn?
You're a great dancer.	**Du tanzt großartig.**
	Doo tunntst GROHS-urr-tigg.
I don't know that dance!	**Diesen Tanz kenne ich nicht!**
	Dee-sen tunnts KEN-neh ee[ch] nee[ch]t!
Do you like this song?	**Magst du dieses Lied?**
	MAHGGST doo dee-ses leed?
You have nice eyes!	**Du hast wunderschöne Augen!**
	Doo hahsst VOON-dehr-sh[oe]h-neh ow-ghenn!

For a full list of features, see p122.

| May I have your phone number? | **Gibst du mir deine Telefonnummer?** |
| | *Gheebst doo mere dye-neh tehleh-PHON-noommer?* |

GETTING CLOSER

You're very attractive.

Du siehst unglaublich gut aus.
Doo seehst oon-gloub-li[ch] GOOT ous.

I like being with you.

Ich bin gern mit dir zusammen.
Ee[ch] bin ghern mitt deer tsoo-SAHMM-en.

I like you.

Ich mag dich.
Ee[ch] MAHGG di[ch].

I want to hold you.

Ich möchte dich in den Arm nehmen.
Ee[ch] m[oe][ch]-teh di[ch] inn dehn AHRRM neh-men.

Kiss me.

Küss mich.
K[UE]SS mee[ch].

May I give you ____

Darf ich dich ____
Dharff ee[ch] di[ch] ____

a hug?

umarmen?
oomm-AHRR-men?

a kiss?

küssen?
K[UE]SS-en?

Would you like ____

Möchtest du gern ____
M[oe][ch]-test doo ghern ____

a back rub?

eine Rückenmassage?
eye-neh R[UE]K-ken-mah-ssah-sheh?

NIGHTLIFE

a massage?	**eine Massage?**
	eye-neh ma-SSAH-sheh?

GETTING INTIMATE

Would you like to come inside?	**Möchtest du mit reinkommen?**
	M[oe][ch]-test doo mitt RYNE-kom-men?
May I come inside?	**Darf ich noch mit reinkommen?**
	Dharrf ee[ch] no[ch] mitt RYNE-kom-men?
Let me help you out of that.	**Lass mich dir damit helfen.**
	Lahss mee[ch] deer dah-mitt HELL-fen.
Would you help me out of this?	**Könntest du mir damit bitte behilflich sein?**
	K[oe]nn-test doo mere dah-mitt bit-eh beh-HILLF-li[ch] syne?
You smell so good.	**Du riechst so gut.**
	Doo REE[CH]ST soh goot.
You're beautiful / handsome.	**Du bist wunderschön / sehr gut-aussehend.**
	Doo bisst voohn-dehr-SH[OE]HN / sehr GOOT-ous-seh-hend.
May I?	**Darf ich?**
	DHARRF ee[ch]?
OK?	**OK?**
	Okay?
Like this?	**So?**
	Soh?
How?	**Wie?**
	Vee?

HOLD ON A SECOND

Please don't do that.

Das möchte ich nicht.
Dahs M[OE][CH]-teh ee[ch] ni[ch]t.

Stop, please.

Hör bitte auf.
H[oe]hr bit-eh OUF.

Do you want me to stop?

Soll ich aufhören?
Sohll ee[ch] OUF-h[oe]h-ren?

Let's just be friends.

Lass uns einfach Freunde sein.
Lahss oonns aihn-fah[ch] FROYN-deh syne.

Do you have a condom?

Hast du ein Kondom?
Hahsst doo aihn con-DOHM?

Are you on birth control?

Nimmst du die Pille?
Nimmst doo dee PILL-eh?

I have a condom.

Ich habe ein Kondom.
Ee[ch] hah-beh aihn con-DOHM.

Do you have anything you should tell me first?

Sollte ich vorher noch etwas wissen?
Soll-teh ee[ch] fohr-hehr noh[ch] at-vahs VISS-en?

BACK TO IT

That's it.

Genau so.
Gheh-NOW soh.

That's not it.

Nicht so.
Ni[ch]t SOH.

Here.

Hier.
Hear.

There.

Da.
Dahh.

For a full list of features, see p122.
For a full list of body parts, see p219.

More.	**Weiter.**
	VYE-tehr.
Harder.	**Härter.**
	H[AE]RR-tehr.
Faster.	**Schneller.**
	SHNELL-ehr.
Deeper.	**Tiefer.**
	TEE-fehr.
Slower.	**Langsamer.**
	LUNG-sah-mehr.
Easier.	**Sanfter.**
	SAHNNF-tehr.

COOLDOWN

You're great.	**Du bist fantastisch.**
	Doo bisst fahn-TAHSS-tish.
That was great.	**Das war fantastisch.**
	Dahs vahr fahn-TAHSS-tish.
Would you like ____	**Möchtest du gern ____**
	M[oe][ch]-test doo ghern ____
a drink?	**etwas zu trinken?**
	at-vahs tsoo TRING-ken?
a snack?	**einen Imbiss?**
	eye-nen IMM-biss?
a shower?	**duschen?**
	DOO-shen?
May I stay here?	**Kann ich hierbleiben?**
	Khann ee[ch] HEAR-blye-ben?
Would you like to stay here?	**Möchtest du bleiben?**
	M[oe][ch]-test doo BLYE-ben?
I'm sorry. I have to go now.	**Es tut mir leid. Ich muss jetzt gehen.**
	As toot mere LYDE. Ee[ch] mooss yetst gheh-hen.
Where are you going?	**Wohin gehst du?**
	Voh-hinn GHEHST doo?

I have to work early.	**Ich muss früh arbeiten.**
	Ee[ch] mooss fr[ue]h ARR-byten.
I'm flying home in the morning.	**Ich fliege morgen früh nach Hause.**
	Ee[ch] flee-gheh morr-ghenn fr[ue]h nah[ch] HOW-seh.
I have an early flight.	**Mein Flug geht frühmorgens.**
	Mine floog gheht fr[ue]h-MORR-ghenns.
I think this was a mistake.	**Ich glaube, das war ein Fehler.**
	Ee[ch] GLOU-beh, dahs vahr aihn FEH-lehr.
Will you make me breakfast too?	**Bekomme ich auch ein Frühstück?**
	Beh-com-meh ee[ch] OU[CH] aihn FR[UE]H-sht[ue]ck?
Stay. I'll make you breakfast.	**Geh nicht. Ich mach dir Frühstück.**
	Gheh ni[ch]t. Ee[ch] mah[ch] deer FR[UE]H-sht[ue]ck.

IN THE CASINO

How much is this table?	**Wie hoch ist der Einsatz an diesem Tisch?**
	Vee hoh[ch] isst der AIHN-sahtts un dee-sem tish?
Deal me in.	**Ich bin dabei.**
	Ee[ch] bin dah-BYE.
Put it on red!	**Setzen Sie das auf Rot!**
	Set-senn zee dahs ouf ROHHT!
Put it on black!	**Setzen Sie das auf Schwarz!**
	Set-senn zee dahs ouf SHVAHRRZ!
Let it ride!	**Los geht's!**
	Lohs GHEHTS!
21!	**21!**
	aihn-oonnd-TSVAHNN-tsigg!

Snake-eyes!	**Schlangenaugen!**
	SHLAHNG-en-ow-ghenn!
Seven.	**Sieben.**
	Zee-ben.

For a full list of numbers, see p7.

Damn, eleven.	**Elf, verdammt.**
	ELLF, fehr-DAHMMT.
I'll pass.	**Ich passe.**
	Ee[ch] PAHSS-eh.
Hit me!	**Karte!**
	KAHRR-teh!
Split.	**Split.**
	Split.
Are the drinks complimentary?	**Sind die Getränke gratis?**
	Sinnd dee ghe-trank-eh GRAH-tees?
May I bill it to my room?	**Kann ich die Kosten über mein Zimmer abrechnen?**
	Khann ee[ch] dee coss-ten [ue]h-behr mine TSIMMER up-re[ch]-nen?
I'd like to cash out.	**Ich möchte meinen Gewinn aus-zahlen lassen.**
	Ee[ch] m[oe][ch]-teh my-nen gheh-VINN ous-tsah-len lahss-en.
I'll hold.	**Ich schiebe.**
	Ee[ch] SHEEH-beh.
I'll see your bet.	**Ich gehe mit.**
	Ee[ch] gheh-heh MITT.
I call.	**Ich will sehen.**
	Ee[ch] vill SEH-hen.
Full house!	**Full House!**
	Full HOUSE!
Royal flush.	**Royal Flush.**
	Royal FLUSH.
Straight.	**Straße.**
	SHTRAH-sseh.

UNIQUELY GERMAN NIGHTLIFE EXPERIENCES

Cabaret

Very popular among visitors to Berlin is the kind of nightspot depicted in the musical *Cabaret*, with floor-show patter and acts spiced with political and social barbs. Cabaret life in decadent interwar Berlin became an indelible part of the city's image. These emporiums of schmaltz have been reborn in the reunified Berlin. Many of today's cabaret shows are more reminiscent of Broadway blockbusters than of the smoky, intimate cellar revues of the 1920s.

German Techno Clubs

Germany is the birthplace of techno, an umbrella term for various kinds of electronic music. The most celebrated DJs include Berlin's Paul von Dyk; Cologne's Schneider TM; and Dr. Motte, founder of the annual Love Parade in Berlin, the world's largest electronic-music event. Today most major German cities have thriving electronic club music scenes, and on any given weekend many of the world's top DJs are spinning in the clubs of Berlin.

The Reeperbahn

The garish, neon-lit Reeperbahn in the St. Pauli district earned Hamburg its reputation as "Sin City Europe." A red-light district since the 1860s, the Reeperbahn is also a major tourist attraction, and home to much of the city's other nightlife as well. Sex shops, strip joints, and peep shows rub shoulders with some of the city's best bars and clubs. The district is liveliest between midnight and 5am, when you'll find thousands of the women (and men in drag) who inspired the Hamburg beer St. Pauli Girl strutting their stuff.

Beer Halls

They've been described as a permanent Oktoberfest and as beer gardens with roofs. Either way, beer halls are a proud German tradition. Here are a few of the best:

Auerbachs Keller, Leipzig   The most famous tavern in eastern Germany, this is where Goethe staged the debate between Faust and Mephistopheles. The tavern dates from 1530 and has a series of murals depicting the Faust legend.

Hofbräuhaus am Platzl, Munich   The Hofbräuhaus is the world's most famous beer hall and can accommodate some 4,500 beer drinkers on any given night. Music from live bands and huge mugs of beer served at wooden tables combine to produce the best of Bavarian nightlife.

Zum Roten Ochsen, Heidelberg   Over the years, the "Red Ox" has drawn beer drinkers from Mark Twain to Bismarck. Students have been getting plastered here since 1703, and the tradition continues unabated.

Ratskeller, Bremen   Traditionally, a *Ratskeller* is a beer hall in the basement of the city hall. One of the best of these is in Bremen. It serves top-notch German and international food and some of the best suds along the Rhine, as well as one of the longest lists of vintage wines from the country's vineyards.

PERFORMING ARTS

The land of Bach and Beethoven is today home to some of the world's finest orchestras and opera houses. A recent survey of European music critics about the best orchestras in Europe, for example, awarded four of the ten top slots to German orchestras. A performance at any of the following venues is certain to be world-class:

Berliner Philharmonisches Orchester   The Berlin Philharmonic, directed by Simon Rattle, is one of the world's premiere orchestras. Its home, the Philharmonie, in the Kulturforum at Potsdamer Platz, is a significant piece of modern architecture, worth a visit even if you do not attend a performance. None of the 2,218 seats are more than 30m (98ft) from the rostrum. www.berlin-philharmonic.com.

Semperoper (Semper Opera House), Dresden   One of the most exquisite opera houses in the world, the Semperoper has counted Wagner and Weber among its conductors. Destroyed in the war, its Renaissance façade and original interior paintings have been masterfully restored. Most importantly, the renovations have also reestablished the fine acoustics for which the opera house was known. Seats are extremely difficult to get; purchase tickets far in advance. www.semperoper.de.

Festspielhaus, Bayreuth   Richard Wagner himself designed the Festspielhaus for the performance of his operas. A huge stage and flawless acoustical balance make it the perfect venue for the performances at the annual Wagner festival: the orchestra never overwhelms the singers. Under the direction of Wagner's grandson Wolfgang, the current opera productions boast exciting avant-garde staging and some of the best musicians and singers in the world. There's an 8-year waiting list for tickets to the festival operas, but they can sometimes be booked as part of a package tour. www.bayreuther-festspiele.de.

Gewandhaus Orchester, Leipzig   Founded in 1781 but now housed in a GDR-era building, the famous Gewandhaus Orchestra saw some of its glory days under the baton of Felix Mendelssohn, who died in Leipzig in 1847. It is now directed by Italian conductor Riccardo Chailly, and has recently released recordings of Mendelssohn, Brahms, and Schumann symphonies. Concerts, ballets, organ recitals, and other events are staged here. www.gewandhaus.de.

RECOMMENDED FILMS

Das Leben der Anderen (The Lives of Others) (2006)   Powerful yet understated Oscar-winning drama about envy, betrayal, and the East German secret police. Directed by Florian von Donnersmarck.

Lola Rennt (Run Lola Run) (1998)   The stylish, high-energy suspense of Lola's run through Berlin, set to furious techno, is iconic of the city in the years following reunification. Directed by Tom Tykwer.

Goodbye, Lenin! (2003)   A hilariously ironic depiction of life in the former East Germany immediately after the fall of the Wall. Directed by Wolfgang Becker.

NIGHTLIFE

Der Himmel über Berlin (Wings of Desire) (1987)   In a masterpiece inspired by the poetry of Rilke, two angels wander Berlin in the final days of the Cold War. Directed by Wim Wenders.

Nirgendwo in Afrika (Nowhere in Africa) (2001)   Based on a true story, follows the trial of a German-Jewish family that seeks refuge from the Nazis in Kenya. Directed by Caroline Link.

Sonnenallee (1999)   Seriocomic snapshot of life in East Berlin; a quintessential work of *Ostalgie* (nostalgia for the DDR). Directed by Leander Haussmann.

Sophie Scholl: The Last Days (2005)   A beautifully acted portrait of the final days in the life of Sophie Scholl, a member of the underground anti-Nazi resistance who was caught and executed in 1943 at the age of 21. Directed by Marc Rothemund.

Metropolis (1927)   This silent film about a futuristic industrial dystopia is a classic work of German Expressionism. Directed by Fritz Lang.

RECOMMENDED BOOKS

The Tin Drum, by Günter Grass. Nobel Prize winner's masterpiece deals with the German psyche coming to terms with World War II.

The Berlin Stories, by Christopher Isherwood. Decadence in Weimar Berlin; the stories that inspired Cabaret.

Complete Grimm Tales, by Jakob and Wilhelm Grimm. The classic Grimm Brothers fairy tales are, after the Bible, the second-most-translated book in the world.

The Magic Mountain, by Thomas Mann. Philosophical and sprawling *Bildungsroman* (novel of education) influenced by Nietzsche.

The Last Days of Hitler, by Hugh Trevor-Roper. An insightful reconstruction of the twilight of the Third Reich.

A Triumph Abroad, by Mark Twain. Comical account of the American humorist's travels through Germany; a highlight is the section on "The Awful German Language."

Collected Poems, by Paul Celan. Holocaust survivor Celan was one of the greatest German-language poets of the twentieth century; many of his poems deal with his experience at Auschwitz.

CHAPTER ELEVEN

HEALTH & SAFETY

This chapter covers the terms you'll need to maintain your health and safety—including the most useful phrases for the pharmacy, the doctor's office, and the police station.

AT THE PHARMACY

Please fill this prescription.	**Ich möchte das Rezept hier ein-lösen.** *Ee[ch] m[oe][ch]-teh dahs reh-tseppt hear AIHN-l[oe]h-sen.*
Do you have something for ____	**Haben Sie etwas gegen ____** *Hah-ben zee at-vahs ghe-ghenn ____*
a cold?	**eine Erkältung?** *eye-ne air-KELL-toong?*
a cough?	**Husten?** *WHO-stenn?*
I need something ____	**Ich brauche etwas ____** *Ee[ch] brow-[ch]eh at-vahs ____*
to help me sleep.	**zum Einschlafen.** *tsoomm AIHN-shlah-fen.*
to help me relax.	**zum Entspannen.** *tsoomm ent-SHPAHNN-en.*
I want to buy ____	**Ich hätte gern ____** *Ee[ch] hat-eh ghern ____*
condoms.	**Kondome.** *con-DOH-meh.*
an antihistamine.	**ein Antihistamin.** *aihn un-tee-his-tah-MEEN.*
antibiotic cream.	**eine antibiotische Salbe.** *eye-ne un-tee-bee-OH-tish-eh SULL-beh.*

215

aspirin.	**Aspirin.**
	ahss-pee-REEN.
non-aspirin pain reliever.	**ein aspirinfreies Schmerzmittel.**
	aihn ahss-pee-REEN-frye-ess SHMEHRTTS-mittel.
medicine with codeine.	**ein Medikament mit Kodein.**
	aihn meh-dee-kah-meant mitt koh-deh-EEN.
insect repellant.	**ein Insektenschutzmittel.**
	aihn in-SECK-ten-shoohts-mittel.
I need something for ____	**Ich brauche etwas gegen ____**
	Ee[ch] brow-[ch]eh at-vahs gheh-ghenn ____
corns.	**Hühneraugen.**
	H[UE]H-nehr-ow-ghenn.
congestion.	**Verstopfung.**
	fehr-SHTOPP-foong.
warts.	**Warzen.**
	VAHRR-tsenn.
constipation.	**Darmträgheit.**
	DHARRM-tr[ae]hgg-hyte.
diarrhea.	**Durchfall.**
	DOORR[CH]-fahll.
indigestion.	**Verdauungsstörungen.**
	fehr-DOW-oongs-sht[oe]h-roong-en.
nausea.	**Übelkeit.**
	[UE]H-bell-kite.
motion sickness.	**Reisekrankheit.**
	RYE-seh-krahnk-hyte.
seasickness.	**Seekrankheit.**
	SEHH-krahnk-hyte.
acne.	**Akne.**
	AHKK-neh.

AT THE DOCTOR'S OFFICE

I would like to see ____	**Ich brauche einen Termin bei einem ____** *Ee[ch] brow-[ch]eh eye-nen tehr-MEEN bye eye-nem ____*
a doctor.	**Arzt.** *artst.*
a chiropractor.	**Chiropraktiker.** *[ch]ee-roh-PRAHKK-tee-kehr.*
a gynecologist.	**Frauenarzt.** *FROW-en-artst.*
an eye / ears / nose / throat specialist.	**Augenspezialisten / Ohrenspezialisten / Nasenspezialisten / Halsspezialisten.** *OW-ghenn-shpeh-tsee-yah-liss-ten / OH-ren-shpeh-tsee-yah-liss-ten / NAH-senn-shpeh-tsee-yah-liss-ten / HAHLLS-shpeh-tsee-yah-liss-ten.*
a dentist.	**Zahnarzt.** *TSAAHN-artst.*
an optometrist.	**Optiker.** *OPP-tee-kehr.*
Do I need an appointment?	**Benötige ich einen Termin?** *Beh-n[oe]-tiggeh ee[ch] eye-nen tehr-MEEN?*
I have an emergency.	**Das ist ein Notfall.** *Dahs isst aihn NOHT-fahll.*
I need an emergency prescription refill.	**Ich benötige dringend eine erneute Rezepteinlösung.** *Ee[ch] beh-n[oe]h-tigge dring-end eye-neh air-noy-teh reh-TSEPPT-aihn-l[oe]h-soong.*

Please call a doctor.	**Rufen Sie bitte einen Arzt.**
	Roofen zee bit-eh eye-nen ARTST.
I need an ambulance.	**Ich brauche einen Krankenwagen.**
	Ee[ch] brow-[ch]eh eye-nen KRAHNK-en-vah-ghenn.

SYMPTOMS

For a full list of body parts, see p219.

My ____ hurts.	**Mein ____ schmerzt. (sing.) / Meine ____ schmerzen. (pl.)**
	Mine ____ shmehrtst. / My-neh ____ shmehr-tsenn.
My ____ is stiff.	**Mein ____ ist steif. (sing.) / Meine ____ sind steif. (pl.)**
	Mine ____ isst shtyfe. / My-neh ____ sinnd shtyfe.
I think I'm having a heart attack.	**Ich glaube, ich habe einen Herzinfarkt.**
	Ee[ch] glauh-beh, ee[ch] hah-beh eye-nen HERRTS-in-farrkt.
I can't move.	**Ich kann mich nicht bewegen.**
	Ee[ch] khann mee[ch] nee[ch]t beh-VEH-ghenn.
I fell.	**Ich bin gestürzt.**
	Ee[ch] bin ghe-SHT[UE]RRTST.
I fainted.	**Ich habe das Bewusstsein verloren.**
	Ee[ch] hah-beh dahs beh-VOOSST-syne fehr-loh-ren.
I have a cut on my ____.	**Ich habe eine Schnittwunde in meiner / meinem ____.**
	Ee[ch] hah-beh eye-neh SHNITT-voonn-deh in minor/my-nem ____.
I have a headache.	**Ich habe Kopfschmerzen.**
	Ee[ch] hah-beh COPF-shmair-tsenn.
My vision is blurry.	**Ich sehe verschwommen.**
	Ee[ch] seh-heh fehr-SHVOMM-en.

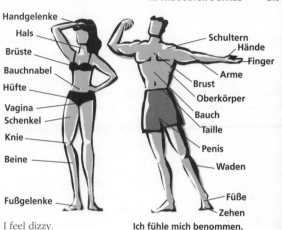

Handgelenke
Hals
Brüste
Bauchnabel
Hüfte
Vagina
Schenkel
Knie
Beine
Fußgelenke

Schultern
Hände
Finger
Arme
Brust
Oberkörper
Bauch
Taille
Penis
Waden
Füße
Zehen

I feel dizzy.	**Ich fühle mich benommen.** *Ee[ch] f[ue]h-leh mee[ch] beh-NOMM-en.*
I think I'm pregnant.	**Ich glaube, ich bin schwanger.** *Ee[ch] glau-beh, ee[ch] bin SHVAHNNG-ehr.*
I don't think I'm pregnant.	**Ich glaube nicht, dass ich schwanger bin.** *Ee[ch] glau-beh NI[CH]T, dahss ee[ch] shvahnng-ehr bin.*
I'm having trouble walking.	**Ich habe Probleme beim Gehen.** *Ee[ch] hah-beh proh-bleh-meh byme GEH-hen.*
I can't get up.	**Ich kann nicht aufstehen.** *Ee[ch] khann ni[ch]t OUF-shteh-hen.*
I was mugged.	**Ich wurde überfallen.** *Ee[ch] voorr-deh [ue]h-behr-FAHLL-en.*

I was raped.	**Ich wurde vergewaltigt.** *Ee[ch] voorr-deh fehr-gheh-VAHLL-tiggt.*
A dog attacked me.	**Ich wurde von einem Hund angegriffen.** *Ee[ch] voorr-deh fonn eye-nem HOONND un-gheh-griff-en.*
A snake bit me.	**Ich wurde von einer Schlange gebissen.** *Ee[ch] voorr-deh fonn eye-nehr SHLUNG-eh gheh-biss-en.*
I can't move my _____ without pain.	**Ich kann mein/meinen/meine _____ nicht schmerzfrei bewegen.** *Ee[ch] khann mine/my-nen/my-neh _____ ni[ch]t shmehrts-frye beh-veh-ghenn.*

MEDICATIONS

I need morning-after pills.	**Ich brauche Pillen für den Morgen danach.** *Ee[ch] brau-[ch]eh PILL-en f[ue]hr dehn morr-ghenn dah-NAH[CH].*
I need birth control pills.	**Ich brauche Antibabypillen.** *Ee[ch] brau-[ch]eh un-tee-BEH-bee-pill-en.*
I lost my eyeglasses and need new ones.	**Ich habe meine Brille verloren und benötige eine neue.** *Ee[ch] hah-beh my-neh BRILL-eh fehr-loh-ren oonnd beh-n[oe]h-tigge eye-neh NOY-eh.*
I need new contact lenses.	**Ich benötige neue Kontaktlinsen.** *Ee[ch] beh-n[oe]h-tigge noye konn-TAHKKT-lin-sen.*

I need erectile dysfunction pills.	**Ich benötige Pillen gegen Erektionsstörungen.**
	Ee[ch] beh-n[oe]h-tigge pill-en gheh-ghenn eh-rekk-tsee-YOHNS-sht[oe]h-roong-en.
Please fill this prescription.	**Ich möchte das hier abholen.**
	Ee[ch] m[oe][ch]-teh dahs hear UP-hoh-len.
I need a prescription for ____.	**Ich benötige ein Rezept für ____.**
	Ee[ch] beh-N[OE]-tiggeh aihn reh-TSEPT f[ue]hr ____.
I am allergic to ____	**Ich bin allergisch gegen ____**
	Ee[ch] bin ah-LERR-ghish gheh-ghenn ____
penicillin.	**Penizillin.**
	penn-ee-tsee-LEAN.
antibiotics.	**Antibiotika.**
	un-tee-bee-YOH-tee-kah.
sulfa drugs.	**schwefelhaltige Medikamente.**
	SHVEHH-fell-hahll-tiggeh meh-dee-kah-menn-teh.
steroids.	**Steroide.**
	shteh-roh-EE-deh.
I have asthma.	**Ich habe Asthma.**
	Ee[ch] hah-beh USST-mah.

DENTAL PROBLEMS

I have a toothache.	**Ich habe Zahnschmerzen.**
	Ee[ch] hah-beh TSAAHN-shmehrts-en.
I chipped a tooth.	**Ich habe einen abgebrochenen Zahn.**
	Ee[ch] hah-beh eye-nen up-gheh-broh[ch]en-en TSAAHN.
My bridge came loose.	**Meine Brücke hat sich gelöst.**
	My-neh BR[UE]KKEH hut see[ch] gheh-l[oe]hst.

I lost a crown.	**Ich habe eine Krone verloren.** *Ee[ch] hah-beh eye-ne KROH-ne* *fehr-loh-ren.*
I lost a denture plate.	**Ich habe eine Zahnprotese ver-** **loren.** *Ee[ch] hah-beh eye-ne TSAAHN-* *proh-teh-se fehr-loh-ren.*

AT THE POLICE STATION

I'm sorry, did I do something wrong?	**Verzeihung, habe ich etwas falsch** **gemacht?** *Fehr-TSYE-oong, hah-beh ee[ch]* *at-vahs FAHLLSH gheh-mah[ch]t?*
I am _____	**Ich bin _____** *ee[ch] bin _____*
an American.	**Amerikaner (m.) / Amerikanerin (f.).** *ah-meh-ree-KAH-nehr /* *ah-meh-ree-KAH-nehr-in.*
British.	**Brite (m.) / Britin (f.).** *BREE-teh / BREE-tin.*
a Canadian.	**Kanadier (m.) / Kanadierin (f.).** *kah-NAH-dee-er / kah-NAH-* *dee-er-in.*
Irish.	**Ire (m.) / Irin (f.).** *EE-re / EE-rin.*
an Australian.	**Australier (m.) / Australierin (f.).** *ous-TRAH-lee-er / ous-TRAH-* *lee-er-in.*
a New Zealander.	**Neuseeländer (m.) /** **Neuseeländerin (f.).** *noy-SEHH-lander / noy-SEHH-* *lander-in.*
The car is a rental.	**Das Auto ist ein Mietwagen.** *Dahs ou-toh isst aihn MEET-vah-* *ghenn.*

Listen Up: Police Lingo

Führerschein, Fahrzeug- und Versicherungspapiere, bitte.	Your license, registration and insurance, please.
F[ue]h-rehr-shine, faahr-tsoygg oonnd fehr-SI[CH]-eh-roongs-pah-peer-eh, bit-eh.	
Die Strafe beträgt 10 €. Sie können direkt bezahlen.	The fine is €10. You can pay me directly.
Dee shtrah-feh beh-tr[ae]hggt tsehn OY-roh. Zee k[oe]nn-en dee-RECKT beh-tsah-len.	
Ihren Ausweis, bitte?	Your passport please?
Eehren OUS-vise, bit-eh?	
Wohin sind Sie unterwegs?	Where are you going?
Voh-hinn sinnd zee oonn-ter-VEHGGS?	
Warum haben Sie es denn so eilig?	Why are you in such a hurry?
Vah-roomm hah-ben zee as denn soh EYE-ligg?	

Do I pay the fine to you?	**Zahle ich die Strafe direkt an Sie?**
	Tsah-leh ee[ch] dee shtrah-feh dee-reckt un Zee?
Do I have to go to court?	**Komme ich vor Gericht?**
	Com-meh ee[ch] fohr ghe-RI[CH]T?
When?	**Wann?**
	Vahnn?

I'm sorry, my German isn't very good.	**Verzeihung, mein Deutsch ist nicht besonders gut.** *Fehr-TSYE-oong, mine doytsch isst ni[ch]t beh-sonn-dehrs GOOT.*
I need an interpreter.	**Ich benötige einen Dolmetscher.** *Ee[ch] beh-n[oe]h-tiggeh eye-nen DOLL-match-ehr.*
I'm sorry, I don't understand the ticket.	**Verzeihung, ich verstehe den Strafzettel nicht.** *Fehr-TSYE-oong, ee[ch] fair-shteh-heh dehn SHTRAHF-tsettel ni[ch]t.*
May I call my embassy?	**Darf ich meine Botschaft anrufen?** *Dharrf ee[ch] my-neh BOHT-shahfft unroofen?*
I was robbed.	**Ich wurde ausgeraubt.** *Ee[ch] voorr-deh OUS-gheh-raubt.*
I was mugged.	**Ich wurde überfallen.** *Ee[ch] voorr-deh [ue]h-behr-FAHLL-en.*
I was raped	**Ich wurde vergewaltigt.** *Ee[ch] voorr-deh fehr-gheh-VAHLL-tiggt.*
Do I need to make a report?	**Muss ich eine Aussage machen?** *Mooss ee[ch] eye-neh OUS-sah-gheh mah-[ch]en?*
Somebody broke into my room.	**In mein Zimmer wurde eingebrochen.** *Inn mine tsimmer voorr-deh AIHN-gheh-broh-[ch]en.*
Someone stole my purse / wallet.	**Meine Handtasche / Geldbörse wurde gestohlen.** *My-neh HAHND-tah-sheh / GELLD-b[oe]r-seh voorr-deh gheh-shtoh-len.*

HEALTH FAST FACTS

Dietary Restrictions   Vegetarian restaurants and organic food (known as Bio) shops are ubiquitous in major cities. Vegetarians will generally do better at ethnic restaurants than at traditional German restaurants. Travelers who keep kosher will have a much easier time in large cities than in the countryside. Synagogues in major cities should have information about kosher restaurants, or you can check www.shamash.org/kosher.

Drugstores   Pharmaceuticals are sold at an *Apotheke*. For cosmetics and toiletries, go to a *Drogerie*. German pharmacies take turns staying open at night, on Sundays, and on holidays, and each *Apotheke* posts a schedule of those in the area that are open off-hours.

Emergencies   Call ⓒ 112 for an ambulance or other emergency medical assistance.

Precautions   Travelers to Germany do not require shots, and food and tap water are generally safe. Do not, however, drink from mountain streams.

If you suffer from epilepsy, diabetes, or heart problems, wear a **MedicAlert** identification tag (ⓒ 888/633-4298; www.medicalert.org), which will immediately alert doctors to your condition. Pack prescription medications in your carry-on luggage, and carry prescription medications in their original containers (to show customs officials as well as physicians, if necessary). Bring enough medications to last the duration of your trip, and know the generic name of medications, as the German pharmacist may not be familiar with a particular brand.

What to Do If You Get Sick   German medical facilities are among the best in the world, and most German doctors speak good English. Your hotel should be able to put you in touch with a reliable doctor. If not, contact your embassy or consulate: each one maintains a list of English-speaking doctors. Medical and hospital services aren't free, so be sure that you have appropriate insurance coverage before you travel.

HEALTH & SAFETY

SAFETY FAST FACTS

Drugs & Alcohol   Drinking laws are flexible, enforced only if a problem develops. Public drunkenness, however, is very much frowned upon. Officially, you must be 18 to consume any kind of alcoholic beverage, but bars and cafes rarely request proof of age. Drinking while driving is treated as a very serious offense, and penalties for illegal drug possession are also severe.

Embassies & Consulates   The consular section of the **U.S. Embassy** in Berlin is at Clayallee 170 in Dahlem (℃ **030/8329233** is answered Monday-Friday 2-4pm; fax 030/8305 1215; U-Bahn Dahlem-Dorf). There are U.S. consulates in Düsseldorf, at Willi-Becker-Allee 10 (℃ **0211/788-8927;** fax 0211/788-8938); in Frankfurt, at Gießenerstr. 30 (℃ **069/75350;** fax 069/75352277); in Hamburg, at Alsterufer 28 (℃ **411/71100;** fax 41/327933); in Leipzig, at Wilhelm-Seyfferth-Strasse 4 (℃ **0341/213840**); and in Munich, at Königinstr. 5 (℃ **089/28880;** fax 089/280-9998).

The **Canadian Embassy** in Berlin is at Lepiziger Platz 17 (℃ **030/203120;** U-Bahn Potsdamer Platz). There are Canadian consulates in Düsseldorf, at Benrather Strasse 8 (℃ **0211/172-170;** fax 0211/359 165); in Hamburg, at Ballindamm 35 (℃ **040/460-0270;** fax 040/46002720); in Munich, at Tal 29 (℃ **089/2199 570;** fax 089/21995757); and in Stuttgart, at Lange Strasse 51 (℃ **0711/223-9678;** fax 0711/223-9679).

Lost & Stolen Credit Cards   Tell all of your credit card companies the minute you find out that your wallet has been lost or stolen. Most credit card companies have an emergency toll-free number to call if your card is lost or stolen; they may be able to wire you a cash advance immediately or deliver an emergency credit card in a day or two. Visa's emergency number outside the U.S. is ℃ **410/581-3836** or in Germany ℃ **800/811-8440.** American Express cardholders should call collect ℃ **336/393-1111.** MasterCard holders should call collect ℃ **314/542-7111.**

Police   The emergency number for the police is **110**; the number for the fire department is **112**.

Theft Pickpocketing and petty theft are not as common as in many other parts of Europe, but they do occur, so exercise precaution. Cell phones and bicycles seem to be particularly favored targets of petty theft in Germany, so always keep an eye on your cell phone and be sure to properly lock any bicycle you rent.

Violence Overall, the security risk to travelers in Germany is low. Germany does, however, experience frequent political demonstrations that have on occasion turned into riots. Exercise particular caution on May 1, as May Day rioting is relatively frequent in major cities, especially in Berlin.

In certain regions, mostly in the former East Germany, dark-skinned foreign visitors may feel threatened by small but aggressive neo-Nazi groups. Harassment and attacks by skinheads on non-white foreigners have led some to dub the eastern suburbs of Berlin "no-go zones" for visitors who appear "foreign."

Women & Safety Germans aren't big on street sexual harassment: Standards of public behavior are quite reserved, and women traveling on their own will generally be left alone by strangers. If, however, you are faced with a persistent harasser who won't go away when ignored, call out a loud and public "Lass mich in Ruhe" (leave me alone), which should summon the attention of passersby.

INSURANCE MATTERS

Check your existing insurance policies before you buy travel insurance; it's likely you already have partial or complete coverage for your trip.

Trip-Cancellation Insurance helps you get your money back if you have to back out of a trip, if you have to return home early, or if your travel supplier goes bankrupt. Permissible reasons for cancellation can range from sickness to natural disasters to the State Department declaring your destination unsafe for travel. Read the fine print.

Protect yourself further by paying for the insurance with a credit card; by law, consumers can get their money back on goods and services not received if they report the loss within 60 days after the charge is listed on their credit card statement. For more information, contact one of the following recommended insurers (they also offer comprehensive packages including medical and lost-baggage coverage): **Access America** (© 866/807-3982; www.accessamerica.com); **Travel Guard International** (© 800/826-4919; www.travelguard.com); **Travel Insured International** (© 800/243-3174; www.travelinsured. com); and **Travelex Insurance Services** (© 888/457-4602; www.travelex-insurance.com).

Lost-Luggage Insurance is useful if you plan to check items worth more than the airlines' standard liability policy, which is limited to approximately $9.05 per pound, up to some $635 per checked bag on international flights (including U.S. portions of international trips).

Medical Insurance is a safety net, as most health plans (including Medicare and Medicaid) do not provide coverage for overseas treatment, and the ones that do often require you to pay for services upfront and reimburse you only after you return home. If you feel you need travel insurance as a backup, contact **MEDEX Assistance** (© 410/453-6300; www.medexassist.com) or **Travel Assistance International** (© 800/821-2828; www.travelassistance.com).

CHAPTER TWELVE

HISTORIC TIMELINE

Germanic Tribes (100 B.C. to 800 A.D.)
The land that will become Germany is controlled by a number of pagan tribes, who are generally war-like and nomadic. By the third century A.D., prominent Germanic tribes, such as the Franks and the Saxons, begin to distinguish themselves as the dominant forces in the region.

58 B.C. The Romans reach the banks of the Rhine; finding a common enemy, the Germanic tribes join forces for the first time.

9 A.D. German tribes fend off the incursion of the Roman Empire in the battle of Teutoburg Forest; centuries of mutual antagonism and skirmishes between the Romans and the Germanic tribes ensue.

Fifth Century Frankish King Clovis establishes the Merovingian dynasty and allies with the Catholic Church, spreading Christianity throughout the region.

768 Charlemagne becomes king of the Franks.

Holy Roman Empire (800-1806)
Expanding throughout much of modern Europe, the Franks form an empire allied with the Catholic Church; the German King and the Pope are to be the political leaders of the region for centuries to come.

800 The Pope crowns Charlemagne emperor, effectively founding the Holy Roman Empire.

843 With the Treaty of Verdun, Charlemagne's bickering grandsons split their empire into three kingdoms that foreshadow future border disputes between France and Germany.

962 German King Otto I "the Great" reunifies the kingdoms.

1075 Chafing at secular rulers' power over the clergy, the Pope demands more autonomy from the Holy Roman Empire, sparking nearly fifty years of civil war in Germany.

1122 The Diet of Worms restores the peace by setting up checks and balances between the church and the monarchy.

14th century Black Death pandemic sweeps Europe, decimating the population.

1356 Treaty of the Golden Bull officially establishes the political structure of the Holy Roman Empire, which now includes 7 principalities.

1517 German monk Martin Luther posts his 95 Theses challenging the practices of the Catholic Church, which sets off the Protestant Reformation.

1618 The Thirty Years' War, a religious conflict between Protestants and Catholics, begins.

1648 The Peace of Westphalia ends the Thirty Years' War and divides Germany into numerous independent states dominated by the Austrian Hapsburg Monarchy and the Kingdom of Prussia.

18th century With Frederick the Great at the reins, the Kingdom of Prussia becomes the ascendant power in Germany.

1806 Napoleon defeats the Holy Roman Empire and redraws the map of the region, effectively taking the first steps toward a unified Germany.

Prussia and the foundation of the German Empire (1814-1914)

Having risen under the reign of Frederick II, Prussia emerges from the Napoleonic Wars as the dominant power in Germany and eventually unites the various German principalities to create the German Empire.

1815 Congress of Vienna, dividing the spoils of Napoleon's defeat, establishes the German Confederation (*Deutscher Bund*), composed of 39 independent states and largely dominated by Prussia.

1862 King Wilhelm I of Prussia appoints Otto von Bismarck as Prime Minister; Bismarck immediately implements expansionist policies aimed at bringing Germany under Prussian control, resulting in the Franco-Prussian war.

1871   German Empire is formed under Wilhelm I after the French defeat in the Franco-Prussian War.

Late 19th century   Germany industrializes at breakneck pace.

World War I (1914-1918)

The bloody conflict, fought between the Entente Powers (composed principally of the Russian Empire, France, Britain, and Italy) and the Central Powers (the Austro-Hungarian, German, and Ottoman empires as well as Bulgaria) defines the brutal nature of modern warfare. In all, more than 9 million soldiers and civilians die.

1914   After the assassination of Austria's crown prince in Sarajevo, the Austro-Hungarian Empire declares war on Serbia, effectively beginning World War I. Almost all the major European powers are quickly drawn into the conflict through a network of pre-existing alliances and treaties. Germany, allying with the Austro-Hungarian Empire, declares war on Russia and invades France.

1917   After German submarines sink seven American merchant ships, the U.S. abandons its previous isolationism and joins the war on the side of the Entente Powers.

1918   Badly outnumbered by Allied troops, Germany begins to view a loss in WWI as inevitable. The Kaiser proclaims a parliamentary democracy to abdicate the responsibility of handling the peace negotiations.

1919   The Treaty of Versailles ends WWI, declares Germany responsible for the war, and demands massive reparations payments from the Germans.

Weimar Republic (1919-1933)

Germany attempts to establish a liberal democracy under the Weimar constitution. Though German culture flourishes, the Republic is plagued by hyperinflation and unemployment and burdened by war reparations payments. Exploiting public discontent and simmering resentments from WWI, The Nazi party and its charismatic leader, Adolf Hitler, rise to power.

1919   The liberal Weimar constitution is signed.

1922-23 Inflation becomes so severe that it takes a wheelbarrow of money to pay for a loaf of bread.

1933 After the Nazis take control of Parliament in the 1932 elections, President Paul von Hindenburg reluctantly appoints Adolf Hitler Chancellor.

Third Reich (1933-1945)

The totalitarian Nazi state, which is based on principles of Aryan racial purity and anti-communism and fueled by a desire to avenge German territorial losses in WWI, quickly dissolves the political freedoms granted under the Weimar Republic. Envisioning itself as heir to the German Empire, it re-militarizes the country and begins a hostile, expansionist campaign against the other European powers.

1933 The Reichstag is set on fire, providing a ruse for Hitler to issue an emergency "Enabling Act" that gives his government nearly unlimited powers.

1939 Hitler invades Poland; Britain and France respond by declaring war, and World War II begins.

1940-45 Hitler establishes death camps; eventually approximately six million Jews will die either in the camps or under the Third Reich's racist policies.

1941 Hitler invades the Soviet Union and, after the bombing of Pearl Harbor, declares war on the U.S.

1942 The tide of war begins to turn in the Allies' favor after Hitler's defeat at the Battle of Stalingrad.

1945 Germany surrenders and Hitler commits suicide, ending WWII; the Allies and the Soviet Union partition Germany into four zones.

Division and Reunification (1945-present)

Split between East and West, Germany becomes the focal point of the Cold War. As the U.S. Marshall Plan pumps economic aid into West Germany, East Germans increasingly flood to the West. To stem the emigration, East Germany builds the Berlin Wall, which becomes the symbol of the Iron Curtain. The collapse of the Soviet Union in the late 1980s leads to German reunification.

Though the scars of division persist, Germany reemerges in the 1990s as a major economic power and an important leader in the European Union.

1948 In the first major crisis of the Cold War, the Soviets blockade West Berlin, and the Western Allies respond by airlifting food and supplies in the Berlin Airlift.

1949 The sectors of Germany controlled by France, Britain, and the U.S. merge to form the democratic Federal Republic of Germany (FRG, or West Germany); the Soviet sector establishes the centralized German Democratic Republic (GDR, or East Germany).

1961 East Germany constructs the Berlin Wall to halt the flood of East Germans escaping the GDR's Communist regime by fleeing to the West.

1989 The Berlin Wall falls after East Germany, wracked by massive demonstrations, eases border restrictions.

1990 East and West Germany are united under Chancellor Helmut Kohl.

1999 German government returns to the new capital, Berlin.

1999 The Euro becomes the official currency of Germany and other European nations.

2005 Germany elects its first female Chancellor, Angela Merkel.

2007 Germany holds the rotating presidencies of both the European Union and the G8.

GERMAN PHILOSOPHY AND SCIENCE

Philosophers

Germany is known as the land of *Dichter und Denker* (poets and philosophers), and German thinkers have written some of the most influential (as well as some of the most convoluted and abstruse) texts in Western philosophy.

- **Immanuel Kant** (1724-1804) developed theories of the role of rationality in ethics that influenced succeeding generations of philosophers.

- **Georg Wilhelm Friedrich Hegel** (1770-1831), a thinker associated with German Idealism, sought to create a new form for philosophy based on the concepts of speculative reasoning and internal dialectic.
- Kantian philosopher **Arthur Schopenhauer** (1788-1860) took the physical world as his main subject in *The World as Will and Representation*.
- Often called the father of Communism, the revolutionary **Karl Marx** (1818-1883) posited that all of history could be explained as a struggle between classes. The political economist's best-known work is *Das Kapital*.
- **Friedrich Nietzsche** (1844-1900) began his career as a philologist but soon invented a vaunting and aphoristic style for philosophy. Famous for his concepts of the will to power and the *Übermensch*, he declared that God was dead, slain at the hand of man.
- **Martin Heidegger** (1889-1976) is widely considered one of the most difficult of the German philosophers. His *Being and Time* attempted to define the very nature of existence.
- **Walter Benjamin** (1891-1940) was a lyrical cultural critic. His famous, Marxist-inflected essay "The Work of Art in the Age of Mechanical Reproduction" looked at the altered role of art in society in the wake of the industrial revolution.
- **Leo Strauss** (1899-1973) fled Germany in the Nazi years and took up a post at the University of Chicago, where he influenced a generation of students who were to become American neoconservative political theorists.
- **Theodor Adorno** (1903-1969) was a sociologist and musicologist who examined how capitalist culture had influenced artistic and musical culture.
- **Hannah Arendt** (1904-1975) was a political theorist who took power, authority, and totalitarianism as her primary themes. While covering the Nürnberg trials of Nazi war

criminals for the *New Yorker*, she coined the now-famous phrase "the banality of evil."

- **Jürgen Habermas** (1929-present) is a social critic, political theorist, and influential commentator on contemporary politics.

Scientists

Germany's tradition of investigative thought has led to many advances in the sciences, particularly in the field of physics.

- **Max Planck** (1858-1947) is credited as the father of quantum theory.
- **Werner Heisenberg** (1907-1955) was awarded the Nobel Prize for the creation of quantum mechanics. Today he is a household name for his Uncertainty Principle, which postulated that two paired quantities cannot be determined simultaneously.
- **Albert Einstein** (1879-1955) was a humble patent clerk before hitting upon his special theory of relativity, which reconciled electromagnetism and mechanics, and his general theory of relativity, which developed a new theory of gravitation.
- Other notable German scientists include **Daniel Gabriel Fahrenheit** (1686-1736), after whom the temperature scale is named; **Wilhelm Conrad Runtgen** (1845-1923), who invented the x-ray; and **Hans Geiger** (1882-1945), the inventor of the Geiger counter. Germany also boasts numerous automotive pioneers, including **Gottlieb Daimler** (1834-1900), **Karl Benz** (1844-1929), and **Rudolf Diesel** (1858-1913).

HISTORY OF GERMAN MUSIC

The greatness of German music grew in part out of the fragmented political situation. The many small principalities and bishoprics that split up the German-speaking world meant that there were many courts to offer patronage to musicians, both composers and instrumentalists. As a result, the German-speaking nations produced more composers of indisputable greatness than any other.

Baroque Music

The greatest composer of the Baroque era was **Johann Sebastian Bach** (1685-1750). Bach produced many church cantatas, especially for St. Thomas Church in Leipzig, where he served as cantor. His compositions were technically outstanding, vigorous, and profound. Little of his music was published during his lifetime, but after his death, his influence steadily grew, and his organ works became especially renowned. The Brandenburg Concertos are highly recommended.

Bach's contemporary, **Georg Frideric Handel** (1685-1759), was another great composer. He first rose to prominence as musician of the court of Hannover, a post that he left to become composer at the court of St. James in England. He was a leading composer of operas and instrumental music for the court. Listen to his oratorio, *Messiah*.

The Classical Period

Wolfgang Amadeus Mozart (1756-91), although an Austrian, cannot be omitted from any discussion of German music. With their contemporary themes and lively musical characterizations, his operas paved the way for later composers. **Franz Josef Haydn** (1732-1809), another Austrian, also exerted great influence on German music, especially on instrumental music. Listen to Mozart's *The Marriage of Figaro and Don Giovanni* and Haydn's "Drum Roll" Symphony no. 103.

The 19th Century and Romanticism

The 19th century was rich in musical genius. **Ludwig van Beethoven** (1770-1827) ushered in Romanticism. His intense, emotion-driven works included symphonies, piano concertos, piano sonatas, and quartets. He greatly expanded and developed the orchestra. Tragically, he completely lost his hearing in 1819. However, the chamber music he wrote thereafter shows an even greater depth and complexity than his previous compositions. Listen to symphonies no. 5 and no. 9.

Other great composers of the era include **Franz Schubert** (1797-1828), the ethereal **Felix Mendelssohn** (1809-47), **Robert Schumann** (1810-56), who drew inspiration from the poetry of Heine and Goethe, and **Johannes Brahms** (1833-97), who imbued Classical forms with Romantic emotion. Listen to Schubert's *Lieder*, Mendelssohn's "Overture" to *A Midsummer Night's Dream*, Schumann's "Scenes from Childhood," and Brahms's *German Requiem*.

The giant of the 19th century opera world was **Richard Wagner** (1813-83). His influence can best be heard in the music of the later Romantic composer **Richard Strauss** (1864-1949), whose operas carry Wagner's ideas of character development to greater psychological depth. Listen to Wagner's *The Ring of the Nibelungs* and Strauss's *Salome*.

The 20th Century

Musical experimentation flourished in early 20th century Germany. Austrian-born **Arnold Schoenberg** (1874-1952) developed the 12-tone system of musical structure. **Kurt Weill** (1900-50) and **Paul Hindemith** (1895-1963) tried to reach a more popular audience. During the Nazi era, many composers fled Germany. Others, like **Hans Pfitzner** (1869-1949) and **Richard Strauss** (1864-1949), remained in an uneasy relationship with the Nazis. Listen to Schoenberg's *Five Pieces for Orchestra*, Weill's *Threepenny Opera*, and Hindemith's *Mathis der Maler*. The music of Pfitzner is still heard in such operas as *Palestrina* from 1917 and *Das Herz* from 1931.

Today, at the beginning of the 21st century, important composers such as **Karlheinz Stockhausen** (b. 1928) and **Hans Werner Henze** (b. 1926) carry on the traditions of Germany's musical past. Listen to Stockhausen's *Gesang der Jünglinge* (Songs of the Youths). Henze has won cultural awards around the world for such compositions as *The English Cat* (1980) and *La Cubana* (1973).

GERMAN ART HISTORY

Romanesque (11th & 12th C)

Artistic expression in medieval Germany was largely church-related. Because Mass was said in Latin, the illiterate masses had to learn Bible lessons via the art on the church walls. *Bas reliefs* (sculptures that project slightly from a flat surface) and wall paintings depicted key tales to inspire faith in God and fear of sin. The best surviving works of this era are primarily found in churches in Cologne: the superb 11th-century carved doors on St. Maria im Kapitol, the intricate carved *The Shrine of the Magi* reliquary in the Cologne Cathedral, and the wall paintings of St. Maria Lyskirchen.

Gothic (13th-15th C)

Late medieval German art continued to be largely ecclesiastical, including stained glass, church facades, and massive wooden altarpieces festooned with statues and carvings. In Gothic painting and sculpture, figures tended to be more natural looking than in the Romanesque, but remained highly stylized, with features and rhythmic gestures exaggerated for symbolic or emotional emphasis. Many fine examples of Gothic art survive in Germany. Exemplary Gothic stained glass can be found in Rothenburg's St. Jakobskirche and Cologne's St. Gereon's Sacristy.

The premier German painter of the Gothic era, **Stephan Lochner**, painted dainty figures against gold backgrounds. His works include the Cologne Cathedral's *Altar of the City Patrons* (ca. 1440) and the Wallraf-Richartz Museum's *Madonna in the Rose Garden* (1450).

Tilman Riemenschneider (1460-1531), Germany's genius Gothic woodcarver, was the first to refrain from painting his sculptures. Some of his best works remain in Würzburg, including statues in the Mainfränkisches Fortress and three sandstone tombs in the Dom St. Kilian. The *Tomb of Heinrich II* in Bamberg's Kaiserdom and the massive altarpieces in Creglingen's Herrgottskirche are considered his masterpieces.

Renaissance (Late 15th-16th C)

Renaissance means "rebirth"—in this case, of Classical ideals. During this era, humanistic thinkers rediscovered the wisdom of ancient Greece and Rome, while artists strove for greater naturalism, using newly developed techniques such as linear perspective to achieve new heights of realism. For the most part Germany was no hotbed of Renaissance art. Most Protestant Reformation movements played down the role of art in worship, and some of the stricter sects outright condemned it as idolatry. This situation left artists with private patronage as their main revenue source, which resulted in lots of portraits, a few landscapes, and little else. Masters include:

- **Albrecht Dürer** (1471-1528) Ingenious painter, superb illustrator, and one of the greatest draftsmen ever, Dürer was the most important Renaissance artist outside Italy. He was the first to paint stand-alone self-portraits (including one in Munich's Alte Pinakothek), as well as watercolors and gouaches for their own sake rather than merely as sketches. His works grace Berlin's Gemäldegalerie and the Germanisches Nationalmuseum in his native Nürnberg.

- **Matthias Grünewald** (1470-1528) A retro foil to Dürer, Grünewald adopted and adapted Renaissance techniques and compositions to pump up the emotional intensity of his paintings, while keeping a distinctly Gothic look. You can see his paintings in the Alte Pinakothek in Munich and the village church in Stupach.

- **Lucas Cranach the Elder** (1472-1553) Cranach melded Renaissance sensibilities with a still somewhat primitive, medieval look. He helped popularize landscape painting and invented the full-length portrait. Cranach also did the woodcuts for the first German translation of the New Testament. Today, his landscape *Rest on the Flight into Egypt* is in Berlin's Gemäldegalerie, and his portraits *The Duke* and *The Duchess* are in Dresden's Gemäldegalerie Alte Meister.

- **Hans Holbein the Younger** (1497-1543) Second only to Dürer in the German Renaissance, Holbein spent most of his career in Basel and later as a court painter in London. Germany preserves precious little of his work, but you can see the *Portrait of Georg Gisze* in Berlin's Gemäldegalerie and a Nativity in the Freiburg Cathedral.

Baroque & Rococo (16th-18th C)

The baroque is more theatrical and decorative than the Renaissance. It mixes super-realism based on the use of peasant models and the exaggerated *chiaroscuro* ("light and dark") of Caravaggio with compositional complexity and explosions of furious movement and color. Rococo is later baroque art run amok, a frothy chaos of curlicues. Most baroque and rococo art in Germany consists of stuccoes and frescoes decorating churches, rather than freestanding artworks. Artists from this period include:

- **Andreas Schlüter** (1660-1714) He came back from Italy crazy about baroque and proceeded to make sculptures in the style, which can now be found at Berlin's Schloss Charlottenburg.
- **Balthasar Permoser** (1651-1732) He studied in Salzburg and Florence before bringing the baroque style of Italy's Bernini back with him to Dresden, where as court sculptor he created the stone pulpit in the Katholische Hofkirche and sculptures adorning the Zwinger.

Romantic (19th C)

The Romantics felt that the classically minded Renaissance had gotten it wrong and the excessively exuberant German baroque was way over the top. The Gothic Middle Ages became their inspiration, and with a surge of Teutonic national pride, the Brothers Grimm collected folktales, builders created fantasy castles, and artists set up easels in the forests and on mountaintops. The Romantics held a suspicion of progress and a deep respect for nature, human rights, and the nobility of the peasantry. Their paintings tended to be heroic, historic, and dramatic.

The best examples from this period include:

- **Adam Elsheimer** (1578-1610) Elsheimer created tiny paintings that bridged the gap from late Renaissance Mannerism (a style characterized by twisting figures in exaggerated positions), through baroque, to proto-Romantic. His *Flight into Egypt* resides in Munich's Alte Pinakothek.

- **Caspar David Friedrich** (1774-1840) Greatest of the German Romantics, Friedrich specialized in majestic landscapes that combined closely examined detail with dramatically exaggerated proportions, often with pro-Protestant, anti-Catholic undertones. Dresden's Gemäldegalerie Alte Meister houses his famous *Cross in the Mountains*.

Early 20th Century

Until Hitler, Germany was one of Europe's hotbeds of artistic activity, a crucible of the modern that gave rise to several important movements whose influences echoed through international 20th-century art. But the Nazis outlawed and confiscated "degenerate" modern art (partly because many of the artists were non-Aryan), devastating the German art scene.

Almost all the artists listed below are represented at Cologne's Museum Ludwig, save Höch and Grosz, who you can find at Berlin's Neue Nationalgalerie alongside Schmidt-Rottluff, Nolde, Dix, and Beckmann. At least one artist from every movement is at Stuttgart's Staatsgalerie, and there are also good modern collections at Düsseldorf's Kunstsammlung Nordrhein-Westfalen and Dresden's Albertinum. Munich's Pinakothek der Moderne is strong on expressionist artists. The major artists and movements of the early 20th century include:

Expressionism Very broadly, expressionism describes art in Germany up through World War I—and beyond—that abandoned realism to embrace exaggeration, visible artistry (thick paint, obvious brushstrokes, and strong colors) and, most importantly, abstraction—all to try to "express" the emotions or philosophy of the artist himself. Pure expressionism fell into two main groups:

Die Brücke, founded in 1905 in Dresden, turned its back on the modernizing 20th century and sought inspiration instead in folk art, medieval examples, and "unspoiled" landscapes. Its greatest members were **Ernst Kirchner** (1880-1938) and **Karl Schmidt-Rottluff** (1884-1976), although impressionist **Emil Nolde** (1867-1956) also later joined for a while. They have their own Brücke Museum in Berlin.

Der Blaue Reiter group was set up in Munich in 1911 by Russian-born **Wassily Kandinsky** (1866-1944), **Franz Marc** (1880-1916), and **August Macke** (1887-1914) to oppose the cultural insularity and anti-modern stance of Die Brücke. The "Blue Riders" embraced international elements, modern abstraction techniques, spontaneity, and vibrant colors to evoke a visceral intensity in their work.

Dadaism   The nonsense word "Dada" was first adopted by a group of disillusioned artists in Zürich in 1916, but the movement quickly spread to Germany. Dadaists were by turns abstract, nihilistic, and anti-art. The movement's proponents included **Hannah Höch** (1889-1978), who collaged photographs and magazine cutouts to make social statements; **George Grosz** (1893-1959), who was more strictly a painter, and later moved on to the Neue Sachlichkeit movement; and **Kurt Schwitters** (1887-1948), who later started his own splinter group called "Merz," which experimented with abstract and Russian constructivist elements. Both **Max Ernst** (1891-1976) and Alsatian **Jean "Hans" Arp** (1887-1966) started as Blaue Reiter expressionists and, after their Dada collage period, ended up in Paris as surrealists—Ernst as a painter, Arp as a sculptor of amorphous shapes.

Neue Sachlichkeit (New Objectivity)   This 1920s Berlin movement opposed the elitism and abstraction of the expressionists with caricature-filled depictions of harsh colors and harsher subjects—sex, violence, and the plight of the urban worker. Proponents included **Otto Dix** (1891-1969), who started as an expressionist but quickly became one of the most scathing

New Objectivity painters; **George Grosz**; and **Max Beckmann** (1884-1950), who was also originally an expressionist.

Post-World War II Art

Germany hasn't had any single school or style to define its art since World War II, although terms such as *neo-expressionism* (an anti-abstract, anti-minimalist, anti-conceptual trend that grounds itself more in tradition and figurative art) are often bandied about. There have been, however, several important artists. Germany's best museum for post-World War II art is Berlin's Hamburger Bahnhof, where you can find works by all three artists listed below. All three are also represented in Stuttgart's Staatsgalerie and Bonn's Kunstmuseum. In addition, Munich's Pinakothek der Moderne has a Kiefer and Cologne's Museum Ludwig has Beuys and Baselitz. Notable post-World War II artists include:

- **Josef Beuys** (1921-1986) An iconoclast who made constructivist sculpture from trash, he helped form the Fluxus group, which rejected the growing commercial gallery scene, and participated in performance art happenings. Once, he memorably strutted around a stage lecturing on art to a dead rabbit in his hand.
- **Anselm Kiefer** (b. 1945) Ignoring the 20th-century tendency for abstraction and minimalism, Kiefer made a return to huge, mixed-media figurative art with a strong historical bent—the bleak landscape of post-World War II Germany.
- **Georg Baselitz** (b. 1938) Baselitz is a figurative painter— and a sculptor, since the 1980s—and an important neoexpressionist with a penchant for portraying people upside down.

GUIDE TO GERMAN ARCHITECTURE

When considering a building's style, particularly for structures built before the 20th century, keep in mind that very few buildings were actually built in one style. A large, expensive structure—such as a church, usually the most significant building in any town—often took centuries to complete, during which time tastes would change and plans would be altered.

Romanesque (10th-12th C)

Romanesque architects concentrated on building large churches with wide aisles to accommodate the masses. The Romanesque took its inspiration from ancient Rome—hence the name—where early Christians had adapted the *basilica*, ancient Roman law buildings, to become churches.

Identifiable Features

- **Rounded arches** allowed architects to open up wide naves and spaces.
- **Thick walls, infrequent and small windows, and huge piers:** Necessary to support the weight of all that masonry.
- **Tall towers on the façades.**
- **Dual chancels.** Some Romanesque churches have chancels at both the west and east ends.
- **Blind arcades.** Decorative arches on piers or columns attached to a wall.
- **Dwarf gallery.** Line of small, open arches on the exterior.

Best Examples

- **Mainz's Dom**   Looks more like a castle fortress than a church, with two massive towers and four smaller ones.
- **Worms's Dom St. Peter**   Another fortress of God, it has two imposing facades sprouting rounded towers and dwarf galleries.
- **Speyer's Kaiserdom**   The largest cathedral in Germany, this four-towered basilica also houses the largest and best Romanesque crypt in Germany.

Gothic (13th-16th C)

By the 12th century, engineering developments freed architects from constructing the heavy, thick walls of Romanesque structures. As a result, ceilings began to soar, walls began to thin, and windows began to proliferate.

Instead of dark, somber, relatively unadorned Romanesque interiors that forced the eyes of the faithful toward the altar, where the priest stood droning on in unintelligible Latin, the Gothic interior enticed the churchgoers' gaze upward to high ceilings filled with light. The priests still conducted Mass in Latin, but now peasants could "read" the Gothic comic books of stained-glass windows.

From the exterior, the squat and brooding Romanesque fortresses of Christianity were replaced by graceful buttresses and soaring spires, which rose from town centers like beacons of religion. German Hallenkirchen, or "Hall Churches," spread from Westphalia throughout southern Germany. Their aisles and transept are about the same height as the nave, giving the Hallenkirche an airy, boxy look.

Identifiable Features

- **Pointed arches.** The most significant development of the Gothic era.
- **Cross vaults.** The ceiling arches to a point in the center, creating four or more sail shapes.
- **Façade flanked by two towers.**
- **Flying buttresses.** Freestanding external pillars connected by thin, graceful stone arms.
- **Spires.**
- **Gargoyles.** These wide-mouthed creatures are actually drain spouts.
- **Tracery.** Delicate, lacy spider webs of curlicues at pointy ends of windows and lower intersections of cross vaulting.
- **Stained glass.** Often filled with Bible stories.
- **Choir screen.** Often decorated with carvings or tombs.
- **Half-timbered houses.** These are houses made of exposed cross timbers, with the triangular sections between the beams filled in with plaster, and often painted.

Best Examples

- **Cologne Cathedral** The façade is Germany's keynote example of flamboyant Gothic, the impossibly huge interior a soaring void of arches and light. It also contains some fantastic Gothic stained glass, paintings, and carved choir stalls.
- **Freiburg Cathedral** This cathedral is a remarkable Gothic construct, centered on an enormous single tower with great gargoyles.
- **Ulm Münster** Ulm's Münster sports the world's tallest spire—although it did take 500 years to complete, so the 1890 finishing is neo-Gothic. Inside, there are five airy aisles with no transept.
- **Hallenkirchen** The best of Germany's tall, airy Hall Churches are **Nördlingen's St. Georgenkirche**, Munich's **Frauenkirche**, **Dinkelsbühl's Georgenkirche**, and **Nürnberg's St.-Lorenz-Kirche.**
- **Backsteingotik** (Northern Brick Gothic) East of the Elbe and along the Baltic, the use of brick forced Gothic architecture to be simple and monumental. Lübeck's **Marienkirche** and **Rathaus** (town hall) are both models for other brick churches and secular architecture, including **Schwerin's Dom** and **Stralsund's St. Nikolaikirche.**
- Gothic towns The best-preserved Gothic town centers include Rothenburg ob der Tauber, Goslar, Regensburg, and Tübingen.

Renaissance (Late 15th Through Mid-17th C)

Germany was so busy with the Reformation that the country had little time for the Renaissance, which really only had an effect in southern Germany, where transalpine influences from Italy were felt. In the far north, a few isolated examples show the Renaissance influence of Flemish and Dutch neighbors.

Identifiable Features

- **Italian Renaissance** Distinguished by the Renaissance ideals of proportion, symmetry, and the Classical orders of columns.

- **Weser Renaissance** This late-16th and early-17th-century style is distinguishable on houses by pinnacled gables, heavy scrollwork, elaborate dormers (an upright window projecting from a sloping roof), rounded pediments (a low-pitched feature above a window, door, or pavilion), and decorative stone bands.

Best Examples

- **Michaelskirche, Munich** The only solidly Renaissance church in Germany, built 1583-97 by the Jesuits to resemble their church in Rome, Michaelskirche has a harmonious statue-studded façade and a huge, cradle-vaulted single nave.
- **Hameln** The Pied Piper town has several fine Weser Renaissance houses, including the Rattenfängerhaus, Hochzeithaus, and Dempterscheshaus.
- **Celle** The preserved town center is Weser Renaissance, entirely built between the 16th and 18th centuries, including the moated Herzogschloss Castle.

Baroque & Rococo (17th-18th C)

More than any other movement, the baroque aimed for a seamless meshing of architecture and art. The stuccoes, sculptures, and paintings of this time were all carefully designed to complement each other—and the space itself—to create a unified whole. This effect was both aesthetic and narrative, the various art forms all working together to tell a single biblical story.

The German baroque only truly flourished in the south and in lower Saxony—especially in Catholic, Counter-Reformation areas—but these regions excelled at it, managing to make Germany's brand of over-the-top, baroque chaos work better than any other country's. Whereas rococo is usually used as a derogatory term for the baroque gone awry into the grotesque, in Germany the rococo actually succeeds—sometimes.

Identifiable Features

- **Classical architecture rewritten with curves.**
- **Complex decoration.** Unlike the Renaissance, the baroque was playful—lots of ornate stucco work, pouty cherubs, airy frescoes, heavy gilding, multicolored marbles, and general frippery.
- **Multiplying forms.** The baroque loved to pile up its forms and elements to create a rich, busy effect.

Best Examples

- **The Residenz, Würzburg**   Balthasar Neumann (1687-1753) designed this sumptuous baroque palace, including the monumental staircase under the world's largest ceiling fresco, the work of Italian master Tiepolo. The palace's chapel is textbook rococo.
- **Wieskirche, near Füssen**   Dominikus Zimmermann (1685-1766) crafted this oval-planned rococo beauty in the middle of a cow pasture.
- **Sans Souci Palace, Potsdam**   Frederick the Great's palace is one of Europe's best examples of rococo, set amid one of the most intricately landscaped of Prussian gardens.
- **Cuvillies' Munich buildings**   Jean Francois de Cuvilles (1698-1767), a French dwarf, was the Elector of Bavaria's court jester until his talent for architecture was recognized. He crafted Munich's greatest rococo monuments, including the jewel box of the Residenz's Alte Residenztheater and the façade of the baroque Theatinerkirche. His masterpiece is Schloss Nymphenburg's Amalienburg hunting lodge.

Neoclassicism & Romantic (Min-18th Through 19th C)

As a backlash against the excesses of the baroque and rococo, by the middle of the 18th century, architects began to turn to the austere simplicity and grandeur of the Classical Age and inaugurated the neoclassical style. Their work was inspired by the rediscovery of Pompeii and other ancient sites. However, many of their interiors continued to be rococo, though more muted than before. The sterility of German neoclassicism didn't last long, though, and the 19th century left the increasingly nationalist German society looking into its own past for inspiration, kicking off the neo-Gothic movement,

Identifiable Features

- **Neoclassical** The classical ideals of mathematical proportion and symmetry, first rediscovered during the Renaissance, are neoclassical hallmarks. Of the classical orders, German neoclassicists preferred the austere, monumental Doric style for their templelike buildings and massive colonnaded porticos.
- **Romantic** Gothic fantasy is the only way to describe this style, which cranked up the defining aspects of the Gothic (spires, tracery, buttresses, and gargoyles) to heights of drama that the Middle Ages never imagined.

Best Examples

- **In Berlin** The Prussians remade Berlin in a neoclassical image, starting with the Brandenburger Tor and moving on to the buildings of Karl Friedrich Schinkel, among which Altes Museum, Schloss Charlottenhof, and Nikolaikirche are his best.
- **In Munich** Ludwig I had Leo von Klenze lay out neoclassical structures across his "new Athens," including those surrounding Königsplatz and the nearby Alte and Neue Pinotheken.
- **Ludwig II's Bavarian fantasies** "Mad" King Ludwig II was the ultimate romantic, building himself a series of faux-medieval castles, including Herrenchiemsee's Neues Schloss and the incomparable fantasy of Neuschwanstein Castle, right out of a brothers Grimm folk tale.

20th Century German Architecture

Germany's take on the early-20th-century Art Nouveau movement was called Jugendstil. The Bauhaus was a 1920s avant-garde school of architecture led by Walter Gropius (1883-1969) that combined industrial-age architecture with art and craft to create functional buildings and furnishings. Among its chief designers and institute teachers were Marcel Breuer, Wassily Kandinsky,

Oskar Schlemmer, and Paul Klee. The Nazis closed the school down in 1933, and it was later reborn in Chicago.

Identifiable Features

- **Jugendstil** This style reacted against the burgeoning culture of mass production by stressing the uniqueness of craft. Practitioners created asymmetrical, curvaceous designs based on organic inspiration (plants and flowers) and used such materials as wrought iron, stained glass, tile, and hand-painted wallpaper.
- **Bauhaus** A use of right angles, concrete, and glass, and an absence of ornamentation, characterize many Bauhaus structures, which otherwise share only a devotion to functionality. In design, the movement is famous for its early plastic and metal tube chairs.

Best Examples

- **Jugendstil** The movement took its name from *Jugend* magazine published in the Schwabing district of Munich, where many buildings in the style survive. Munich is also home to the Jugendstil Museum in the Stuck-Villa, a hybrid neoclassical/Jugendstil structure.
- **Bauhaus** Bauhaus structures pepper Germany in unobtrusive ways, often in city outskirts. One fine example is Berlin's Siemensstadt, the first modern housing complex, built with long "slab" blocks by Walter Gropius. Berlin also has the Bauhaus-Archiv Museum für Gestaltung, devoted to Bauhaus drawings, photographs, and design examples.

DICTIONARY KEY

n	noun	m	masculine
v	verb	f	feminine
adj	adjective	gn	gender neutral
prep	preposition	s	singular
adv	adverb	pl	plural
pron	pronoun		

All verbs are listed in infinitive (to + verb) form, cross-referenced to the appropriate conjugations page. Adjectives are listed first in masculine singular form, followed by the feminine ending.

For food terms, see the Menu Reader (p83) and Grocery section (p89) in Chapter 4, Dining.

A

able, to be able to (can) v
    können **p26**

above adj über

accept, to accept v p20
    akzeptieren

Do you accept credit cards?
    *Akzeptieren Sie
    Kreditkarten?*

accident n der Unfall m

I've had an accident. *Ich
    hatte einen Unfall.*

account n das Konto gn

**I'd like to transfer to / from
    my checking / savings
    account.** *Ich möchte etwas
    auf mein / von meinem
    Girokonto / Sparkonto
    überweisen.*

acne n die Akne f

across prep über p

across the street *auf der
    anderen Straßenseite*

actual adj tatsächlich,
    eigentlich, wirklich

adapter plug n der
    Adapterstecker m

address n die Adresse f

What's the address?
    Wie lautet die Adresse?

admission fee n die
    Eintrittsgebühr f

in advance im Voraus

African-American adj
    afroamerikanisch

afternoon n der Nachmittag m

in the afternoon am
    Nachmittag

age n das Alter gn

What's your age? *Wie alt
    sind Sie? (formal) / Wie alt
    bist du? (informal)*

agency n die Agentur / das
    Büro f/gn

car rental agency die
    Autovermietung f

agnostic adj agnostisch

air conditioning n die
    Klimaanlage f

ENGLISH–GERMAN

Would you lower / raise the air conditioning? *Könnten Sie die Klimaanlage bitte auf eine höhere / niedrigere Temperatur einstellen?*

airport *n der Flughafen m*

I need a ride to the airport. *Ich muss zum Flughafen.*

How far is it from the airport? *Wie weit ist das vom Flughafen entfernt?*

airsickness bag *n die Spucktüte f*

aisle (in store) *n der Gang m*

Which aisle is it in? *In welchem Gang finde ich das?*

alarm clock *n der Wecker m*

alcohol *n der Alkohol m*

Do you serve alcohol? *Haben Sie alkoholische Getränke?*

I'd like nonalcoholic beer. *Ich hätte gerne ein alkoholfreies Bier.*

all *n Alles*

all *adj ganz; alle*

all of the time *die ganze Zeit*

That's all, thank you. *Danke, das ist alles.*

allergic *adj allergisch*

I'm allergic to ____. *Ich bin allergisch gegen ____. See p91 and 221 for common allergens.*

also *auch adv*

altitude *n die Höhe f*

aluminum *n das Aluminium gn*

ambulance *n der Krankenwagen m*

American *n der Amerikaner m, die Amerikanerin f*

amount *n die Menge (things) / der Betrag (money) f/m*

angry *adj wütend*

animal *n das Tier gn*

another *adj noch ein / eine / einen*

answer *n die Antwort f*

answer, to answer (phone call, question) *v p20 beantworten (question) / entgegennehmen (phone call)*

Answer me, please. *Antworten Sie mir bitte.*

antibiotic *n das Antibiotikum gn*

I need an antibiotic. *Ich brauche ein Antibiotikum.*

antihistamine *n das Antihistamin gn*

anxious *adj besorgt*

any *adj beliebig*

anything *n alles / irgend etwas*

anywhere *adv überall / irgendwo*

April *n der April m*

appointment *n der Termin m*

Do I need an appointment? *Benötige ich einen Termin?*

ENGLISH—GERMAN

are *v See* **be, to be p23**

arrive, to arrive *v* ankommen

arrival(s) *n* die Ankunft *f*

art *n* die Kunst *f*

> **exhibit of art** die Kunstausstellung

art *adj* Kunst-

art museum das Kunstmuseum

artist *n* der Künstler *m*, die Künstlerin

Asian *adj* asiatisch

ask for (request) *v* bitten um **p24**

ask a question *v* fragen **p24**

aspirin *n* das Aspirin *gn*

assist *v* helfen **p24**

assistance *n* die Hilfe *f*

asthma *n* das Asthma *gn*

> **I have asthma.** Ich habe Asthma.

atheist *adj* atheistisch

ATM *n* der Geldautomat *m*

> **I'm looking for an ATM.** Ich suche einen Geldautomaten.

attend *v* teilnehmen (meeting) / behandeln (doctor) **p22/24**

audio *adj* Audio-

August *n* der August *m*

aunt *n* die Tante *f*

Australian *n* der Australier *m*, die Australierin

Austrian *n* der Österreicher *m*, die Österreicherin

autumn *n* der Herbst *m*

available *adj* verfügbar

B

baby *n* das Baby *gn*

baby *adj* Baby- / für Babys

> **Do you sell baby food?** Verkaufen Sie Babynahrung?

babysitter *n* der Babysitter *m*

> **Do you have babysitters who speak English?** Haben Sie englischsprachige Babysitter?

back *n* der Rücken *m*

> **My back hurts.** Mein Rücken schmerzt.

back rub *n* die Rückenmassage *f*

backed up (toilet) *adj* verstopft

> **The toilet is backed up.** Die Toilette ist verstopft.

bad *schlecht adj*

bag *n* die Tasche *f*, die Tüte *f*

> **airsickness bag** die Spucktüte
>
> **My bag was stolen.** Meine Tasche wurde gestohlen.
>
> **I lost my bag.** Ich habe meine Tasche verloren.

bag *v* einpacken **p20**

baggage *n* das Gepäck *gn*

baggage *adj* Gepäck-

> **baggage claim** Gepäckausgabe

bait *n* der Köder *m*

balance (on bank account) *n* der Kontostand *m*

balance v *balancieren (something shaky) / begleichen (invoice)*

balcony n *der Balkon m*

bald adj *kahl*

ball (sport) n *der Ball m*

ballroom dancing n *der Gesellschaftstanz m*

band (musical ensemble) n *die Band f*

band-aid n *das Pflaster gn*

bank n *die Bank f*

Can you help me find a bank? *Könnten Sie mir bitte helfen, eine Bank zu finden?*

bar n *die Bar f*

barber n *der (Herren-) Frisör m*

bass (instrument) n *der Bass m*

bath (spa) n *das Bad gn*

bathroom (restroom) n *die Toilette / das WC f/gn*

Where is the nearest public bathroom? *Wo finde ich das nächste öffentliche WC?*

bathtub n *die Badewanne f*

bathe, to bathe oneself v *baden / ein Bad nehmen* **p20, 24**

battery (for flashlight) n *die Batterie f*

battery (for car) n *die Batterie f*

bee n *die Biene f*

I was stung by a bee. *Ich wurde von einer Biene gestochen.*

be, to be v *sein* **p23**

beach n *der Strand m*

beach v *stranden* **p20**

beard n *der Bart m*

beautiful adj *schön*

bed n *das Bett gn*

beer n *das Bier gn*

beer on tap *das Bier vom Fass*

begin v *beginnen / anfangen* **p24**

behave v *sich benehmen* **p24**

well behaved *brav*

behind adv *hinter*

Belgian n *der Belgier m, die Belgierin f*

below adv *unter*

belt n *der Gürtel m*

conveyor belt *das Transportband*

berth n *die Koje f*

best *am besten*

bet, to bet v *wetten* **p20**

better *besser*

big adj *groß* **p11**

bilingual adj *zweisprachig*

bill (currency) n *der (Geld-)Schein m*

bill v *berechnen* **p20**

billion n *die Milliarde f*

biography n *die Biografie f*

bird n *der Vogel m*

birth control n *die Verhütung*

birth control adj Antibaby-
I'm out of birth control pills. Ich habe keine Antibabypillen mehr.
I need more birth control pills. Ich brauche mehr Antibabypillen.

bit (small amount) n ein bisschen gn

black adj schwarz

blanket n die (Bett-)Decke f

bleach n das Bleichmittel gn

blend v mischen

blind adj blind

block v blockieren **p20**

blond(e) adj blond

blouse n die Bluse f **blue** adj blau

blurry adj verschwommen

board n die Tafel f
on board an Bord

board v einsteigen / an Bord gehen **p24**

boarding pass n die Bordkarte f

boat n das Boot gn

bomb n die Bombe f

book n das Buch gn

bookstore n die Buchhandlung f

bordello n der Puff m

boss n der Chef m, die Chefin f

bottle n die Flasche f

May I heat this (baby) bottle someplace? Kann ich dieses (Baby-) Fläschchen irgendwo aufwärmen?

box (seat) n die Loge f

box office n der Kartenverkauf m

boy n der Junge m

boyfriend n der Freund m

braid n der Zopf m

braille, American n die englische Blindenschrift f

brake n die Bremse f
emergency brake die Notbremse

brake v bremsen **p20**

brandy n der Brandy m

brave adj tapfer

bread n das Brot n

break v (zer-)brechen **p24**

breakfast n das Frühstück gn
What time is breakfast? Um wie viel Uhr gibt es Frühstück?

bridge (across a river, dental) n die Brücke f

briefcase n der Aktenkoffer m

bright adj hell

broadband n Breitband-

bronze adj bronzefarben

brother n der Bruder m

brown adj braun

brunette n die Brünette f

Buddhist n der Buddhist m, die Buddhistin f

budget n das Budget gn

buffet n das Buffet gn

bug n der Käfer m, das Insekt gn

burn v brennen p24

> **Can I burn a CD here?** Kann
> ich hier eine CD brennen?

bus n der Bus m

> **Where is the bus stop?**
> Wo ist die nächste
> Bushaltestelle?
> **Which bus goes to ____?**
> Welcher Bus fährt nach
> ____?

business n das Unternehmen
gn

business adj Geschäfts-

> **business center** das
> Geschäftszentrum

busy adj gut besucht
(restaurant), besetzt
(phone)

butter n die Butter f

buy, to buy v kaufen p20

C

café n das Café gn

> **Internet café** das
> Internetcafé

call, to call v rufen (shout)
anrufen (phone) p24

camp, to camp v zelten p20

camper n das Wohnmobil
(van) / der Wohnwagen
(trailer) gn/m

camping adj Camping-

> **Do we need a camping
> permit?** Benötigen wir
> eine Campingerlaubnis?

campsite n der Campingplatz m

can n die Dose f

can (able to) v können p26

Canada n Kanada

Canadian adj kanadisch

cancel, to cancel v stornieren
p20

> **My flight was canceled.**
> Mein Flug wurde storniert.

canvas n die Leinwand f (for
painting), das Segeltuch gn
(material)

cappuccino n der Cappuccino
m

car n das Auto gn

> **car rental agency** die
> Autovermietung
> **I need a rental car.**
> Ich benötige einen
> Mietwagen.

card n die Karte f

> **Do you accept credit
> cards?** Akzeptieren Sie
> Kreditkarten?
> **May I have your business
> card?** Könnte ich bitte Ihre
> Visitenkarte haben?

car seat (child's safety seat) n
der Kindersitz m

> **Do you rent car seats for
> children?** Vermieten Sie
> Kindersitze?

carsickness n die
Autokrankheit f

cash n das Bargeld gn

> **cash only** Nur gegen
> Barzahlung

cash, to cash v *einlösen (check)* **p20**

to cash out (gambling) *auszahlen lassen*

cashmere n *der Kaschmir* m

casino n *das Kasino* gn

cat n *die Katze* f

cathedral n *der Dom* m

Catholic adj *katholisch*

cavity (tooth cavity) n *das Loch* gn

I think I have a cavity. *Ich glaube, ich habe ein Loch im Zahn.*

CD n *die CD* f

CD player n *der CD-Player* m

celebrate, to celebrate v *feiern* **p20**

cell phone n *das Mobiltelefon / das Handy* gn

centimeter n *der Zentimeter* m

chamber music n *die Kammermusik* f

change (money) n *das Wechselgeld* gn

I'd like change, please. *Geben Sie mir bitte Wechselgeld.*

This isn't the correct change. *Das Wechselgeld stimmt leider nicht.*

change (to change money, clothes) v *wechseln* **p20**

changing room n *die Umkleidekabine* f

charge, to charge (money) v *abbuchen* **p20**

charge, to charge (a battery) v *aufladen* **p24**

charmed adj *entzückt*

charred (meat) adj *verkohlt*

charter, to charter v *chartern* **p22**

cheap adj *billig*

check n *der Scheck* m

Do you accept travelers' checks? *Akzeptieren Sie Reiseschecks?*

check, to check v *überprüfen / sich vergewissern* **p20**

checked (pattern) adj *kariert*

check-in n *der Check-In* m

What time is check-in? *Um wie viel Uhr wird eingecheckt?*

check-out n *der Check-Out* gn

check-out time *Uhrzeit für das Auschecken*

What time is check-out? *Um wie viel Uhr wird ausgecheckt?*

check out, to check out v *auschecken* **p20**

cheese n *der Käse* m

chicken n *das Hähnchen* gn

child n *das Kind* gn

children n *Kinder* gn

Are children allowed? *Sind Kinder erlaubt?*

Do you have children's programs? *Haben Sie ein Programm für Kinder?*

Do you have a children's menu? *Haben Sie ein Kindermenü?*

chiropractor n der
  Chiropraktiker m
church n die Kirche f
cigar n die Zigarre f
cigarette n die Zigarette f
  a pack of cigarettes eine
  Schachtel Zigaretten
cinema n das Kino gn
city n die Stadt f
claim n die Reklamation f
  I'd like to file a claim.
  Ich möchte etwas
  reklamieren.
clarinet n die Klarinette f
class n die Klasse f
  business class die
  Businessklasse
  economy class die
  Economyklasse
  first class die Erste Klasse
classical (music) adj klassisch
clean adj sauber
clean, to clean v reinigen p20
  **Please clean the room
  today.** Reinigen Sie bitte
  heute das Zimmer.
clear v räumen p20
clear adj klar
climbing n das Klettern gn
climb, to climb v klettern
  (mountain) / steigen
  (stairs) p20, 24
  to climb a mountain
  bergsteigen
  to climb stairs Treppen
  steigen

close, to close v schließen
  p24
close (near) nah
closed adj geschlossen
cloudy adj bewölkt
clover n der Klee m
go clubbing, to go clubbing v
  einen Nachtclub besuchen
  p20
coat n die Jacke f
coffee n der Kaffee m
  iced coffee der Eiskaffee
cognac n der Kognak m
coin n die Münze f
cold n die Erkältung f
  I have a cold. Ich habe eine
  Erkältung.
cold adj kalt
  I'm cold. Mir ist kalt.
  It's cold out. Es ist kalt
  draußen.
coliseum n die Sporthalle f
collect adj unfrei
  **I'd like to place a collect
  call.** Ich möchte ein R-
  Gespräch führen.
collect, to collect v sammeln
  p20
college n die Hochschule f
color n die Farbe f
color v färben p20
computer n der Computer m
concert n das Konzert gn
condition n der Zustand m
  in good / bad condition in
  gutem / schlechtem Zustand

ENGLISH–GERMAN

condom *n das Kondom gn*
Do you have a condom?
Hast du ein Kondom?
not without a condom *nicht ohne Kondom*
condor *n der Kondor m*
confirm, to confirm *v bestätigen* **p20**
I'd like to confirm my reservation. *Ich möchte meine Reservierung bestätigen.*
confused *adj verwirrt*
congested *adj überfüllt*
connection speed *n die Verbindungs-geschwindigkeit f*
consequently *folglich adv*
consistent *konsequent adj*
constipated *adj verstopft*
I'm constipated. *Ich habe Verstopfung.*
contact lens *n die Kontaktlinse f*
I lost my contact lens. *Ich habe meine Kontaktlinse verloren.*
continue, to continue *v fortsetzen* **p20**
convertible *n das Cabrio gn*
cook, to cook *v kochen*
I'd like a room where I can cook. *Ich hätte gerne ein Zimmer mit Kochgelegenheit.*
cookie *n der Keks m*
copper *adj Kupfer-*

corner *n die Ecke f*
on the corner *an der Ecke*
correct *v korrigieren*
correct *adj richtig*
Am I on the correct train? *Bin ich im richtigen Zug?*
cost, to cost *v kosten* **p20**
How much does it cost? *Wie viel kostet das?*
Costa Rican *adj costa-ricanisch*
costume *n das Kostüm gn*
cotton *n die Baumwolle f*
cough *n der Husten m*
cough *v husten* **p20**
counter (in bar) *n die Theke f*
country-and-western *n die Country-Musik f*
court (legal) *n das Gericht gn*
court (sport) *n der Platz m*
courteous *adj zuvorkommend*
cousin *n der Cousin m, die Cousine f*
cover charge (in bar) *n der Eintrittspreis m*
cow *n die Kuh f*
crack (in glass object) *n der Sprung m*
craftsperson *n der Handwerker m, die Handwerkerin f*
cream *n die Sahne f*
credit card *n die Kreditkarte f*
Do you accept credit cards? *Akzeptieren Sie Kreditkarten?*

crib n das Kinderbett gn
crown (dental) n die Krone f
curb n der Bordstein m
curl n die Locke f
curly adj gelockt
currency exchange n die Geldwechselstube f

Where is the nearest currency exchange? Wo finde ich die nächste Geldwechselstube?

current aktuell adj
current (water) n die Strömung f
customs n der Zoll m
cut (wound) n der Schnitt m

I have a bad cut. Ich habe eine tiefe Schnittwunde.

cut, to cut v schneiden p24
cybercafé n das Internetcafé gn

Where can I find a cybercafé? Wo finde ich ein Internetcafé?

Czech n der Tscheche m, die Tschechin f

D

damaged adj beschädigt
Damn! expletive Verdammt!
dance v tanzen p20
danger n die Gefahr f
Danish n der Däne m, die Dänin f
dark n die Dunkelheit f
dark adj dunkel
daughter n die Tochter f
day n der Tag m

the day before yesterday vorgestern

these last few days die letzten paar Tage

dawn n die Morgendämmerung f

at dawn bei Tagesanbruch

dazzle v blenden
deaf adj taub
deal (bargain) n das Schnäppchen gn

What a great deal! Was für ein großartiges Schnäppchen!

deal (cards) v geben p24

Deal me in. Ich bin dabei.

December n der Dezember m
declined adj abgelehnt

Was my credit card declined? Wurde meine Kreditkarte nicht akzeptiert?

declare v verzollen (customs) p20

I have nothing to declare. Ich habe nichts zu verzollen.

deep adj tief
delay n die Verspätung f

How long is the delay? Wie viel beträgt die Verspätung?

delighted adj erfreut
democracy n die Demokratie f
dent v verbeulen p20

He / She dented the car. Er / Sie hat das Auto verbeult.

dentist n der Zahnarzt m

denture n das Gebiss gn

  denture plate die Zahnprothese

departure n die Abreise f

designer n der Designer m, die Designerin f

dessert n die Nachspeise f

  dessert menu die Dessertkarte

destination n das Ziel gn

diabetic adj Diabetiker-

dial (a phone) v wählen p20

  dial direct durchwählen

diaper n die Windel f

  Where can I change a diaper? Wo kann ich hier Windeln wechseln?

diarrhea n der Durchfall m

dictionary n das Wörterbuch gn

different (other) adj anders

difficult adj schwierig

dinner n das Abendessen gn

directory assistance (phone) n die Telefonauskunft f

disability n die Behinderung f

disappear v verschwinden p20

disco n die Disko f

disconnected adj unterbrochen

  Operator, I was disconnected. Vermittlung, mein Gespräch wurde unterbrochen.

discount n der Preisnachlass m

  Do I qualify for a discount? Bekomme ich einen Preisnachlass?

dish n das Gericht gn

dive v tauchen p20

  scuba dive tauchen (mit Atemgerät)

divorced adj geschieden

dizzy adj benommen

do, to do v tun p24

doctor n der Arzt m, die Ärztin f

doctor's office n die Arztpraxis f

dog n der Hund m

  service dog der Blindenhund

dollar n der Dollar m

dome n die Kuppel f

door n die Tür f

double adj Doppel-

  double bed das Doppelbett

  double vision doppelt sehen

down adj abwärts

download v herunterladen p24

downtown n das Stadtzentrum gn

dozen n das Dutzend gn

drain n der Abfluss m

drama n das Drama gn

drawing (work of art) n die Zeichnung f

dress (garment) n das Kleid gn

dress (general attire) n die Kleidung f

What's the dress code? Welche Kleidung ist vorgeschrieben?

dress v anziehen p24, 29

Should I dress up for that affair? Muss ich mich dafür herausputzen?

dressing (salad) n das Dressing gn

dried adj getrocknet / Trocken-

drink n das Getränk gn

I'd like a drink. Ich hätte gerne etwas zu trinken.

drink, to drink v trinken p24

drip v tropfen p20

drive v fahren p24

driver n der Fahrer m

driving range n die Driving Range f

drum n die Trommel f

dry adj trocken

This towel isn't dry. Dieses Handtuch ist nicht trocken.

dry, to dry v trocknen p20

I need to dry my clothes. Ich muss meine Kleidung trocknen.

dry cleaner n die chemische Reinigung f

dry cleaning n das chemische Reinigen gn

duck n die Ente f

Dutch n der Niederländer m, die Niederländerin f

duty-free adj zollfrei

duty-free shop n der Duty-free-Shop m

DVD n die DVD f

Do the rooms have DVD players? Gibt es auf den Zimmern einen DVD-Player?

Where can I rent DVDs or videos? Wo kann ich DVDs oder Videos ausleihen?

E

early adj früh

It's early. Es ist früh.

eat v essen p24

to eat out auswärts essen

economy n die Wirtschaft f

editor n der Redakteur m, die Redakteurin f

educator n der Erzieher m, die Erzieherin f

eight n acht

eighteen n Achtzehn

eighth n achter

eighty n achtzig

election n die Wahl f

electrical hookup n der Elektroanschluss m

elevator n der Aufzug m

eleven n elf

e-mail n die E-Mail f

May I have your e-mail address? Kann ich Ihre (formal) / deine (informal) E-Mail-Adresse haben?

e-mail message die E-Mail-Nachricht

e-mail, to send e-mail v eine
E-Mail senden p20

embassy n die Botschaft f

emergency n der Notfall m

emergency brake n die
Notbremse f

emergency exit n der
Notausgang m

employee n der Mitarbeiter
m, die Mitarbeiterin f

employer n der Arbeitgeber
m

engine n der Motor m

engineer n der Ingenieur m,
die Ingenieurin f

England n England

English n, adj englisch,
der Engländer m, die
Engländerin f

Do you speak English?
Sprechen Sie Englisch?

enjoy, to enjoy v genießen
p24

enter, to enter v betreten
p24

Do not enter. Kein Eingang.

enthusiastic adj begeistert

entrance n der Eingang m

envelope n das Kuvert gn

environment n die Umwelt f

escalator n die Rolltreppe f

espresso n der Espresso m

exchange rate n der
Wechselkurs m

**What is the exchange rate
for US / Canadian dollars?**
Welcher Wechselkurs gilt
für US-Dollar / kanadische
Dollar?

excuse (pardon) v
entschuldigen p20

Excuse me. Entschuldigung.

exhausted adj erschöpft

exhibit n die Ausstellung f

exit n der Ausgang m

not an exit kein Ausgang

exit v verlassen p24

expensive adj teuer

explain v erklären p20

express adj Express-

express check-in der
Express-Check-In

extra (additional) adj
zusätzlich

extra-large adj besonders
groß

eye n das Auge gn

eyebrow n die Augenbraue f

eyeglasses n die Brille f

eyelash n die Wimper f

F
fabric n der Stoff m

face n das Gesicht gn

faint v ohnmächtig werden
p24

fall (season) n der Herbst m

fall v fallen p24

family n die Familie f

fan n der Ventilator (blower)
/ der Fan (sport) m

far *weit*

> **How far is it to _____?** *Wie weit ist es nach / zur / zum _____?*

fare *n der Fahrpreis m*

fast *adj schnell*

fat *adj beleibt*

father *n der Vater m*

faucet *n der Wasserhahn m*

fault *n der Fehler m*

> **I'm at fault.** *Es war mein Fehler.*
> **It was his fault.** *Es war sein Fehler.*

fax *n das Fax gn*

February *n der Februar m*

fee *n die Gebühr f*

female *adj weiblich*

fiancé(e) *n der Verlobte m, die Verlobte f*

fifteen *adj fünfzehn*

fifth *adj fünfter*

fifty *adj fünfzig m*

find *v finden* **p24**

fine (for traffic violation) *n die Strafe f*

fine *gut*

> **I'm fine.** *Mir geht es gut.*

fire! *n Feuer! gn*

first *adj erste / erster / erstes*

fishing pole *n die Angelrute f*

fitness center *n das Fitness-Center gn*

fit (clothes) *v passen* **p20**

> **Does this look like it fits?** *Passt mir das?*

fitting room *n die Umkleidekabine f*

five *adj fünf*

flight *n der Flug m*

> **Where do domestic flights arrive / depart?** *Wo finde ich den Ankunftsbereich / Abflugbereich für Inlandsflüge?*
> **Where do international flights arrive / depart?** *Wo finde ich den Ankunftsbereich / Abflugbereich für Auslandsflüge?*
> **What time does this flight leave?** *Welche Abflugzeit hat dieser Flug?*

flight attendant *der Flugbegleiter (m) / die Flugbegleiterin (f)*

floor *n die Etage f*

> **ground floor** *das Erdgeschoß*
> **second floor** *das erste Stockwerk*
> **Note that in German, the second floor is called the first, the third is the second, etc.*

flower *n die Blume f*

flush (gambling) *n der Flush m*

flush, to flush *v spülen* **p20**

> **This toilet won't flush.** *Die Toilettenspülung funktioniert nicht.*

flute *n die Flöte f*

food *n das Essen gn*

ENGLISH–GERMAN

foot (body part, measurement) n (der) Fuß
forehead n die Stirn f
formula n die Formel f
  Do you sell infants' formula? Haben Sie Säuglingsanfangsnahrung?
forty adj vierzig
forward adj vorwärts
four adj vier
fourteen adj vierzehn
fourth adj vierter
  one-fourth ein Viertel
fragile adj zerbrechlich
freckle n die Sommersprosse f
French n der Franzose m, die Französin f
fresh adj frisch
Friday n der Freitag m
friend n der Freund m, die Freundin f
front adj Vorder-
  front desk die Rezeption
  front door die Vordertür
fruit n die Frucht f
fruit juice n der Fruchtsaft m
full, to be full (after a meal) adj satt
Full house! n Full House!
fuse n die Sicherung f

G

garlic n der Knoblauch m
gas n das Gas (for cooking) n, das Benzin (for cars) gn
  gas gauge die Tankanzeige
  out of gas kein Benzin mehr

gate (at airport) n das Gate gn
German n der/die Deutsche m/f
gift n das Geschenk gn
gin n der Gin m
girl n das Mädchen gn
girlfriend n die Freundin f
give, to give v geben p24
glass n das Glas gn
  Do you have it by the glass? Schenken Sie das als offenes Getränk aus?
  I'd like a glass please. Ich hätte gerne ein Glas.
glasses (eye) n die Brille f
  I need new glasses. Ich brauche eine neue Brille.
glove n der Handschuh m
go, to go v gehen p24
goal (sport) n das Tor gn
goalie n der Torwart m
gold adj Gold-
golf n das Golf(-spiel) gn
golf, to go golfing v Golf spielen p20
good adj gut
goodbye n der Abschied m
grade (school) n die Note f
gram n das Gramm gn
grandfather n der Großvater m
grandmother n die Großmutter f
grandparents n die Großeltern pl only
grape n die Traube f
gray adj grau

great *adj* großartig

Greek *n* der Grieche *m*, die Griechin *f*

Greek Orthodox *adj* griechisch-orthodox

green *adj* grün

groceries *n* die Lebensmittel *gn*

group *n* die Gruppe *f*

grow, to grow (get larger) *v* wachsen **p24**

  Where did you grow up? *Wo sind Sie (formal) / bist du (informal) aufgewachsen?*

guard *n* der Wachmann *m*

  security guard *der Sicherheitsbeamte*

guest *n* der Gast *m*

guide (of tours) *n* der Fremdenführer / die Fremdenführerin *m/f*

guide (publication) *n* der Reiseführer *m*

guide, to guide *v* führen **p20**

guided tour *n* die Fremdenführung *f*

guitar *n* die Gitarre *fs* Fitnessstudio *gn*

gynecologist *n* der Frauenarzt *m*

H

hair *n* das Haar *gn*, die Haare *pl*

haircut *n* der Haarschnitt *m*

  I need a haircut. *Ich muss mir die Haare schneiden lassen.*

  How much is a haircut? *Wie viel kostet ein Haarschnitt?*

hairdresser *n* der Frisör *m*, die Frisörin *f*

hair dryer *n* der Haartrockner *m*

half *n* die Hälfte *f*

  one-half *halb-*

hallway *n* der Gang *m*

hand *n* die Hand *f*

handicapped-accessible *adj* behindertengerecht

handle, to handle *v* handhaben **p20**

handsome *adj* gut aussehend

hangout (hot spot) *n* der Treff *m*

hang out (to relax) *v* entspannen / abhängen (slang) **p20, 24**

hang up (to end a phone call) *v* auflegen **p20**

hanger *n* der Kleiderbügel *m*

happy *adj* fröhlich

hard *adj* schwierig (difficult), hart (firm)

hat *n* der Hut *m*

have *v* haben **p24**

hazel *adj* nussbraun

headache *n* die Kopfschmerzen *pl*

headlight *n* der Scheinwerfer *m*

headphones *n* der Kopfhörer *m*

hear *v* hören **p20**

hearing-impaired *adj* hörgeschädigt

heart *n das Herz gn*
heart attack *n der Herzinfarkt m*
hello *n Hallo*
Help! *n Hilfe!*
help, to help *v helfen* **p24**
hen *n die Henne f*
her *adj ihr*
herb *n das Kraut gn*
here *n hier*
high *adj hoch*
highlights (hair) *n die Strähnchen pl*
highway *n die Autobahn f*
hike, to hike *v wandern* **p20**
him *pron ihm / ihn*
hip-hop *n Hiphop*
his *adj sein / seine*
historical *adj historisch*
history *n die Geschichte f*
hobby *n das Hobby gn*
hold, to hold *v halten* **p24**
to hold hands *Händchen halten*
Would you hold this for me? *Könnten Sie (formal) / Kannst du (informal) das bitte für mich halten?*
hold, to hold (to pause) *v innehalten* **p24**
Hold on a minute! *Einen Moment bitte!*
I'll hold. *Ich warte.*
hold, to hold (gambling) *v schieben*
holiday *n der Feiertag m*

home *n das Zuhause gn, das Haus gn*
homemaker *n die Hausfrau f*
horn *n die Hupe f*
horse *n das Pferd gn*
hostel *n die Jugendherberge f*
hot *adj heiß*
hot chocolate *n die heiße Schokolade f*
hotel *n das Hotel gn*
Do you have a list of local hotels? *Haben Sie eine Liste der örtlichen Hotels?*
hour *n die Stunde f*
hours (at museum) *n die Öffnungszeiten pl*
how *adv wie*
humid *adj feucht*
hundred *n Hundert*
hurry *v sich beeilen* **p29**
I'm in a hurry. *Ich bin in Eile.*
Hurry, please! *Beeilung, bitte!*
hurt, to hurt *v verletzen* **p20**
Ouch! That hurts! *Autsch! Das tut weh!*
husband *n der Ehemann m*

I
I *pron ich*
ice *n das Eis gn*
identification *n die Papiere pl*
indigestion *n die Verdauungsstörung f*
inexpensive *adj günstig*

infant n das Kleinkind gn
Are infants allowed? Sind Kleinkinder erlaubt?
information n die Information f
information booth n der Informationsstand m
insect repellent n das Insektenschutzmittel gn
inside drinnen
insult v beleidigen p20
insurance n die Versicherung f
intercourse (sexual) n der (Geschlechts-)Verkehr m
interest rate n der Zinssatz m
intermission n die Pause f
Internet n das Internet gn
High-speed Internet Hochgeschwindigkeits-Internet
Do you have Internet access? Haben Sie einen Internetanschluss?
Where can I find an Internet café? Wo finde ich ein Internetcafé?
interpreter n der Dolmetscher / die Dolmetscherin m/f
I need an interpreter. Ich benötige einen Dolmetscher.
introduce, to introduce v vorstellen p20

I'd like to introduce you to ____. Ich möchte Sie (formal) / dich (informal) mit _____ bekannt machen.
Ireland n Irland
Irish n der Ire m, die Irin f
is v See be (to be) p23
Italian n der Italiener m, die Italienerin f

J
jacket n die Jacke f
January n der Januar m
Japanese adj japanisch
jazz n der Jazz m
Jewish adj jüdisch
jog, to run v joggen p20
juice n der Saft m
June n der Juni m
July n der Juli m

K
keep, to keep v behalten p24
kid n das Kind gn
Are kids allowed? Sind Kinder erlaubt?
Do you have kids' programs? Haben Sie ein Programm für Kinder?
Do you have a kids' menu? Haben Sie ein Kindermenü?
kilo n das Kilo gn
kilometer n der Kilometer m
kind (type) n die Art f
What kind is it? Um welche Art handelt es sich?

kiss *n* der Kuss *m*
kitchen *n* die Küche *f*
know, to know (something)
v (etwas) wissen p27
know, to know (someone) *v*
(jemanden) kennen p26
kosher *adj* koscher

L
lactose-intolerant *adj* mit
Laktoseunverträglichkeit
land, to land *v* landen p20
landscape *n* die Landschaft *f*
language *n* die Sprache *f*
laptop *n* das Notebook *gn*
large *adj* groß
last, to last *v* dauern p20
last *adv* letzter
late *adj* spät
   Please don't be late. *Bitte
   pünktlich sein.*
later *adv* später
   See you later. *Bis später.*
laundry *n* die Wäscherei *f*
lavender *adj* Lavendel-
law *n* das Gesetz *gn*
lawyer *n* der Anwalt / die
Anwältin *m/f*
least *n* das Mindeste *gn*
least *adj* mindestens
leather *n* das Leder *gn*
leave, to leave (depart) *v*
abreisen p20
left *adj* links
   on the left *auf der linken
   Seite*

leg *n* das Bein *gn*
lemonade *n* die Limonade *f*
less *adj* weniger
lesson *n* die
Unterrichtseinheit *f*
license *n* die Lizenz *f*
   driver's license *der
   Führerschein*
life preserver *n* die
Schwimmweste *f*
light *n* (lamp) das Licht *gn*
light *n* (for cigarette) das
Feuer *gn*
   May I offer you a light?
   *Darf ich Ihnen (formal) /
   dir (informal) Feuer
   geben?*
lighter *n* (cigarette) das
Feuerzeug *m*
like, desire *v* gern haben p24
   I would like ____. *Ich hätte
   gerne ____.*
like, to like *v* gefallen p28
   I like this place. *Mir gefällt
   es hier.*
limo *n* die Limousine *f*
liquor *n* das alkoholische
Getränk *gn*
liter *n* der Liter *m*
little *adj* klein (size), gering
(amount)
live, to live *v* leben p20
   Where do you live? *Wo
   wohnen Sie? (formal) / Wo
   wohnst du? (informal)*

living n der Lebensunterhalt m

What do you do for a living? Was machen Sie (formal) / machst du (informal) beruflich?

local adj örtlich

lock n das Schloss gn

lock, to lock v abschließen **p24**

I can't lock the door. Die Tür lässt sich nicht abschließen.

I'm locked out. Ich bin ausgesperrt.

locker n der Spind m

storage locker der Aufbewahrungsschrank

locker room die Umkleide

long adv lang

For how long? Für wie lange?

long adj lang

look, to look v (to observe) umsehen **p24**

I'm just looking. Ich sehe mich nur um.

Look here! Schau her!

look, to look v (to appear) aussehen **p24**

How does this look? Wie sieht das aus?

look for, to look for (to search) v suchen **p20**

I'm looking for a porter. Ich suche einen Träger für mein Gepäck.

loose adj locker

lose, to lose v verlieren **p24**

I lost my passport. Ich habe meinen Pass verloren.

I lost my wallet. Ich habe meine Geldbörse verloren.

I'm lost. Ich habe mich verirrt.

lost See **lose** verlieren

loud adj laut

loudly adv laut

lounge n das Foyer gn

lounge, to lounge v faulenzen **p20**

love n die Liebe f

love, to love v lieben **p20**

to love (family) lieben

to love (a friend) mögen

to love (a lover) lieben

to make love miteinander schlafen

low adj niedrig

lunch n das Mittagessen gn

luggage n das Gepäck gn

Where do I report lost luggage? Wo kann ich verloren gegangenes Gepäck melden?

Where is the lost luggage claim? Wo finde ich die Ausgabe für verloren gegangenes Gepäck?

M

machine n die Maschine f

made of adj aus

magazine n die Zeitschrift f

maid (hotel) *n das Zimmermädchen gn*

maiden *adj Mädchen-*
That's my maiden name. *Das ist mein Mädchenname.*

mail *n die Post f*
air mail *die Luftpost*
registered mail *das Einschreiben*

mail *v versenden* p20

make, to make *v machen* p20

makeup *n das Make-up gn*

make up, to make up (apologize) *v wiedergutmachen* p20

make up, to make up (apply cosmetics) *v schminken* p20

male *n der Mann m*

male *adj männlich*

mall *n das Einkaufszentrum gn*

man *n der Mann m*

manager *n der Manager / die Managerin m/f*

manual (instruction booklet) *n das Handbuch gn*

many *adj viele*

map *n die Karte f*

March (month) *n der März m*

market *n der Markt m*
flea market *Flohmarkt*
open-air market *der Freiluftmarkt*

married *adj verheiratet*

marry, to marry *v heiraten* p20

massage, to massage *v massieren* p20

match (sport) *n das Spiel gn*

match *n das Streichholz gn*
book of matches *das Streichholzbriefchen*

match, to match *v passen* p20
Does this match my outfit? *Passt das zu meinem Outfit?*

May (month) *n der Mai m*

may *v aux dürfen* p24
May I? *Darf ich?*

meal *n die Mahlzeit f*

meat *n das Fleisch gn*

meatball *n die Frikadelle f*

medication *n das Medikament gn*

medium (size) *adj mittel*

medium rare (meat) *adj halb gar*

medium well (meat) *adj medium*

member *n das Mitglied gn*

menu *n die Speisekarte f*
May I see a menu? *Könnte ich bitte die Speisekarte bekommen?*
children's menu *Kindermenü*
diabetic menu *Diabetikermenü*
kosher menu *koscheres Menü*

metal detector *n der Metalldetektor m*

meter *n der Meter m*

middle *adj* Mittel-
midnight *n* Mitternacht *f*
military *n* das Militär *gn*
milk *n* die Milch *f*
  milk shake *der Milchshake*
milliliter *n* der Milliliter *m*
millimeter *n* der Millimeter *m*
minute *n* die Minute *f*
  in a minute *sofort*
miss, to miss (a flight) *v*
  verpassen **p20**
missing *adj* fehlend
mistake *n* der Fehler *m*
moderately priced *adj* der
  mittleren Preiskategorie
mole (facial feature) *n* das
  Muttermal *gn*
Monday *n* der Montag *m*
money *n* das Geld *gn*
  money transfer *die*
  Überweisung
month *n* der Monat *m*
morning *n* der Morgen *m*
  in the morning *morgens*
mosque *n* die Moschee *f*
mother *n* die Mutter *f*
mother, to mother *v*
  bemuttern **p20**
motorcycle *n* das Motorrad *gn*
mountain *n* der Berg *m*
  mountain climbing *das*
  Bergsteigen
mouse *n* die Maus *f*
mouth *n* der Mund *m*
move, to move *v* bewegen **p20**
movie *n* der Film *m*
much *n* viel

mug, to mug (someone) *v*
  überfallen **p24**
  mugged *adj* überfallen
museum *n* das Museum *gn*
music *n* die Musik *f*
  live music *die Livemusik*
musician *n* der Musiker *m*,
  die Musikerin *f*
muslim *adj* muslimisch
mustache *n* der Schnurrbart *m*
mystery (novel) *n* der
  Mystery-Roman *m*

N
name *n* der Name *m*
  My name is ___. *Ich heiße*
  ___.
  What's your name? *Wie*
  heißen Sie? (formal) / Wie
  heißt du? (informal)
napkin *n* die Serviette *f*
narrow *adj* schmal
nationality *n* die Nationalität *f*
nausea *n* die Übelkeit *f*
near *adj* nähe
nearby *adj* in der Nähe
neat (tidy) *adj* ordentlich
need, to need *v* benötigen
  p20
neighbor *n* der Nachbar *m*,
  die Nachbarin *f*
nephew *n* der Neffe *m*
network *n* das Netzwerk *gn*
new *adj* neu
newspaper *n* die Zeitung *f*
newsstand *n* der
  Zeitungsstand *m*

ENGLISH—GERMAN

New Zealand n Neuseeland
New Zealander adj der Neuseeländer m, die Neuseeländerin f
next prep neben
  next to neben
  the next station der nächste Halt
nice adj nett
niece n die Nichte f
night n die Nacht f
  at night nachts
  per night pro Übernachtung
nightclub n der Nachtclub m
nine adj neun
nineteen adj neunzehn
ninety adj neunzig
ninth adj neunter
no adv nein
noisy adj laut
none n keiner, keine, kein
nonsmoking adj Nichtraucher-
  nonsmoking area der Nichtraucherbereich
  nonsmoking room das Nichtraucherzimmer
noon n der Mittag m
Norwegian n der Norweger m, die Norwegerin f
nose n die Nase f
novel n der Roman m
November n der November m
now adv jetzt
number n die Nummer f

  Which room number? Welche Zimmernummer?
  May I have your phone number? Kann ich bitte Ihre Telefonnummer haben?
nurse n der Krankenpfleger m, die Krankenpflegerin f
nurse v stillen p20
  Do you have a place where I can nurse? Haben Sie einen Raum zum Stillen?
nursery n die Kinderkrippe f
  Do you have a nursery? Haben Sie eine Kinderkrippe?
nut n die Nuss f

O
o'clock adv Uhr
  two o'clock zwei Uhr
October n der Oktober m
offer, to offer v anbieten p24
officer n der Polizist m, die Polizistin f
oil n das Öl gn
okay adv OK, in Ordnung
old adj alt
olive n die Olive f
one adj ein / eine
one way (traffic sign) adj Einbahnstraße
open (business) adj geöffnet
  Are you open? Haben Sie geöffnet?
opera n die Oper f

operator (phone) n die Vermittlung f

optometrist n der Optiker m, die Optikerin f

orange (color) adj orange

orange juice n der Orangensaft m

order, to order (demand) v befehlen p24

order, to order (request) v bestellen p20

organic adj Bio-

Ouch! interj Au!

outside n draußen

overcooked adj zerkocht

overheat, to overheat v überhitzen p20

The car overheated. Das Auto hat sich überhitzt.

overflowing adv überlaufend

oxygen tank n die Sauerstoffflasche f

P

package n das Paket gn

pacifier n der Schnuller m

page, to page (someone) v anpiepen p20

paint, to paint v streichen p24

painting n das Gemälde gn

pale adj blass

paper n das Papier gn

parade n der Umzug m

parent n der Elternteil m

park n der Park m

park, to park v parken p20

no parking das Parkverbot

parking fee die Parkgebühr

parking garage das Parkhaus

partner n der Partner m, die Partnerin f

party n die Partei f

party n die Party f

political party die Partei

pass, to pass v passen p20

I'll pass. Ich passe.

passenger n der Passagier m

passport n der Ausweis m

I've lost my passport. Ich habe meinen Ausweis verloren.

pay, to pay v bezahlen p20

peanut n die Erdnuss f

pedestrian adj Fußgänger-

pediatrician n der Kinderarzt m, die Kinderärztin f

Can you recommend a pediatrician? Können Sie mir einen Kinderarzt empfehlen?

permit n die Genehmigung f

Do we need a permit? Benötigen wir eine Genehmigung?

permit, to permit v erlauben p20

phone n das Telefon gn

May I have your phone number? Kann ich bitte Ihre Telefonnummer haben?

Where can I find a public phone? *Wo finde ich eine Telefonzelle?*
phone operator *die Vermittlung*
Do you sell prepaid phones? *Verkaufen Sie Prepaid-Telefone?*
phone *adj Telefon-*
Do you have a phone directory? *Haben Sie ein Telefonbuch?*
phone call *n der Telefonanruf m*
I need to make a collect phone call. *Ich möchte ein R-Gespräch führen.*
an international phone call *ein Auslandsgespräch*
photocopy, to photocopy *v (foto-)kopieren* **p20**
piano *n das Klavier gn*
pillow *n das Kissen gn*
down pillow *das Daunenkissen*
pink *adj rosa*
pizza *n die Pizza f*
place, to place *v platzieren* **p20**
plastic *n der Kunststoff m*
play *n das Theaterstück gn*
play, to play (a game) *v spielen* **p20**
play, to play (an instrument) *v spielen* **p20**
playground *n der Spielplatz m*

Do you have a playground? *Haben Sie einen Spielplatz?*
please (polite entreaty) *adv bitte*
please, to be pleasing to *v gefallen* **p28**
It's a pleasure. *Freut mich.*
plug *n der Stecker m*
plug, to plug *v einstecken* **p20**
point, to point *v zeigen, weisen* **p20, 24**
Would you point me in the direction of ____? *Wie komme ich zu / zum / zur ____?*
poison *n das Gift gn* **police** *n die Polizei f*
police station *n die Polizeiwache f*
Polish *n der Pole m, die Polin f*
pool *n der (Swimming-)Pool m*
pool (the game) *n das Poolbillard gn*
pop music *n die Popmusik f*
popular *adj beliebt*
port (beverage) *n der Portwein m*
port (for ship) *n der Hafen m*
porter *n der Portier m*
portion *n die Portion f*
portrait *n das Porträt gn*

Portuguese *n der Portugiese m, die Portugiesin f*

postcard *n die Postkarte f*

post office *n das Postamt gn*

> **Where is the post office?**
> *Wo befindet sich das Postamt?*

poultry *n das Geflügel gn*

pound *n das Pfund gn*

prefer, to prefer *v bevorzugen* **p20**

pregnant *adj schwanger*

prepared *adj vorbereitet*

prescription *n das Rezept gn*

price *n der Preis m*

print, to print *v drucken* **p20**

private berth / cabin *n eine eigene Kabine f*

problem *n das Problem gn*

process, to process *v verarbeiten* **p20**

product *n das Produkt gn*

professional *adj professionell*

program *n das Programm gn*

> **May I have a program?**
> *Geben Sie mir bitte ein Programm.*

Protestant *n der Protestant m die Protestantin f*

publisher *n der Verleger m die Verlegerin f*

puff *n der Hauch / Zug m*

pull, to pull *v ziehen* **p24**

purple *adj violett*

purse *n die Handtasche f*

push, to push *v drücken* **p20**

put, to put *v setzen, stellen, legen* **p20**

Q

quarter *adj Viertel-*

one-quarter *Viertel-*

quiet *adj ruhig*

R

rabbit *n der Hase m*

radio *n das Radio gn*

> **satellite radio** *das Satellitenradio*

rain, to rain *v regnen* **p20**

> **Is it supposed to rain?** *Soll es regnen?*

rainy *adj regnerisch*

> **It's rainy.** *Es ist regnerisch.*

ramp (wheelchair) *n die Rampe (Rollstuhl) f*

rare (meat) *adj blutig*

rate (for car rental, hotel) *n der Preis m*

> **What's the rate per day?**
> *Wie hoch ist der Preis pro Tag?*
> **What's the rate per week?**
> *Wie hoch ist der Preis pro Woche?*

rate plan (cell phone) *n die Tariftabelle f*

rather *adv lieber*

read, to read *v lesen* **p24**

really *adv wirklich*

receipt *n die Quittung f*

receive, to receive *v erhalten* **p23**

recommend, to recommend *v empfehlen* **p24**

red *adj rot*

redhead n der Rothaarige m, die Rothaarige f

reef n das Riff gn

refill to refill (of beverage) v nachschenken

refill (of prescription) n die erneute Einlösung f

reggae adj Reggae-

relative (family) n der / die Verwandte m/f

remove, to remove v entfernen p20

rent, to rent v mieten p20

I'd like to rent a car. Ich möchte ein Auto mieten.

repeat, to repeat v wiederholen p20

Would you please repeat that? Könnten Sie das bitte wiederholen?

reservation n die Reservierung f

I'd like to make a reservation for ___. Ich möchte eine Reservierung für ___. See p7 for numbers.

restaurant n das Restaurant gn

Where can I find a good restaurant? Wo finde ich ein gutes Restaurant?

restroom n die Toilette f

Do you have a public restroom? Gibt es hier eine öffentliche Toilette?

return, to return (to a place) v zurückkehren p20

return, to return (something to a store) v zurückgeben p24

ride, to ride v fahren (vehicle) / reiten (horse) p23

right adj rechts

___ **is on the right.** ___ befindet sich auf der rechten Seite.

Turn right at the corner. Biegen Sie an der Ecke nach rechts ab.

rights n die Rechte gn, **civil rights** die Bürgerrechte

river n der Fluss m

road n die Straße f

road closed sign n das Straßensperrschild gn

rob, to rob v ausrauben p20

I've been robbed. Ich wurde ausgeraubt.

rock and roll n Rock'n'Roll m

rock climbing n das Felsenklettern gn

rocks (ice) n die Würfel f, pl

I'd like it on the rocks. Ich hätte das gerne auf Eis.

romance (novel) n der Liebesroman m

romantic adj romantisch

room (hotel) n das Zimmer gn

room for one / two Einzelzimmer / Doppelzimmer

room service der Zimmerservice

rose n die Rose f

royal flush *n der Royal Flush m*
rum *n der Rum m*
run, to run *v rennen* **p24**
Russian *n der Russe m, die Russin f*

S

sad *adj traurig*
safe (for storing valuables) *n der Tresor m*
  Do the rooms have safes? *Verfügen die Zimmer über einen Tresor?*
safe (secure) *adj sicher*
  Is this area safe? *Ist dieses Gebiet sicher?*
sail *n das Segel gn*
sail, to sail *v ablegen (start) / segeln (on a sailboat)* **p20**
  When do we sail? *Wann legen wir ab?*
salad *n der Salat m*
salesperson *n der Verkäufer m, die Verkäuferin f*
salt *n das Salz gn*
  Is that low-salt? *Enthält das wenig Salz?*
satellite *n der Satellit m*
  satellite radio *das Satellitenradio*
  satellite tracking *das Navigationssystem*
Saturday *n der Sonntag m*
sauce *n die Soße f*
say, to say *v sagen* **p20**
scan, to scan *v (document) scannen* **p20**

schedule *n der Fahrplan m*
school *n die Schule f*
scooter *n der Roller m*
score *n der Spielstand f*
Scottish *adj schottisch*
scratched *adj zerkratzt*
  scratched surface *die zerkratzte Oberfläche*
scuba dive, to scuba dive *v tauchen (mit Atemgerät)* **p20**
sculpture *n die Skulptur f*
seafood *n die Meeresfrüchte f, pl*
search *n die Suche f*
  hand search *das Abtasten*
search, to search *v suchen* **p20**
seasick *adj seekrank*
  I am seasick. *Ich bin seekrank.*
  seasickness pill *n die Tablette gegen Seekrankheit f*
seat *n der Platz m*
  child seat *der Kindersitz*
second *adj zweiter*
security *n die Sicherheit f*
  security checkpoint *die Sicherheitsschleuse*
  security guard *der Sicherheitsbeamte*
sedan *n die Limousine f*
see, to see *v sehen* **p24**
  May I see it? *Dürfte ich das mal sehen?*
self-serve *adj Selbstbedienungs-*

sell, to sell *v verkaufen* **p20**

seltzer *n das Selters gn*

send, to send *v versenden* **p20**

separated (marital status) *adj getrennt lebend*

September *n der September m*

serve, to serve *v servieren* **p20**

service *n der Service m*

services (religious) *n der Gottesdienst m*

service charge *n die Servicegebühr f*

seven *adj sieben*

seventy *adj siebzig*

seventeen *adj siebzehn*

seventh *adj siebter*

sew, to sew *v nähen* **p20**

sex (gender) *n das Geschlecht gn*

sex, to have (intercourse) *v Sex haben* **p24**

shallow *adj seicht*

sheet (bed linen) *n das Bettlaken gn*

shellfish *n das Schalentier gn*

ship *n das Schiff gn*

ship, to ship *v versenden* **p20**

How much to ship this to
_____? *Wie viel kostet der Versand hiervon nach _____?*

shipwreck *n das Schiffswrack gn*

shirt *n das Hemd gn*

shoe *n der Schuh m*

shop *n das Geschäft gn*

shop *v einkaufen* **p20**

I'm shopping for
mens' clothes. *Ich bin auf der Suche nach Herrenbekleidung.*
I'm shopping for
womens' clothes. *Ich bin auf der Suche nach Damenbekleidung.*
I'm shopping for
childrens' clothes. *Ich bin auf der Suche nach Kinderbekleidung.*

short *adj kurz*

shorts *n die kurze Hose f*

shot (liquor) *n der Kurze m*

shout *v rufen* **p24**

show (performance) *n die Vorstellung f*

What time is the show?
Wann beginnt die Vorstellung?

show, to show *v zeigen* **p20**

Would you show me?
Könnten Sie mir das bitte zeigen?

shower *n die Dusche f*

Does it have a shower? *Gibt es eine Dusche?*

shower, to shower *v duschen* **p20, 29**

shrimp *n die Garnele f*

shuttle bus *n der Pendelbus m*

sick *adj krank*
  I feel sick. *Mir ist schlecht.*
side *n die Beilage f*
  on the side (e.g., salad dressing) *dazu*
sidewalk *n der Gehweg m*
sightseeing *n das Sightseeing gn*
sightseeing bus *n der Sightseeing-Bus m*
sign, to sign *v unterschreiben* **p24**
  Where do I sign? *Wo muss ich unterschreiben?*
silk *n die Seide f*
silver *adj Silber-*
sing, to sing *v singen* **p24**
single (unmarried) *adj ledig*
  Are you single? *Sind Sie ledig?*
single (one) *adj Einzel-*
  single bed *das Einzelbett*
sink *n das Waschbecken gn*
sister *n die Schwester f*
sit, to sit *v sitzen*
six *adj sechs*
sixteen *adj sechzehn*
sixty *adj sechzig*
size (clothing, shoes) *n die Kleidergröße f*
skin *n die Haut f*
sleeping berth *n das Schlafabteil gn*
slow *adj langsam*
slow, to slow *v verlangsamen* **p20**

Slow down! *Fahren Sie bitte langsamer.*
slow(ly) *adv langsam*
  Speak more slowly. *Sprechen Sie bitte etwas langsamer.*
small *adj klein*
smell, to smell *v riechen*
smoke, to smoke *v rauchen* **p20**
smoking *n das Rauchen gn*
  smoking area *Raucherbereich*
  No Smoking *Rauchen verboten*
snack *n der Imbiss m*
Snake eyes! *n Schlangenaugen!*
snorkel *n der Schnorchel m*
sock *n die Socke f*
soda *n die Limonade f*
  diet soda *die Diätlimonade*
soft *adj weich*
software *n die Software f*
sold out *adj ausverkauft*
some *adj etwas (uncountable) / einige (countable)*
someone *n jemand*
something *n etwas m*
son *n der Sohn m*
song *n das Lied gn*
soon *adv bald*
sorry *adj leid*
  I'm sorry. *Tut mir leid.*
spa *n das Heilbad m*
Spain *n Spanien*

Spanish *n der Spanier m, die Spanierin f*

spare tire *n der Reservereifen m*

speak, to speak *v sprechen* p24

> **Do you speak English?** *Sprechen Sie Englisch?*
>
> **Would you speak louder, please?** *Könnten Sie bitte etwas lauter sprechen?*
>
> **Would you speak slower, please?** *Könnten Sie bitte etwas langsamer sprechen?*

special (featured meal) *n die Spezialität f*

specify, to specify *v angeben* p24

speed limit *n die Geschwindigkeitsbegrenzung f*

> **What's the speed limit?** *Welche Geschwindigkeitsbegrenzung gilt hier?*

speedometer *n der Tacho m*

spell, to spell *v buchstabieren* p20

> **How do you spell that?** *Wie schreibt sich das?*

spice *n das Gewürz gn*

spill, to spill *v verschütten* p20

split (gambling) *n der Split m*

sports *n der Sport m*

spring (season) *n der Frühling m*

stadium *n das Stadion gn*

staff (employees) *n die Mitarbeiter pl*

stamp (postage) *n die Briefmarke f*

stair *n die Stufe f*

> **Where are the stairs?** *Wo finde ich das Treppenhaus?*
>
> **Are there many stairs?** *Gibt es viele Stufen?*

stand, to stand *v stehen* p24

start, to start (commence) *v beginnen*

start, to start (a car) *v anlassen* p24

state *n der Staat (gov.) / der Status (status) m*

station *n der Bahnhof m*

> **Where is the nearest_____?** *Wo ist die nächste _____?*
>
> **gas station** *Tankstelle*
> **bus station** *Bushaltestelle*
> **subway station** *U-Bahn-Haltestelle*
>
> **Where is the nearest train station?** *Wo ist der nächste Bahnhof?*

stay, to stay *v Aufenthalt, bleiben* p24

> **We'll be staying for ____ nights.** *Wir bleiben ____ Nächte.* See numbers, p7.

steakhouse *n das Steakhaus gn*

steal, to steal *v stehlen*

stolen *adj gestohlen*

stop *n die Haltestelle f*

Is this my stop? *Ist das hier meine Haltestelle?*

I missed my stop. *Ich habe meine Haltestelle verpasst.*

stop, to stop *v anhalten*

Please stop. *Halten Sie bitte an.*

STOP (traffic sign) *STOP*

Stop, thief! *Haltet den Dieb!*

store *n das Lager gn*

straight *adj gerade (street) / glatt (hair)*

straight ahead *geradeaus*

straight (drink) *pur*

Go straight. *Gehen Sie geradeaus*

straight (gambling) *n der Straight m*

street *n die Straße f*

across the street *gegenüber*

down the street *am Ende der Straße*

Which street? *Welche Straße?*

How many more streets? *Wie viele Straßen noch?*

stressed *adj gestresst*

striped *adj gestreift*

stroller *n der Kinderwagen m*

Do you rent baby strollers? *Vermieten Sie Kinderwagen?*

substitution *n der Ersatz m*

subway *n die U-Bahn f*

subway line *die U-Bahn-Linie*

subway station *die U-Bahn-Haltestelle*

Which subway do I take for ____? *Mit welcher U-Bahn komme ich zu / zur / zum ____?*

subtitle *n die Untertitel m, pl*

suitcase *n der Koffer m*

suite *n die Suite f*

summer *n der Sommer m*

sun *n die Sonne f*

sunburn *n der Sonnenbrand m*

I have a bad sunburn. *Ich habe einen starken Sonnenbrand.*

Sunday *n der Sonntag m*

sunglasses *n die Sonnenbrille f*

sunny *adj sonnig*

It's sunny out. *Draußen scheint die Sonne.*

sunroof *n das Sonnendach gn*

sunscreen *n die Sonnencreme f*

Do you have sunscreen SPF ____? *Haben Sie Sonnencreme mit Lichtschutzfaktor ____?* See numbers p7.

supermarket *n der Supermarkt m*

surf *v surfen p20*

surfboard *n das Surfbrett gn*

suspiciously *adv verdächtig*

swallow, to swallow *v schlucken p20*

sweater *n der Pullover m*

ENGLISH—GERMAN

Swedish *n der* Schwede *m*, die Schwedin *f*

swim, to swim *v* schwimmen **p24**

> Can one swim here? *Kann man hier schwimmen?*

swimsuit *n der* Badeanzug *m*

swim trunks *n die* Badehose *f*

Swiss *n der* Schweizer *m*, die Schweizerin *f*

symphony *n die* Symphonie *f*

T

table *n der* Tisch *m*

> table for two *der* Tisch *für zwei*

tailor *n der* Schneider *m* die Schneiderin *f*

> Can you recommend a good tailor? *Können Sie mir einen guten Schneider empfehlen?*

take, to take *v* nehmen, bringen **p24**

> Take me to the station. *Bringen Sie mich bitte zum Bahnhof.*

> How much to take me to _____? *Wieviel kostet die Fahrt zu / zur / zum _____?*

takeout menu *n das* Essen zum Mitnehmen *gn*

talk, to talk *v* sprechen **p24**

tall *adj* groß

tanned *adj* gebräunt

taste (flavor) *n der* Geschmack *m*

taste *n* (discernment) *der* Geschmack *m*

taste, to taste *v* schmecken **p20**

tax *n die* Steuer *f*

> value-added tax (VAT) *Mehrwertsteuer (MwSt.)*

taxi *n das* Taxi *gn*

> Taxi! *Taxi!*

> Would you call me a taxi? *Könnten Sie mir bitte ein Taxi rufen?*

tea *n der* Tee *m*

team *n das* Team *gn*

Techno *n der* Techno *m*

television *n der* Fernseher *m*

temple *n der* Tempel *m*

ten *adj* zehn

tennis *n das* Tennis *gn*

> tennis court *der* Tennisplatz

tent *n das* Zelt *gn*

tenth *adj* zehnter

terminal *n* (airport) *das* Terminal *gn*

thank you *danke*

that (near) *adj* diese / dieser / dieses

that (far away) *adj* jene / jener / jenes

theater *n das* Theater *gn*

them (m/f) *sie*

there (demonstrative) *adv* da (nearby), dort (far)

> Is / Are there _____ over there? *Tatsächlich _____ dort drüben?*

these *adj* diese

thick adj dick

thin adj dünn

third adj dritter

thirteen adj dreizehn

thirty adj dreißig

this adj diese / dieser / dieses

those jene / jener / jenes adj

thousand Eintausend

three drei

Thursday n der Donnerstag m

thus (therefore) also adv

ticket n das Ticket gn

 ticket counter der Kartenschalter

 one-way ticket das einfache Ticket

 round-trip ticket das Hin- und Rückreiseticket

tight adj eng

time n die Zeit f

 Is it on time? Ist er (train, bus) pünktlich? / Ist es (plane, ship) pünktlich?

 At what time? Um wie viel Uhr?

 What time is it? Wie spät ist es?

timetable n (train) der Fahrplan m

tip (gratuity) das Trinkgeld gn

tire n der Reifen m

 I have a flat tire. Ich habe einen platten Reifen.

tired adj müde

today n heute

today's special n das Menü gn

toilet n die Toilette f

 The toilet is overflowing. Die Toilette läuft über.

 The toilet is backed up. Die Toilette ist verstopft.

toilet paper n das Toilettenpapier gn

 You're out of toilet paper. Sie haben kein Toilettenpapier mehr.

toiletries n die Hygieneartikel m, pl

toll n die Gebühr f

tomorrow n morgen

ton n die Tonne f

too (excessively) adv zu

too (also) adv auch

tooth n der Zahn m

 I lost my tooth. Ich habe einen Zahn verloren.

toothache n die Zahnschmerzen m, pl

 I have a toothache. Ich habe Zahnschmerzen.

total n die Gesamtsumme f

 What is the total? Wie hoch ist die Gesamtsumme?

tour n der Ausflug m

 Are guided tours available? Werden Fremdenführungen angeboten?

 Are audio tours available? Werden Audioführungen angeboten?

towel n das Handtuch gn

May we have more towels? *Könnten wir bitte mehr Handtücher bekommen?*

toy n *das Spielzeug* gn

toy store n *das Spielwarengeschäft* gn

Do you have any toys for the children? *Haben Sie Kinderspielzeug?*

traffic n *der Verkehr* m

How's traffic? *Wie ist der Verkehr?*

traffic rules *die Verkehrsregeln*

trail n *der Weg* m

Are there trails? *Gibt es dort Wege?*

train n *der Zug* m

express train *der Expresszug*

local train *der Nahverkehrszug*

Does the train go to ____? *Fährt der Zug nach / zum _____?*

May I have a train schedule? *Könnte ich bitte einen Zugfahrplan bekommen?*

Where is the train station? *Wo finde ich den Bahnhof?*

train, to train v *trainieren* p20

transfer, to transfer v *überweisen* p24

I need to transfer funds. *Ich möchte eine Überweisung tätigen.*

transmission n *das Getriebe* gn

automatic transmission *das Automatikgetriebe*

standard transmission *das Schaltgetriebe*

travel, to travel v *reisen* p20

travelers' check n *der Reisescheck* m

Do you cash travelers' checks? *Kann ich mir hier Reiseschecks auszahlen lassen?*

trillion n *die Billion* f

trim, to trim (hair) v *schneiden* p24

trip n *die Reise* f

triple adj *dreifach*

trumpet n *die Trompete* f

trunk n *der Koffer* m (luggage) *der Kofferraum* m (car)

try, to try (attempt) v *versuchen* p20, *ausprobieren* p20

try, to try on (clothing) v *anprobieren* p20

try, to try (food) v *probieren*

Tuesday n *der Dienstag* m

Turkish n *der Türke* m, *die Türkin* f

turn, to turn v *abbiegen* (car) / *sich wenden* (person) p24

to turn left / right *links / rechts abbiegen*

to turn off / on *ausschalten / einschalten* **p20**

twelve *adj zwölf*

twenty *adj zwanzig*

twine *n die Paketschnur f*

two *adj zwei*

U

umbrella *n der Regenschirm m*

uncle *n der Onkel m*

undercooked *adj noch nicht durch*

understand, to understand *v verstehen* **p24**

I don't understand. *Ich verstehe nicht.*

Do you understand? *Verstanden?*

underwear *n die Unterwäsche f*

university *n die Universität f*

up *adv aufwärts*

update, to update *v aktualisieren* **p20**

upgrade *n die höhere Kategorie f*

upload, to upload *v hochladen* **p24**

upscale *adj gehoben*

us *pron uns*

USB port *n der USB-Anschluss m*

use, to use *v verwenden* **p20**

V

vacation *n der Urlaub m*

on vacation *im Urlaub*

to go on vacation *in Urlaub gehen*

vacancy *n das freie Zimmer (hotel) gn*

van *n der Kleinbus m, der Van m*

VCR *n der Videorekorder m*

Do the rooms have VCRs? *Gibt es auf den Zimmern einen Videorekorder?*

vegetable *n das Gemüse gn*

vegetarian *n der Vegetarier m, die Vegetarierin f*

vending machine *n der Automat m*

version *n die Version f*

very *sehr*

video *n das Video gn*

Where can I rent videos or DVDs? *Wo kann ich Videos oder DVDs ausleihen?*

view *n die Aussicht f*

beach view *die Aussicht auf den Strand*

city view *die Aussicht auf die Stadt*

vineyard *n das Weingut gn*

vinyl *n das Vinyl gn*

violin *n die Geige f*

visa *n das Visum gn*

Do I need a visa? *Benötige ich ein Visum?*

vision *n die Sicht f*

visit, to visit *v besuchen* **p20**

visually-impaired *adj sehbehindert*

vodka *n der Wodka m*
voucher *n der Gutschein m*

W

wait, to wait *v warten* **p20**
　Please wait. *Warten Sie bitte.*
　How long is the wait? *Wie lange muss ich warten? (sing.) / Wie lange müssen wir warten? (pl.)*
waiter *n der Kellner m, die Kellnerin f*
waiting area *n der Wartebereich m*
wake-up call *n der Weckruf m*
wallet *n die Geldbörse f*
　I lost my wallet. *Ich habe meine Geldbörse verloren.*
　Someone stole my wallet. *Meine Geldbörse wurde gestohlen.*
walk, to walk *v gehen* **p24**
walker (ambulatory device) *n die Gehhilfe f*
walkway *n der Fußgängerweg m*
　moving walkway *der Fahrsteig*
want, to want *v wollen* **p25**
war *n der Krieg m*
warm *adj warm*
watch, to watch *v zusehen* **p24**
water *n das Wasser gn*

　Is the water potable? *Ist das Wasser trinkbar?*
　Is there running water? *Gibt es fließend Wasser?*
wave, to wave *v winken* **p20**
waxing *n das Enthaaren (mit Wachs) gn*
wear, to wear *v tragen* **p24**
weather forecast *n der Wetterbericht m*
Wednesday *n der Mittwoch m*
week *n die Woche f*
　this week *diese Woche*
　last week *letzte Woche*
　next week *nächste Woche*
weigh *v wiegen* **p24**
　I weigh ____. *Ich wiege ____.*
　It weighs ____. *Das wiegt ____. See p7 for numbers.*
weights *n die Gewichte gn, pl*
welcome *adv willkommen*
　You're welcome. *Gern geschehen.*
well *adv gut*
　well done (meat) *gut durch*
　well done (task) *gut gemacht*
　I don't feel well. *Ich fühle mich nicht gut.*
western *adj westlich, abendländisch*
whale *n der Wal m*
what *adv welche / welcher / welches*

What sort of ___? *Welche Art von ___?*

What time is ___? *Wann gibt es ___?*

See p3 for questions.

wheelchair *n der Rollstuhl m*

wheelchair access *der Zugang per Rollstuhl*

wheelchair ramp *die Rampe für Rollstuhlfahrer*

power wheelchair *der elektrisch betriebene Rollstuhl*

wheeled (luggage) *adj mit Rollen*

when *adv wann*

See p3 for questions.

where *adv wo*

Where is ___? *Wo ist ___?*

See p3 for questions.

which *adv welche / welcher / welches*

Which one? *Welche / Welcher / Welches?*

See p3 for questions.

white *adj weiß*

who *adv wer*

whose *adj wessen / dessen*

wide *adj breit*

widow, widower *n die Witwe f, der Witwer m*

wife *n die Ehefrau f*

wi-fi *n das Wi-Fi gn*

window *n das Fenster gn, der Schalter m*

drop-off window *Abgabeschalter*

pickup window *Abholschalter*

windshield *n die Frontscheibe f*

windshield wiper *n der Scheibenwischer m*

windy *adj windig*

wine *n der Wein m*

winter *n der Winter m*

wiper *n der Wischer m*

with *prep mit*

withdraw *v abheben p24*

I need to withdraw money. *Ich möchte Geld abheben.*

without *prep ohne*

woman *n die Frau f*

work, to work *v arbeiten (person), funktionieren (device) p20*

___ doesn't work. *___ funktioniert nicht.*

workout *n das Training m*

worse *schlimmer*

worst *am schlimmsten*

write, to write *v schreiben p24*

Would you write that down for me? *Könnten Sie mir das bitte aufschreiben?*

writer *n der Autor m*

X

x-ray machine *n das Röntgengerät gn*

Y

yellow *adj gelb*
yes *adv ja*
yesterday *n gestern*
  the day before yesterday
   vorgestern
yield sign *n das Schild*
  „Vorfahrt gewähren" gn
you *pron Sie / du / ihr*
  you (singular, informal) *du*
  you (singular, formal) *Sie*
  you (plural informal) *ihr*
  you (plural formal) *Sie*
your, yours *adj Ihr / Ihre*
  (formal); dein / deine
  (informal)
young *adj jung*

Z

zoo *n der Zoo m*

A

abbiegen (car) *to turn* v **p24**

abbiegen *to turn* v **p24**

> **Biegen Sie links / rechts ab.** *Turn left / right.*

abbuchen *to charge (money)* v **p20**

das Abendessen gn *dinner* n

der Abfluss m *drain* n

abgelehnt *declined* adj

> **Ihre Kreditkarte wurde abgelehnt.** *Your credit card was declined.*

abheben *to withdraw* v **p24**

die Abhebung f *withdrawal* n

ablegen *to sail* v **p20**

> **Wann legen wir ab?** *When do we sail?*

die Abreise f *departure* n

abreisen *to leave (depart)* v **p20**

abschließen *to lock* v **p22**

abwärts *down* adv

acht *eight* adj

achter *eighth* adj

> **drei Achtel** *three eighths*

achtzehn *eighteen* adj

achtzig *eighty* adj

der Adapterstecker m *adapter plug* n

der Adler m *eagle* n

die Adresse f *address* n

> **Wie lautet die Adresse?** *What's the address?*

Afro- *afro* adj

afroamerikanisch *African American* adj

die Agentur / das Büro f/gn *agency* n

der Agnostiker m, **die Agnostikerin** f *agnostic* n

die Akne f *acne* n

der Aktenkoffer m *briefcase* n

aktualisieren *to update* v **p20**

aktuell *current* adj

akzeptieren *to accept* v **p20**

> **Wir akzeptieren Kreditkarten.** *Credit cards accepted.*

der Alkohol m *alcohol* n

die Allergie f *allergy* n

allergisch *allergic* adj

> **Ich bin allergisch gegen ____.** *I'm allergic to ____.*

alles / irgend etwas *anything* n

also *thus, therefore* adv

alt *old* adj

das Alter gn *age* n

> **Wie alt sind Sie? (formal) / Wie alt bist du? (informal)** *What's your age?*

das Aluminium gn *aluminum* n

am besten *best. See* **gut**

am schlimmsten *worst. See* **schlecht**

am wenigsten *least. See* **wenig**

der Amerikaner m, **die Amerikanerin** f *American* n

amerikanisch *American adj*

an Bord *on board*

anbieten *to offer v* **p24**

anders *different (other) adj*

angeben *to specify v* **p24**

die Angelegenheit *f matter, affair*

Kümmern Sie sich um Ihre eigenen Angelegenheiten. *Mind your own business.*

die Angelrute *f fishing pole n*

anhalten *to stop v* **p24**

Halten Sie bitte an. *Please stop.*

ankommen *to arrive v* **p24**

die Ankunft *f arrival n*

anlassen *to start (a car) v*

anpiepen *to page (someone) v* **p20**

anrufen *to call (to phone) v* **p24**

Antibaby- *birth control adj*

Ich habe keine Antibabypillen mehr. *I'm out of birth control pills.*

das Antibiotikum *gn antibiotic n*

das Antihistamin *gn antihistamine n*

die Antwort *f answer n*

Ich benötige eine Antwort. *I need an answer.*

antworten (auf eine Frage) *to answer (respond to a question) v* **p20**

Antworten Sie mir bitte. *Answer me, please.*

der Anwalt / die Anwältin *m/f lawyer n*

anziehen *to dress v* **p24 p29**

der April *m April n*

arbeiten (person) *to work v* **p20**

der Arbeitgeber *m employer n*

die Art *f kind (sort, type) n*

Um welche Art handelt es sich? *What kind is it?*

der Arzt *m / die Ärztin f doctor n*

die Arztpraxis *f doctor's office n*

asiatisch *Asian adj*

das Aspirin *gn aspirin n*

das Asthma *gn asthma n*

Ich habe Asthma. *I have asthma.*

atheistisch *atheist adj*

auch *too (also) adv*

Audio- *audio adj*

das Audio *gn audio n*

der Aufenthalt *m wait n*

aufladen *to charge (a battery) v* **p24**

auflegen *hang up (to end a phone call) v* **p24**

aufwärts *up adv*

der Aufzug *m elevator n*

das Auge *gn eye n*

die Augenbraue *f eyebrow n*

der August *m August n*

aus *made of adj*

auschecken to check out (of hotel) v **p20**

der Ausflug m tour n

ausrauben, stehlen to rob v, to steal v **p20, 24**

die Ausrüstung f equipment n

ausschalten to turn off (lights) v **p20**

aussehen to look (appear) v **p24**

die Aussicht f view n

die Aussicht auf den Strand beach view

die Aussicht auf die Stadt city view

die Ausstellung f exhibit n

Australien Australia n

australisch Australian adj

ausverkauft sold out adj

auswärts essen to eat out

der Ausweis m passport n

auszahlen lassen to cash out (gambling)

auszahlen to cash v

das Auto gn car n

die Autovermietung car rental agency

die Autobahn f highway n

die Autokrankheit f carsickness n

der Autor / die Autorin m/f writer n

die Autovermietung f car rental agency

Autsch! Ouch! interj

B

das Baby gn baby n

Baby-, für Babys for babies adj

Kinderwagen baby stroller

Babynahrung baby food

der Babysitter m babysitter n

das Bad gn bath, spa n

der Badeanzug m swimsuit n

baden to bathe v **p20, 29**

die Badewanne f bathtub n

das Badezimmer gn bathroom n, bath n

der Bahnhof m station n

Wo finde ich die nächste Tankstelle? Where is the nearest gas station?

balancieren (something shaky) / begleichen (invoice) to balance v **p20, 24**

bald soon adv

der Balkon m balcony n

der Ball m ball (sport) n

die Band f band n

Bank- bank adj

das Bankkonto bank account

die Bankkarte bank card

die Bank f bank n

die Bar f bar n

die Pianobar piano bar

die Single-Bar singles bar

das Bargeld gn cash n

Nur gegen Barzahlung. Cash only.

der Bass m bass (instrument) n

die **Batterie** f battery (for flashlight) n

die **Batterie** f battery (for car) n

die **Baumwolle** f cotton n

bearbeiten to process (a transaction) v **p20**

sich **beeilen** to hurry v **p20**, **35**

begeistert enthusiastic adj

beginnen to begin v, to start (commence) v **p24**

behalten to keep v **p24**

die **Behinderung** f disability n

die **Behinderung** f handicap n

das **Bein** gn leg n

beleibt fat adj

beleidigen to insult v **p20**

der **Belgier** m, die **Belgierin** f Belgian n

beliebig any adj

beliebt popular adj

bemuttern to mother v **p20**

sich **benehmen** to behave v **p24**

benommen dizzy adj

das **Benzin** gn gas n

berechnen to bill v **p20**

der **Berg** m mountain n

das **Bergsteigen** mountain climbing

das **Bergsteigen** gn mountain climbing n

beschädigt damaged adj

besetzt busy adj (phone line), occupied adj

besorgt anxious adj

Ich brauche ein Antibiotikum. I need an antibiotic.

besser better. See gut

bestätigen to confirm v **p20**

die **Bestätigung** f confirmation n

bestellen (restaurant) to order v **p20**

besuchen to visit v **p20**

betreten to enter v **p24**

Kein Eingang. Do not enter. **Zutritt verboten.** Entry forbidden.

das **Bett** gn bed n

das **Bettlaken** gn sheet (bed linen) n

die **Beule** f dent n

bevorzugen to prefer v **p20**

bevorzugt preferably adj

bewegen to move v **p20**

bewölkt cloudy adj

bezahlen to pay v **p20**

die **Biene** f bee n

das **Bier** gn beer n

das **Bier vom Fass** beer on tap, draft beer

billig cheap adj

billig cheap
billiger cheaper
am billigsten cheapest

die **Billion** f trillion n

Bio- organic adj

Bis später. See you later.

bitte please (polite entreaty) adv

blass pale adj

blau *blue adj*
bleiben *to stay v* **p24**
das Bleichmittel *gn bleach n*
blenden *to dazzle, to blind v* **p15**
blind *blind adj*
der Block *m block n*
blockieren *to block v* **p20**
der Blonde *m*, **die Blondine** *f blond(e) n*
die Blume *f flower n*
die Bluse *f blouse n*
blutig *rare (meat) adj*
das Boot / Schiff *gn boat n / ship n*
die Bordkarte *f boarding pass n*
der Bordstein *m curb n*
die Botschaft *f embassy n*
der Brandy *m brandy n*
brauchen *to need v* **p20**
braun *brown adj*
brav *well behaved adj*
breit *wide adj*
Breitband- *broadband n*
die Bremse *f brake n*
bremsen *to brake v* **p20**
das Bremslicht *brake light*

  die Motorkontrollleuchte *check engine light*
  der Scheinwerfer *headlight*
  die Ölkontrollleuchte *oil light*

brennen *to burn v* **p24**
die Briefmarke *f stamp (postage) n*
die Brille *f eyeglasses n*

bronzefarben *bronze (color) adj*
das Brot *gn bread n*
die Brücke *f bridge (across a river) n / bridge (dental structure) n*
der Bruder *m brother n*
der Brünette *m*, **die Brünette** *f brunette n* **p106**
buchstabieren *to spell v* **p20**

  Wie schreibt sich das? *How do you spell that?*

der Buddhist *m*, **die Buddhistin** *f Buddhist n*
das Budget *gn budget n*
das Buffet *gn buffet n*
der Bus *m bus n*

  die Bushaltestelle *bus stop*
  der Pendelbus *shuttle bus*
  der Sightseeing-Bus *sightseeing bus*

die Butter *f butter n*

C
das Cabrio *gn convertible n*
das Café *(coffee house) n*
der Campingplatz *m campsite n*
der Cappuccino *m c cappuccino n*
die CD *f CD n*
Charter- *charter adj*

  der Charterflug *charter flight*

chartern *to charter (transportation) v* **p20**
der Check-In *check-in n*

der Curbside-Check-In *curbside check-in*
der elektronische Check-In *electronic check-in*
der Express-Check-In *express check-in*

der Chef *m*, **die Chefin** *f boss n*
die chemische Reinigung *f dry cleaner n*
der Chiropraktiker *m chiropractor n*
der Computer *m computer n*
die Country-Musik *f country-and-western adj*
der Cousin *m*, **die Cousine** *f cousin n*
die Creme *f cream n*
cremefarben *off-white adj*

D
da *there (nearby) adv (demonstrative)*
das Dach *gn roof n*
das Sonnendach *sunroof*
die Damentoilette *women's restroom*
der Däne *m*, **die Dänin** *f Danish n*
danke *thank you*
Darf ich Ihnen ____ vorstellen? *I'd like to introduce you to ____.*
das *this n*
dauern *to last v p20*
die Dauerwelle *f permanent (hair)*

die (Bett-)Decke *f blanket n*
dein *your, yours adj sing (informal)*
die Demokratie *f democracy n*
der Designer *m*, **die Designerin** *f designer n*
der Deutsche *m*, **die Deutsche** *f German n*
der Dezember *m December n*
Diabetiker- *diabetic adj*
dick *thick adj*
der Dienstag *m Tuesday n*
diese *these adj pl*
diese *those (near) adj pl*
diese *those adj pl*
dieser / diese / dieses *that (near) adj*
dieser / diese / dieses *this adj*
die Disko *f disco n*
der Dollar *m dollar n*
der Dolmetscher / die Dolmetscherin *m/f interpreter n*
der Dom *m cathedral n*
der Donnerstag *m Thursday n*
Doppel- *double adj*
dort drüben *over there adv*
dort *there (far) adv (demonstrative)*
der Download *m download n*
das Drama *gn drama n*
draußen *outside n*
drei *three adj*
dreifach *triple adj*

dreißig *thirty adj*

dreizehn *thirteen adj*

das Dressing *gn dressing (salad) n*

drinnen *inside adj*

dritter *third adj*

die Driving Range *f driving range n*

drucken *to print v* **p20**

drücken *to push v* **p20**

du *you pron sing (informal)*

dunkel *dark adj*

die Dunkelheit *f darkness n*

dünn *thin (fine, skinny, slender) adj*

der Durchfall *m diarrhea n*

durchwählen *to dial direct*

die Dusche *f shower n*

duschen *to shower v* **p20, 29**

das Dutzend *gn dozen n*

die DVD *f DVD n*

E

die Ecke *f corner n*

an der Ecke *on the corner*

die Ehefrau *f wife n*

der Ehemann *m husband n*

eigentlich / wirklich *actual adv*

ein / eine *one adj*

eine E-Mail senden *to send e-mail v*

einen Nachtclub besuchen *to go clubbing v* **p20**

einfach *single adj / simple adj*

ohne Eis *straight up (drink)*

das einfache Ticket *one-way ticket*

der Eingang *m entrance n*

einkaufen *to shop v* **p20**

das Einkaufszentrum *gn mall n*

einpacken *to bag v* **p20**

einstecken *to plug v* **p20**

einsteigen / an Bord gehen *to board v* **p24**

das Eis *gn ice n*

die Eismaschine *ice machine*

der Elefant *m elephant n*

der Elektroanschluss *m electrical hookup n*

elf *eleven adj*

die E-Mail *f e-mail n*

Kann ich Ihre (formal) / deine (informal) E-Mail-Adresse haben? *May I have your e-mail address?*

die E-Mail-Nachricht *e-mail message*

empfehlen *to recommend v* **p24**

eng *tight adj*

England *England n*

der Engländer *m*, **die Engländerin** *f English n*

englisch *English adj*

die englische Blindenschrift *f braille (American) n*

die Ente *f duck n*

entfernen *to remove v* **p20**

das Enthaaren (mit Wachs) *gn waxing n*

entschuldigen to excuse (pardon) v **p20**

> **Verzeihung.** Excuse me.

entspannen / abhängen (slang) to hang out (relax) v **p20, 24**

entzückt charmed adj

er he pron

erbitten to request, demand v **p24**

die Erdnuss f peanut n

erfreut delighted adj

erhalten to receive v **p24**

die Erkältung f cold (illness) n

erklären to explain v **p20**

erlauben to permit v **p20**

die erneute Einlösung f refill (of prescription) n

der Ersatz m substitution n

erschöpft exhausted adj

erster first adj

der Erzieher m, **die Erzieherin** f educator n

der Esel m donkey n

das Essen gn food n

essen to eat v **p24**

das Essen zum Mitnehmen takeout menu

die Etage f floor n

> **das erste Stockwerk** ground floor, first floor

etwas bit (small amount) n

etwas (uncountable) / einige (countable) some adj

etwas gn something n

Express- express adj

> **der Express-Check-In** express check-in

F

fahren to drive v **p24**

fahren to ride v **p24**

der Fahrer m driver n

der Fahrplan m schedule n, timetable (train) n

der Fahrpreis m fare n

fallen to fall v **p24**

die Familie f family n

die Farbe f color n

färben to color v **p20**

faulenzen to lounge v **p20**

das Fax gn fax n

der Februar m February n

fehlend missing adj

der Fehler m fault n

> **Es war mein Fehler.** I'm at fault.
>
> **Es war sein Fehler.** It was his fault.

der Fehler m mistake n

feiern to celebrate v **p20**

der Feiertag m holiday n

der Fels m rock n

> **auf Eis** on the rocks

das Fenster gn window n

der Fernseher m television n

> **das Kabelfernsehen** cable television
>
> **das Satellitenfernsehen** satellite television

das Festival gn festival n

feucht humid adj

das Feuer gn fire n

das Feuer *gn light (for cigarette) n*

Darf ich Ihnen (formal) / dir (informal) Feuer geben? *May I offer you a light?*

das Feuerzeug *gn lighter (cigarette) n*

der Film *m movie n*

finden *to find v p24*

das Fitness-Center *gn fitness center n*

das Fitnessstudio *gn gym n*

die Flasche *f bottle n*

das Fleisch *gn meat n*

die Flöte *f flute n*

der Flug *m flight n*

der Flugbegleiter / die Flugbegleiterin *m / f flight attendant*

der Flughafen *m airport n*

der Fluss *m river n*

folglich *consequently adv*

das Format *gn format n*

die Formel *f formula n*

der Fortschritt *m advance n*

fortsetzen *to continue v p20*

(foto-)kopieren *to photocopy v p20*

das Foyer *gn lounge n*

fragen *to ask v p20*

der Franzose *m,* **die Französin** *f French n*

französisch *French adj*

die Frau *f woman n*

der Frauenarzt / die Frauenärztin *m/f gynecologist n*

das freie Zimmer (hotel) *gn vacancy n*

der Freitag *m Friday n*

der Fremdenführer / die Fremdenführerin *m/f guide (of tours) n*

die Fremdenführung *f guided tour n*

die Freude *f pleasure n*

Freut mich. *It's a pleasure.*

der Freund *m /* **die Freundin** *f friend n*

der Freund *m boyfriend n*

die Freundin *f girlfriend n*

die Frikadelle *f meatball n*

frisch *fresh adj*

der Frisör *m,* **die Frisörin** *f hairdresser n*

fröhlich *happy adj*

die Frontscheibe *f windshield n*

die Frucht *f fruit n*

der Fruchtsaft *m fruit juice n*

früh *early adj*

der Frühling *m spring (season) n*

das Frühstück *gn breakfast n*

führen *to guide v p20*

Full House! *Full house! n*

fünf *five adj*

fünfter *m fifth adj*

fünfzehn *m fifteen adj*

fünfzig *fifty adj*

(der) Fuß *m foot (body part) n*

Fußgänger- *pedestrian adj*

die **Fußgängerzone** pedestrian shopping district

der **Fußgängerweg** m walkway n

der **Fahrsteig** moving walkway

G

der **Gang** m aisle (in store) n / hallway n

ganz all adj

die **ganze Zeit** all the time

Das ist alles. That's all.

die **Garnele** f shrimp n

das **Gas** (for cooking) / das **Benzin** (for cars) gn gas n

die **Tankanzeige** gas gauge

kein Benzin mehr out of gas

der **Gast** m guest n

geben to deal (cards) v **p24**

Ich bin dabei. Deal me in.

geben to give v **p24**

das **Gebiss** gn dentures, denture plate n

gebräunt tanned adj

die **Gebühr** f fee n

die **Gebühr** f toll n

der **Gedanke** m thought n

die **Gefahr** f danger n

gefallen to please v to be pleasing to v **p24**

das **Geflügel** gn poultry n

gehen to go v **p24**

die **Gehhilfe** f walker (ambulatory device) n

gehoben upscale adj

Geht es Ihnen (formal) / dir (informal) gut? Are you okay?

der **Gehweg** m sidewalk n

die **Geige** f violin n

gelb yellow adj

der **(Geld-)Schein** m bill (currency) n

das **Geld** gn money n

die **Überweisung** money transfer

der **Geldautomat** m ATM n

die **Geldbörse** f wallet n

die **Geldwechselstube** f currency exchange n

gelockt curly adj

das **Gemälde** gn painting n

das **Gemüse** gn vegetable n

die **Genehmigung** f permit n

genießen to enjoy v **p24**

geöffnet open (business) adj

Gepäck- baggage adj

die **Gepäckausgabe** baggage claim

das **Gepäck** gn baggage, luggage n

das **verloren gegangene Gepäck** lost baggage

gerade straight adj

das **Gericht** gn court (legal) n

das **Gericht für Verkehrsdelikte** traffic court

das **Gericht** gn dish n

die **Gesamtsumme** f total n

Wie hoch ist die Gesamtsumme? *What is the total?*

Ich arbeite bei ____. *I work for ____.*

das Geschäft *gn shop n, store n*

das Zelt *gn tent n*

Geschäfts- *business adj*

das Geschäftszentrum *business center*

das Geschenk *gn gift n*

die Geschichte *f history n*

geschieden *divorced adj*

das Geschlecht *gn sex (gender) n*

der (Geschlechts-) Verkehr *m intercourse (sexual) n*

geschlossen *closed adj*

der Geschmack *m taste (discernment) n*

der Geschmack *m taste, flavor n*

der Schokoladengeschmack *chocolate flavor*

der Gesellschaftstanz *m ballroom dancing n*

das Gesicht *gn face n*

gestern *yesterday adv*

gestohlen *stolen adj*

gestreift *striped adj*

gestresst *stressed adj*

das Getränk *gn drink n*

das Gratisgetränk *complimentary drink*

getrennt lebend *separated (marital status) adj*

das Getriebe *gn transmission n*

das Automatikgetriebe *automatic transmission*

das Schaltgetriebe *standard transmission*

getrocknet / Trocken- *dried adj*

die Gewichte *gn, pl weights n*

das Gewürz *gn spice n*

Gibt es hier ____? *Is / Are there ____?*

Gibt es hier eine öffentliche Toilette? *Do you have a public restroom?*

das Gift *gn poison n*

der Gin *m gin n*

die Gitarre *f guitar n*

das Glas *gn glass (drinking) n*

Schenken Sie das als offenes Getränk aus? *Do you have it by the glass?*

Ich hätte gerne ein Glas. *I'd like a glass please.*

das Gold *gn gold n*

golden *gold (color) adj*

golden *golden adj*

Golf spielen *to go golfing v p24*

das Golf (-spiel) *gn golf n*

der Golfplatz *golf course*

der Gottesdienst *m service (religious) n*

das Gramm *gn gram n*

grau *gray adj*

der Grieche *m,* **die Griechin** *f Greek n*

griechisch *Greek adj*
griechisch-orthodox *Greek Orthodox adj*
groß *big adj, large adj*
  groß *big, large*
  größer *bigger, larger*
  am größten *biggest, largest*
Großartig! *Great! interj*
die Großmutter *f grandmother n*
der Großvater *m grandfather n*
grün *green adj*
die Gruppe *f group n*
günstig *inexpensive adj*
der Gürtel *m belt n*
  das Transportband *conveyor belt*
gut aussehend *handsome adj*
gut besucht *busy (restaurant) adj*
gut *fine adj*
  Mir geht es gut. *I'm fine.*
gut *good adj*
gut *well adv*
  Gute Nacht. *Good night.*
  Guten Abend. *Good evening.*
  Guten Morgen. *Good morning.*
  Guten Tag. *Good afternoon.*
der Gutschein *m voucher n*
  der Essensgutschein *meal voucher*
  der Zimmergutschein *room voucher*

H
das Haar *gn hair n*
der Haarschnitt *m haircut n*
der Haartrockner *m hair dryer n*
haben *to have v p24*
  Sex haben *to have sex (intercourse)*
der Hafen *port (for ship mooring) n*
das Hähnchen *gn chicken n*
halb *half adj*
halb gar *medium rare (meat) adj*
halbes Pfund *half-pound*
die Hälfte *f half n*
Hallo *hello n*
halten *to hold v p24*
  Händchen halten *to hold hands*
die Haltestelle *f stop n*
  die Bushaltestelle *bus stop*
Haltet den Dieb! *Stop, thief!*
die Hand *f hand n*
das Handbuch *gn manual (instruction booklet) n*
handhaben *to handle v p20*
  Vorsicht! *Handle with care*
der Handschuh *m glove n*
die Handtasche *f purse n*
  Ich habe meine Geldbörse verloren. *I lost my wallet.*
  Meine Geldbörse wurde gestohlen. *Someone stole my wallet.*
das Handtuch *gn towel n*
hart *hard (firm) adj*

der Hase *m hare (bunny) n*
der Hauch / Zug *m puff n*
die Hausfrau *f homemaker n*
die Haut *f skin n*
das Heilbad *gn spa n*
heiraten *to marry v* **p20**
heiß *hot adj, warm adj*
die heiße Schokolade *f hot chocolate n*
helfen *to help / to assist v* **p24**
hell *bright adj*
das Hemd *gn shirt n*
der Herbst *m autumn (fall season) n*
der (Herren-) Frisör *m barber n*
die Herrentoilette *men's restroom*
herunterladen *to download v* **p24**
das Herz *gn heart n*
der Herzinfarkt *m heart attack n*
heute *today n*
hier *here adv*
die Hilfe *f assistance n*
die Hilfe *f help n*
Hilfe! *Help! n*
das Hin- und Rückreiseticket *round-trip ticket*
hinter *behind adj*
der Hiphop *hip-hop n*
historisch *historical adj*
das Hobby *gn hobby n*
hoch *high adj*

hoch *high adj*
höher *higher*
am höchsten *highest*
hochladen *to upload v* **p24**
die Hochschule *f college n, high school n*
die Höhe *f altitude n*
die höhere Kategorie *f upgrade n*
hören *to hear v*
hören *to listen v* **p20**
hörgeschädigt *hearing-impaired adj*
die Hose *f pair of pants n*
   die Badehose *swim trunks n*
   die kurze Hose *shorts*
das Hotel *gn hotel n*
der Hund *m dog n*
   der Blindenhund *service dog*
hundert *hundred adj*
die Hupe *f horn n*
der Husten *m cough n*
husten *to cough v* **p20**
der Hut *m hat n*
die Hygieneartikel *m, pl toiletries n*

I
Ich hätte gern etwas zu trinken. *I'd like a drink.*
ich *I pron*
ihr *you pron pl (informal)*
Ihr *you pron (formal)*
ihr / ihre *her / their adj*
im Voraus *in advance adv*
der Imbiss *m snack n*

der **Impressionismus** m
Impressionism n
in der Nähe near, nearby adj
nah near adj
näher nearer (comparative)
am nächsten nearest
(superlative)
die **Information** f information
n
der **Informationsstand** m
information booth n
der **Ingenieur** m, die
Ingenieurin f engineer n
innehalten, warten to hold
(to pause) v, to wait v
p24, 20
das **Insektenschutzmittel** gn
insect repellent n
das **Internet** gn Internet n
**Wo finde ich ein
Internetcafé?** Where can I
find an Internet café?
das **Internetcafé** gn
cybercafé n
der **Ire** m, die **Irin** f Irish n
irisch Irish adj
Irland Ireland n
italienisch Italian adj
der **Italiener** m, die
Italienerin f Italian n

J
ja yes adv
die **Jacke** f coat n
die **Jacke** f jacket n
das **Jahr** gn year n

**Wie alt sind Sie? (formal) /
Wie alt bist du? (informal)**
What's your age?
der **Januar** m January n
der **Jazz** m jazz n
jemand someone n
jener / jene / jenes that (far
away) adj
jetzt now adv
das **Joggen** jogging n
jüdisch Jewish adj
die **Jugendherberge** f hostel
n
der **Juli** m July n
jung young adj
der **Junge** m boy n, kid n
der **Juni** m June n

K
der **Käfer** m bug n
der **Kaffee** (beverage) m
coffee n
der Eiskaffee iced coffee
der Espresso m espresso n
das Internetcafé Internet
café
kahl bald adj
kalt cold adj
Kanada m Canada n
kanadisch Canadian adj
kariert checked (pattern) adj
die **Karte** f card n
die Kreditkarte credit card
**Akzeptieren Sie
Kreditkarten?** Do you
accept credit cards?
die Visitenkarte business
card

die **Karte** *f map n*
  der **Straßenatlas** *road map*
der **Kartenschalter** *ticket counter*
der **Kartenverkauf** *m box office n*
der **Kaschmir** *m cashmere n*
der **Käse** *m cheese n*
das **Kasino** *gn casino n*
der **Katholik** *m*, die **Katholikin** *f Catholic n*
die **Katze** *f cat n*
kein *none, no adj adv*
  keine freien Zimmer *no vacancy*
der **Keks** *m cookie n*
der **Kellner** / die **Kellnerin** *m / f waiter n*
kennen *to know (someone) v* **p24**
das **Kennwort** *gn password n*
das **Kilo** *gn kilo n*
die **Kinder** *gn, pl children n pl*
der **Kinderarzt** / die **Kinderärztin** *pediatrician n*
das **Kinderbett** *gn crib n*
die **Kinderkrippe** *f nursery n*
der **Kinderwagen** *m stroller n*
das **Kino** *gn cinema n*
die **Kirche** *f church n*
das **Kissen** *gn pillow n*
  das **Daunenkissen** *down pillow*
klar *clear adj*
die **Klarinette** *f clarinet n*

die **Klasse** *f class n*
  die **Businessklasse** *business class*
  die **Economyklasse** *economy class*
  die **Erste Klasse** *first class*
klassisch *classical (music) adj*
das **Klavier** *gn piano n*
das **Kleid** *gn dress (garment) n*
der **Kleiderbügel** *m hanger n*
die **Kleidergröße** *f size (clothing, shoes) n*
die **Kleidung** *f dress (general attire) n*
klein *little adj, small adj*
  klein *small, little*
  kleiner *smaller, littler*
  am kleinsten *smallest, littlest*
der **Kleinbus** *m van n*
das **kleine Mädchen** *gn little girl n*
das **Kleinkind** *gn infant n*
Kletter- *climbing adj*
  die **Kletterausrüstung** *climbing gear*
klettern (mountain) / **steigen (stairs)** *to climb v* **p20, 24**
  bergsteigen *to climb a mountain*
das **Klettern** *gn climbing n*
  das **Felsenklettern** *rock climbing*
die **Klimaanlage** *f air conditioning n*
der **Knoblauch** *m garlic n*
kochen *to cook v* **p20**

die **Kochgelegenheit** f *kitchenette* n

der **Köder** m *bait* n

der **Koffer** m *suitcase / trunk (luggage)* n

der **Kofferraum** m *trunk (of car)* n

der **Kognak** m *cognac* n

die **Koje** f *berth* n

das **Kondom** gn *condom* n

Hast du ein Kondom? *Do you have a condom?*

nicht ohne Kondom *not without a condom*

können *to be able to (can)* v, *may* v aux **p26**

Kann ich ____? *May I ____?*

konsequent *consistent(ly)* adj/adv

der **Kontakt für den Notfall** m *emergency contact* n

das **Konto** gn *account* n

der **Kontostand** m *balance (on bank account)* n

das **Konzert** gn *concert* n

der **Kopfhörer** m *headphones* n

korrekt *correct* adj

korrigieren *to correct* v **p20**

das **koschere Essen** *kosher meal*

kosten *to cost* v **p20**

kosten *to taste* v, *to try (food)* v **p20**

das **Kostüm** gn *costume* n

krank *sick* adj

der **Krankenpfleger / die Krankenpflegerin** m/f *nurse* n

der **Krankenwagen** m *ambulance* n

kratzen *to scratch* v **p20**

der **Kratzer** m *scratch* n

das **Kraut** gn *herb* n

das **Kreditinstitut** gn *credit bureau* n

der **Krieg** m *war* n

die **Krone** f *crown (dental)* n

der **Kubismus** m *Cubism* n

die **Küche** f *kitchen* n

die **Kuh** f *cow* n

Kunst- *art* adj

das **Kunstmuseum** *art museum*

der **Handwerker** m, die **Handwerkerin** f *craftsperson / artisan* n

die **Kunst** f *art* n

die **Kunstausstellung** *exhibit of art*

der **Künstler / die Künstlerin** m/f *artist* n

der **Kunststoff** m *plastic* n

kupferfarben *copper* adj

die **Kuppel** f *dome* n

kurz *short* adj

der **Kurze** m *shot (liquor)* n

der **Kuss** m *kiss* n

das **Kuvert** gn *envelope* n

L

laktoseunverträglich *lactose-intolerant* adj

das Lämpchen *light (on car dashboard)*

landen *to land v* **p20**

langsamer werden *to slow v* **p24**

das Laufband *gn treadmill n*

laufen *to walk v* **p24**

laut *loud, noisy adj*

das Leben *gn life n*

Was machen Sie (formal) / machst du (informal) beruflich? *What do you do for a living?*

leben *to live v* **p20**

Wo wohnen Sie? (formal) / Wo wohnst du? (informal) *Where do you live?*

die Lebensmittel *gn, pl groceries n*

das Leder *gn leather n*

ledig *single (unmarried) adj*

Sind Sie ledig? *Are you single?*

leid *sorry adj*

Tut mir leid. *I'm sorry.*

letzter / letzte / letztes *last adv*

das Licht *gn light (lamp) n*

die Liebe *f love n*

lieben *to love v* **p20**

das Lied *gn song n*

die Limonade *f soda n*

die Diätlimonade *diet soda*

die Limousine *f sedan n*

links *left adj*

das Loch *gn cavity (tooth cavity) n*

die Locke *f curl n*

locker *loose adj*

die Loge *f box (seat) n*

die Luftpost *air mail*

der Expressversand *express mail*

der Versand erster Klasse *first class mail*

das Einschreiben *registered mail*

Wo befindet sich das Postamt? *Where is the post office?*

M

machen *to do v, to make v* **p20**

das Mädchen *gn girl n*

die Mahlzeit *f meal n*

das Essen für Diabetiker *diabetic meal*

der Mai *m May (month) n*

das Make-up *gn makeup n*

die Mama *f mom n, mommy n*

der Manager / die Managerin *m / f manager n*

der Mann *m man n*

männlich *male adj*

der Markt *m market n*

der Flohmarkt *flea market*

der Freiluftmarkt *open-air market*

der März *m March (month) n*

die Maschine *f machine n*

das Röntgengerät *x-ray machine*

der Automat *vending machine*

massieren *to massage* v **p20**

die Maus *f mouse* n

medium *medium well (meat)* adj

die Medizin *f medicine* n, *medication* n

die Meeresfrüchte *f, pl seafood* n

die Menge (things) / der Betrag (money) *f / m amount* n

das Menü *gn today's special* n

messen *to measure* v **p24**

der Metalldetektor *m metal detector* n

der Meter *m meter* n

mieten *to rent* v

das Militär *gn military* n

die Milliarde *f billion* n

der Milliliter *m milliliter* n

der Millimeter *m millimeter* n

mindestens *at least* n

die Minibar *f minibar* n

die Minute *f minute* n

sofort *in a minute*

mischen *to blend* v **p15**

mit *with* prep

mit Buffet *buffet-style* adj

mit Rollen *wheeled (luggage)* adj

mit wenig Salz *low-salt*

der Mitarbeiter *m*, die Mitarbeiterin *f employee* n

das Mitglied *gn member* n

die Mitgliedschaft *f membership* n

der Mittag *noon* n

das Mittagessen *gn lunch* n

mittel *medium* adj (size)

Mittel- *middle* adj

Mitternacht *midnight* adv

der Mittwoch *m Wednesday* n

das Mobiltelefon / Handy *cell phone*

Geben Sie mir bitte Ihre Telefonnummer? *May I have your phone number?*

die Telefonvermittlung *f phone operator*

das Prepaid-Telefon *prepaid phones*

der Monat *m month* n

der Montag *m Monday* n

der Morgen *m morning* n

morgens *in the morning*

morgen *gn tomorrow* adv

die Morgendämmerung *f dawn* n

bei Tagesanbruch *at dawn*

die Moschee *f mosque* n

der Motor *m engine* n

das Motorrad *gn motorcycle* n

müde *tired* adj

der Mund *m mouth* n

die Münze *f coin* n

das Museum *gn museum* n

das Musical *gn musical (music genre)* n

die Musik *f music* n

die Popmusik *pop music*

musikalisch *musical adj*

der Musiker / die Musikerin
m / f musician n

der Muslim *m,* **die Muslimin**
f Muslim n

die Mutter *f mother n*

das Muttermal *gn mole
(facial feature) n*

N

der Nachbar *m,* **die**
Nachbarin *f neighbor n*

der Nachmittag *m afternoon
n*

  nachmittags *in the
afternoon*

der Nachname *m last name*

  Ich habe meinen
Mädchennamen behalten.
I kept my maiden name.

Nachschenken *v refill (of
beverage) v*

die Nachspeise *f dessert n*

  die Dessertkarte *dessert
menu*

die Nacht *f night n*

  nachts *at night*

  pro Nacht *per night*

der Nachtclub *m nightclub n*

nah, in der Nähe *close, near
adj*

  nah *close*

  näher *closer*

  am nächsten *closest*

nähen *to sew v* **p20**

der Name *m name n*

  der Vorname *first name*

die Nase *f nose n*

die Nationalität *f nationality n*

neben *next prep*

  der nächste Halt *the next
station*

der Neffe *m nephew n*

nehmen *to take v* **p24**

  Wie lange wird das dauern?
How long will this take?

nett *nice (kind) adj*

das Netzwerk *gn network n*

neu *new adj*

neun *nine adj*

neunter *ninth adj*

neunzehn *nineteen adj*

neunzig *ninety n adj*

Neuseeland *New Zealand n*

der Neuseeländer *m,* **die**
Neuseeländerin *f New
Zealander n*

die Nichte *f niece n*

Nichtraucher- *nonsmoking
adj*

  der Nichtraucherbereich
nonsmoking area

  das Nichtraucherauto
nonsmoking car

  das Nichtraucherzimmer
nonsmoking room

nichts / keine *none n*

der Niederländer *m,* **die**
Niederländerin *f Dutch n*

niedrig *low adj*

  niedrig *low adj*

  niedriger *lower*

  am niedrigsten *lowest*

noch einen / eine / ein
another adj

der Norweger *m*, **die Norwegerin** *f* Norwegian *n*

die Note *f* grade (school) *n*

das Notebook *gn* laptop *n*

der Notfall *m* emergency *n*

der November *m* November *n*

die Nummer *f* number *n*

die Nuss *f* nut *n*

O

die Öffnungszeiten *f, pl* hours (at museum) *n*

ohne without *prep*

ohnmächtig werden to faint *v* **p24**

OK / in Ordnung Okay *adj adv*

der Oktober *m* October *n*

das Öl *gn* oil *n*

die Olive *f* olive *n*

der Onkel *m* uncle *n*

die Oper *f* opera *n*

das Opernhaus *gn* opera house *n*

der Optiker / die Optikerin *m/f* optometrist *n*

orange orange (color) *adj*

der Orangensaft *m* orange juice *n*

die Orgel *f* organ *n*

örtlich local *adj*

der Österreicher *m*, **die Österreicherin** *f* Austrian *n*

P

das Paket *gn* package *n*

das Papier paper *n*

der Papierteller paper plate

die Papierserviette paper napkin

die Papiere *gn, pl* identification *n*

der Park *m* park *n*

Park- parking *adj*

parken to park *v* **p20**

Parkverbot no parking

die Partei *f* political party *n*

der Partner *m*, **die Partnerin** *f* partner *n*

der Passagier *m* passenger *n*

passen to fit (clothes) *v* **p20**

passen to match *v* **p20**

passen to pass (gambling) *v* **p20**

die Pause *f* intermission *n*

das Penthaus *gn* penthouse *n*

die Person *f* person *n*

Person mit Sehbehinderung visually-impaired person

das Personal *gn* staff (employees) *n*

das Pferd *gn* horse *n*

die Pizza *f* pizza *n*

der Platz *m* court (sport) *n*

der Platz *m* seat *n*

der Orchesterplatz orchestra seat

platzieren to place *v* **p20**

der Pole *m*, **die Polin** *f* Polish *n*

die Polizei *f* police *n*

die Polizeiwache *f* police station *n*

der Polizist / die Polizistin
m / f officer n

das Poolbillard *gn pool (the game) n*

der Portier *m porter n*

die Portion *f portion (of food) n*

das Porträt *gn portrait n*

der Portugiese *m,* **die Portugiesin** *f Portuguese n*

der Portwein *m port (beverage) n*

die Post *f mail n/post office n*

die Postkarte *f postcard n*

der Preis eines Gedecks *m cover charge (in bar) n*

der Preis *m price n*
die Eintrittsgebühr *admission fee n*
in der mittleren Preiskategorie *moderately priced*

der Preisnachlass *m discount n*
der Kinderrabatt *children's discount*
der Seniorenrabatt *senior discount*
der Studentenrabatt *student discount*

Privat- *home adj*
die Privatadresse *home address*
die private Telefonnummer *home telephone number*

das Problem *gn problem n*

das Produkt *gn product n*

professionell *professional adj*

das Programm *gn program n*

protestantisch *Protestant adj*

der Puff *m bordello n*

der Pullover *m sweater n*

die Pumpe *f pump n*

Q

das Querformat *gn landscape (painting) n*

die Quittung *f receipt n*

R

das Radio *gn radio n*
das Satellitenradio *satellite radio*

die Rampe für Rollstuhlfahrer *f wheelchair ramp n*

das Rauchen *gn smoking n*
der Raucherbereich *smoking area*
Rauchen verboten *no smoking*

rauchen *to smoke v p20*

räumen *to clear v p20*

die Rechte *gn, pl rights n pl*
die Bürgerrechte *civil rights*

rechts *right adj*
____ **befindet sich auf der rechten Seite.** ____ *is on the right.*
Biegen Sie an der Ecke nach rechts ab. *Turn right at the corner.*
Gehen Sie geradeaus. *Go straight. (giving directions)*

der Redakteur *m,* **die Redakteurin** *f editor n*

der Regenschirm *m umbrella n*

der Reggae *m reggae n*

regnen *to rain v* **p20**

regnerisch *rainy adj*

der Reifen *m tire n*

  der Reservereifen *spare tire n*

die Reise *f trip n*

der Reiseführer *m guide (publication) n*

reisen *to travel v* **p20**

der Reisescheck *m travelers' check n*

die Reklamation *f claim n*

rennen *to run v* **p24**

die Reservierung *f reservation n*

das Restaurant *gn restaurant n*

  das Steakhaus *steakhouse*

das Rezept *gn prescription n*

die Rezeption *f front desk n*

die Richtung *f direction*

  Einbahnstraße *one way (traffic sign)*

riechen *to smell v* **p24**

das Riff *gn reef n*

der Rock'n'Roll *m rock and roll n*

der Roller *m scooter n*

der Rollstuhl *m wheelchair n*

  der Zugang per Rollstuhl *wheelchair access*

  die Rampe für Rollstuhlfahrer *wheelchair ramp*

der elektrisch betriebene Rollstuhl *power wheelchair*

die Rolltreppe *f escalator n*

der Roman *m novel n*

  der Mystery-Roman *mystery novel*

  der Liebesroman *romance novel*

romantisch *romantic adj*

rosa *pink adj*

die Rose *f rose n*

rot *red adj*

rothaarig *redhead adj*

der Royal Flush *royal flush*

der Rücken *m back n*

die Rückenmassage *f back rub n*

rufen *to call (shout) v* **p24**

rufen *to shout v* **p24**

ruhig *quiet adj*

der Rum *m rum n*

der Russe *m,* die Russin *f Russian n*

S

der Saft *m juice n*

sagen *to say v* **p20**

der Salat *m salad n*

das Salz *gn salt n*

sammeln *to collect v* **p20**

der Samstag *m Saturday n*

der Satellit *m satellite n*

das Satellitenradio *satellite radio*

  die Satellitenverfolgung *satellite tracking*

die Sauerstoffflasche f
oxygen tank n

scannen to scan (document)
v **p20**

das Schalentier gn shellfish n

der Schalter m window n

der Abgabeschalter drop-
off window

der Abholschalter pickup
window

Schau her! Look here!

der Scheck m check n

der Scheinwerfer m
headlight n

schieben to hold (gambling)
v **p24**

das Schiffswrack gn
shipwreck n

das Schild „Vorfahrt
gewähren" gn yield sign n

der Schlafwagen m sleeping
car n

Schlangenaugen! Snake
eyes! n

schlecht adj bad adj

schließen to close v **p24**

schlimmer worse See
schlecht

das Schloss gn castle n

das Schloss gn lock n

schlucken to swallow v **p20**

schmal narrow adj

schmerzen to hurt (to feel
painful) v **p20**

Autsch! Das tut weh! Ouch!
That hurts!

die Kopfschmerzen m, pl
headache n

die Zahnschmerzen m, pl
toothache n

Ich habe Zahnschmerzen.
I have a toothache.

schminken to make up
(apply cosmetics) v **p20**

das Schnäppchen gn deal
(bargain) n

schneiden to cut v **p24**

der Schneider / die
Schneiderin m / f tailor n

schnell fast adj

der Schnitt m cut (wound) n

der Schnorchel m snorkel
(breathing tube) n

der Schnuller m pacifier n

schön beautiful adj

schottisch Scottish adj

schreiben to write v **p24**

Könnten Sie mir das bitte
aufschreiben? Would you
write that down for me?

der Schuh m shoe n

die Schule f school n

die Mittelstufe junior high /
middle school

die juristische Fakultät law
school

die medizinische Fakultät
medical school

die Grundschule primary
school

die weiterführende Schule
high school

der Schwan m swan n

schwanger *pregnant adj*
schwarz *black adj*
der Schwede *m*, **die Schwedin** *f Swedish n*
das Schwein *gn pig n*
der Schweizer *m*, **die Schweizerin** *f Swiss n*
die Schwester *f sister n*
schwierig *difficult adj*
schwimmen *to swim v* **p24**
　Schwimmen verboten.
　Swimming prohibited.
die Schwimmweste *f life preserver n*
sechs *six adj*
sechzehn *sixteen adj*
sechzig *sixty adj*
das Segel *gn sail n*
das Segeltuch *gn canvas (fabric) n*
sehen *to see v* **p24**
　Dürfte ich das mal sehen?
　May I see it?
sehr *very*
seicht *shallow adj*
die Seide *f silk n*
das Seil *gn rope n*
sein *to be v* **p23**
sein / seine *his adj*
Selbstbedienungs- *self-serve adj*
das Selters *gn seltzer n*
senden *to send v* **p20**
der September *m September n*
der Service *m service n*
　außer Betrieb *out of service*

die Servicegebühr *f service charge n*
servieren *to serve v* **p20**
die Serviette *f napkin n*
setzen *to put (gambling) v* **p20**
　Setzen Sie das auf Rot / Schwarz! *Put it on red / black!*
　Beeilen Sie sich bitte! *Hurry, please!*
sicher *safe (secure) adj*
die Sicherheit *f security n*
　die Sicherheitsschleuse *security checkpoint*
　der Sicherheitsbeamte *security guard*
die Sicherung *f fuse n*
sie *f she / they*
sie *them pron pl*
Sie *you pron sing/pl (formal)*
sieben *seven adj*
siebter *seventh adj*
siebzehn *seventeen adj*
siebzig *seventy adj*
das Sightseeing *gn sightseeing n*
das Silber *gn silver n*
Silber- *silver adj*
silbern *silver (color) adj*
singen *to sing v* **p24**
sitzen *to sit v* **p24**
die Skulptur *f sculpture n*
die Socke *f sock n*
die Software *f software n*
der Sohn *m son n*
der Sommer *m summer n*

die **Sommersprosse** f freckle n

die **Sonne** f sun n

der **Sonnenbrand** m sunburn n

die **Sonnenbrille** f sunglasses n

die **Sonnencreme** f sunscreen n

sonnig sunny adj

der **Sonntag** m Sunday n

die **Soße** f sauce n

der **Sozialismus** m socialism n

der **Spanier** m, die **Spanierin** f Spanish n

spanisch Spanish adj

spät late adj

Bitte pünktlich sein. Please don't be late.

später later adv

der **Spaziergang** m walk n

der **Specht** m woodpecker n

die **Speisekarte** f menu n

das **Kindermenü** children's menu

das **Diabetikermenü** diabetic menu

die **Spezialität** f special (featured meal) n

das **Spiel** gn match (sport) n

die **Spielekonsole** f game console n

spielen to play (a game) v p20

spielen to play (an instrument) v p20

der **Spielplatz** m playground n

der **Spielstand** m score n

das **Spielwarengeschäft** gn toy store n

das **Spielzeug** gn toy n

der **Spind** m locker n

der **Umkleidesschrank** gym locker

der **Aufbewahrungsschrank** storage locker

der **Split** m split (gambling) n

der **Sport** m sports n

die **Sporthalle** f coliseum n

sprechen to speak v, to talk v p24

Wir sprechen Englisch. English spoken here.

der **Sprung** m crack (in glass object) n

spülen to flush v p20

der **Staat (gov.) / der Status (status)** m state n

das **Stadion** gn stadium n

die **Stadt** f city n

das **Stadtzentrum** gn downtown n

der **Stecker** m plug n

stehen to stand v p24

die **Steuer** f tax n

die **Mehrwertsteuer (MwSt)** value-added tax (VAT)

stillen to nurse v p20

die **Stirn** f forehead n

der **Stoff** m fabric n

STOP STOP (traffic sign)

stornieren to cancel v p20

die **Strafe** f fine (for traffic violation) n

die Strähnchen *gn, pl*
highlights (hair) n
der Strand *m beach n*
stranden *to beach v* **p20**
die Straße *f road n*
die Straße *f street n*
  am Ende der Straße *down*
  the street
  gegenüber *across the street*
streichen *to paint v* **p24**
das Streichholz *gn match*
(fire) n
die Streitkräfte *f pl armed*
forces n pl
die Strömung *f current (water)*
n
die Stufe *f stair n*
die Suche *f search n*
  das Abtasten *hand search*
suchen *to look for (to search)*
v **p20**
die Suite *f suite n*
der Supermarkt *m*
supermarket n
surfen *to surf v* **p20**
  das Surfbrett *surfboard n*
der (Swimming-)Pool *m pool*
(swimming) n
die Symphonie *f symphony n*

T
die Tablette *f pill n*
  die Tablette gegen
  Seekrankheit *f seasickness*
  pill
der Tacho *m speedometer n*
die Tafel *f board n*

der Tag *m day n*
die Tante *f aunt n*
tapfer *brave adj*
die Tariftabelle *f rate plan*
(cell phone) n
  Haben Sie eine Tariftabelle?
  Do you have a rate plan?
die Tasche *f /* die Tüte *f bag n*
tatsächlich *actual adj*
taub *deaf adj*
tauchen *to dive v* **p20**
tauchen (mit Atemgerät) *to*
scuba dive v
  Ich tauche mit Atemgerät.
  I scuba dive.
  schnorcheln *to snorkel v*
tausend *thousand adj*
das Taxi *gn taxi n*
  Taxi! *Taxi!*
  der Taxistand *taxi stand*
der Techno *m techno n*
(music)
der Tee *m tea n*
  Tee mit Milch und Zucker
  tea with milk and sugar
  Tee mit Zitrone *tea with*
  lemon
  Kräutertee *herbal tea*
das Telefon *gn phone n*
Telefon- *phone adj*
der Telefonanruf *m phone*
call n
  das R-Gespräch *collect*
  phone call
  das Auslandsgespräch
  international phone call
  das Ferngespräch *long-*
  distance phone call

die Telefonauskunft *phone directory*
die Telefonauskunft *f directory assistance*
der Tempel *m temple n*
das Tennis *gn tennis n*
der Termin *m appointment n*
das Terminal *gn terminal (airport) n*
teuer *expensive adj*
das Theater *gn theater n*
das Theaterstück *gn play n*
die Theke *f counter (in bar) n*
Ticket *gn ticket n*
tief *deep adj*
das Tier *gn animal n*
der Tisch *m table n*
die Tochter *f daughter n*
die Toilette *f toilet n*
das Toilettenpapier *gn toilet paper n*
die Tonne *f ton n*
das Tor *gn goal (sport) n*
trainieren *to train v* **p20**
das Training *gn workout n*
die Transaktion *f transaction n*
der Transfer *m transfer n*
die Überweisung *money transfer*
transferieren / überweisen *to transfer v* **p20, 24**
die Traube *f grape n*
traurig *sad adj*
der Treff *m hangout (hot spot) n*
Treppen steigen *to climb stairs*

der Tresor *safe (for storing valuables) n*
trimmen *to trim (hair) v* **p20**
trinken *to drink v* **p24**
das Trinkgeld *gn tip (gratuity)*
inklusive Trinkgeld *tip included*
trocken *dry adj*
trocknen *to dry v* **p20**
die Trommel *f drum n*
die Trompete *f trumpet n*
tropfen *to drip v* **p20**
der Truthahn *m turkey*
der Tscheche, die Tschechin *f Czech n*
die Tür *f door n*
das Gate *gate (at airport)*
der Türke *m,* **die Türkin** *f Turkish n*

U
die U-Bahn *f subway n*
die U-Bahn-Linie *subway line*
die U-Bahn-Haltestelle *subway station*
Mit welcher U-Bahn komme ich zu / zur / zum ____? *Which subway do I take for ____?*
die Übelkeit *f nausea n*
über *above adj*
überall / irgendwo *anywhere adv*
überfallen *to mug (assault) v* **p24**

überfallen werden to get mugged

überhitzen to overheat *v* **p20**

die Übernachtung mit Frühstück *f* bed-and-breakfast (B & B) *n*

überprüfen / sich vergewissern to check *v* **p20**

die Uhr *m* clock *n*, watch *n*

Uhr o'clock *adv*

zwei Uhr two o'clock

die Uhrzeit *f* time *n*

die Uhrzeit für das Auschecken check-out time

kein Ausgang not an exit

der Notausgang emergency exit

die Umkleide *f* locker room *n*

die Umkleidekabine *f* changing room *n*

die Umkleidekabine *f* fitting room *n*

umsehen to look (observe) *v* **p24**

die Umwelt *f* environment *n*

der Umzug *m* parade *n*

der Unfall *m* accident *n*

unfrei collect *adj*

die Universität *f* university *n*

unter below *adj*

unterbrechen to disconnect *v* **p24**

das Unternehmen *gn* business *n*

unterschreiben to sign *v* **p24**

Unterschreiben Sie bitte hier. Sign here.

die Untertitel *m, pl* subtitle *n*

die Unterwäsche *f* underwear *n*

die Unze *f* ounce *n*

der Urlaub *m* vacation *n*

im Urlaub on vacation

in Urlaub gehen to go on vacation

der USB-Anschluss *m* USB port *n*

V

der Vater *m* father *n*

der Vegetarier *m*, **die Vegetarierin** *f* vegetarian *n*

das vegetarische Essen vegetarian meal

der Ventilator *m* fan *n*

die Verbindungsgeschwindigkeit *f* connection speed *n*

verdächtig suspiciously *adv*

Verdammt! Damn! expletive

die Verdauungsstörung *f* indigestion *n*

verfügbar available *adj*

verheiratet married *adj*

die Verhütung *f* birth control *n*

Ich nehme die Pille. I'm on birth control.

verkaufen to sell *v* **p20**

der Verkäufer *m*, **die Verkäuferin** *f* salesperson *n*

der Straßenhändler *m*, die Straßenhändlerin *f* street vendor

der Verkehr *m* traffic *n*

Wie ist der Verkehr? *How's traffic?*

Es ist viel Verkehr. *Traffic is terrible.*

die Verkehrsregeln *traffic rules*

der Verkehrsstau *m* congestion (traffic) *n*

verkohlt *charred (meat) adj*

der Verkostungsraum *m* tasting room *n*

verlangsamen *to slow v* **p20**

Fahren Sie bitte langsamer. *Slow down!*

verlieren *to lose v* **p24**

der Verlobte *m*, die Verlobte *f* fiancé(e) *n*

die Vermittlung *f* operator (phone) *n*

verschütten *to spill v* **p20**

verschwinden *to disappear v* **p24**

verschwommen *blurry adj*

versenden *to ship v* **p20**

die Versicherung *f* insurance *n*

die Unfallversicherung *collision insurance*

die Haftpflichtversicherung *liability insurance*

die Version *f* version *n*

die Verspätung *f* delay *n*

verstehen *to understand v* **p24**

Ich verstehe nicht. *I don't understand.*

Verstanden? *Do you understand?*

verstopft *constipated adj*

die Verstopfung *f* congestion / constipation *n*

versuchen *to try (attempt) v* **p20**

der Verwandte *m*, die Verwandte *f* relative *n*

verwenden *to use v* **p20**

verwirrt *confused adj*

verzollen (customs) *to declare v* **p20**

das Video *g n* video *n*

der Videorekorder *m* VCR *n*

viel *a lot n*

viel *much adj*

viel Spaß *have fun* **pvii**

viele *many adj*

vier *four adj*

vierter *fourth adj*

ein Viertel *one quarter, one fourth*

vierzehn *fourteen adj*

vierzig *forty adj*

das Vinyl *g n* vinyl *n*

violett *purple adj*

das Visum *g n* visa *n*

der Vogel *m* bird *n*

voll *full adj*

vorbereitet *prepared adj*

Vorder- *front adj*

vorgestern *the day before yesterday adv*

die letzten paar Tage *these last few days*
vorstellen *to introduce v* **p20**
die Vorstellung *f show (performance) n*
vorwärts *forward adj*

W
der Wachmann *m guard n*
der Sicherheitsbeamte *security guard*
wachsen *to grow (get larger) v* **p24**
Wo sind Sie (formal) / bist du (informal) aufgewachsen? *Where did you grow up?*
die Wahl *f election n*
wählen *to dial (a phone number) v* **p20**
wählen *to vote v* **p20**
wandern *to hike v* **p20**
wenig *little*
wann *when adv*
der Wartebereich *m waiting area n*
die Warze *f wart n*
was *what adv*
Was gibt's? *What's up?*
das Waschbecken *gn sink n*
das Wasser *gn water n*
das heiße Wasser *hot water*
das kalte Wasser *cold water*
der Wasserhahn *m faucet n*
das Wechselgeld *gn change (money) n*
der Wechselkurs *m exchange rate n*

wechseln *to change (money) v / to change (clothes) v* **p20**
der Wecker *alarm clock*
Weckruf *wake-up call n*
der Weg *m trail n*
weiß *white adj*
weich *soft adj*
der Wein *m wine n*
das Weingut *gn vineyard n*
welcher / welche / welches *which adv*
weniger *See wenig*
wer *who adv*
Wem gehört ____? *Whose is ____?*
der Western *western n (movie)*
westlich, abendländisch *western adj*
die Wette *f bet n*
Ich gehe mit. *I'll see your bet.*
wetten *to bet v* **p20**
der Wetterbericht *m weather forecast n*
wie *how adv*
wie (viel) *how (much) adv*
Wie viel? *How much?*
Für wie lange? *For how long?*
wie (viele) *how (many) adv*
wiedergutmachen *to make up (apologize) v* **p20**
wiedergutmachen *to make up (compensate) v* **p20**
wiederholen *to repeat v* **p20**

GERMAN—ENGLISH

Könnten Sie das bitte wiederholen? *Would you please repeat that?*

Auf Wiedersehen *m goodbye n*

wiegen *to weigh v* **p24**

das Wi-Fi *gn wi-fi n*

willkommen *welcome adj*

Gern geschehen. *You're welcome.*

die Wimper *f eyelash n*

die Windel *f diaper n*

die Stoffwindel *cloth diaper*

die Wegwerfwindel *disposable diaper*

windig *windy adj*

windsurfen *to windsurf v*

der Winter *m winter n*

wir *we pron pl*

wirklich *really adj*

die Wirtschaft *f economy n*

das Wischerblatt *gn wiper blade n*

wissen *to know (something) v*

die Witwe *f widow n*

der Witwer *m widower*

Wo ist ___? *Where is ___?*

wo *where adv*

die Woche *f week n*

diese Woche *this week*

letzte Woche *last week*

nächste Woche *next week*

eine Woche *one week*

in einer Woche *a week from now*

der Wodka *m vodka n*

das Wohnmobil (van) / der Wohnwagen (trailer) *gn / m camper n*

wollen *to want v* **p25**

das Wörterbuch *gn dictionary n*

wütend *angry adj*

X

XL- *extra-large adj*

Z

der Zahn *m tooth n*

der Zahnarzt *m dentist n*

zehn *ten adj*

zehnter *tenth adj*

zeichnen *drawing (activity) v* **p20**

die Zeichnung *f drawing (work of art) n*

zeigen *to point v* **p20**

Könnten Sie mir das bitte zeigen? *Would you show me?*

die Zeit *f time n*

die Zeitschrift *f magazine n*

die Zeitung *f newspaper n*

der Zeitungsstand *m newsstand n*

zelten *to camp v* **p20**

der Zentimeter *m centimeter n*

(zer-)brechen *to break v* **p24**

zerbrechlich *fragile adj*

zerkocht *overcooked adj*

zerkratzt *scratched adj*
die Ziege *f goat n*
ziehen *to pull v* **p24**
das Ziel *gn destination n*
die Zigarette *f cigarette n*
  die Schachtel Zigaretten
    pack of cigarettes
die Zigarre *f cigar n*
das Zimmer *gn room (hotel) n*
das Zimmermädchen *gn*
    maid (hotel) n
der Zinssatz *m interest rate n*
Zoll *inch*
der Zoll *m customs n*
der Zoo *m zoo n*
der Zopf *m braid n*
zu *too (excessively) adv*
zu *toward prep*
der Zug *m train n*
  der Expresszug *express*
    train
  der Nahverkehrszug *local*
    train
das Zuhause *gn home n*
zurückgeben *to return*
    (something) v **p24**
zurückkehren *to return (to a*
    place) v **p20**
zusätzlich *extra adj*
zusehen *to watch v* **p24**
der Zustand *m condition n*
  in gutem / schlechtem
    Zustand *in good / bad*
    condition
zuvorkommend *courteous*
    adj

zwanzig *twenty adj*
zwei *two adj*
zweisprachig *bilingual adj*
zweiter *second adj*
zwölf *twelve adj*

NOTES

NOTES

NOTES

NOTES

NOTES